THE
Courage
TO
Love

THE Courage TO Love

*From Abuse to Happiness,
a Healing Memoir*

GUY GIARD

Foreword by Patch Adams, MD

This book is not intended and should not be regarded as a substitute for professional medical advice, a professional medical diagnosis, or medical treatment administered by a health-care professional. If you are experiencing a health problem, you should always seek the advice of your physician or another qualified medical professional. Never disregard professional medical advice, and if you are in need of medical attention of any kind whatsoever, do not hesitate to seek assistance of the relevant support groups.

Author: Giard, Guy (1959–)
Foreword: Hunter Patch Adams, MD (1945–)
Interview: Hunter Patch Adams, MD (1945–)
Series: Guy Giard Love's Healing Journey

ISBN 978-2-925120-08-7 (Ebook English edition)
ISBN 978-2-925120-09-4 (Paperback English edition)
ISBN 978-2-925120-10-0 (Hardcover English edition)
ISBN 978-2-925120-11-7 (Audiobook English edition)

1. Creative Nonfiction 2. Memoir 3. Autobiography 4. Sexual abuse 5. PTSD 6. Therapies 7. Humanitarian Clown 8. Health 9. Vipassana 10. Art 11. Music 12. Laughter yoga

Editor: Jennifer Huston Schaeffer
Cover: MiblArt
Interior design: Eswari Kamireddy
Photo credits back cover : Guy Giard and Leo Ramirez

Legal deposit: National Library and Archives of Quebec 2023
First English edition: 2023
Publisher: Guy Giard
Copyright © 2023 Guy Giard

This book is the expanded English edition of "Le Grincement Des Balançoires" (French), "El Chirrido De Los Columpios" (Spanish) now republished respectively as "Le Courage d'Aimer" (French), "El Coraje De Amar" (Spanish).

We have had the privilege to have Guy on several of our clown trips. He is a big, softhearted soul whose radiant smile has brought much glee and stimulation for the trips. He and I have spoken often, and I truly feel his passion for living radiantly, using clowning as a tool to help midwife a loving world. To hear of his own transformation to bring a loving soul will inspire others to try it on. Let him sparkle your environment.

—PATCH ADAMS, MD, PHYSICIAN, COMEDIAN, SOCIAL ACTIVIST, CLOWN, AUTHOR, AND FOUNDER OF THE GESUNDHEIT! INSTITUTE

To Guy. Never forget that you have a gift. A gift of resilience. And for those who don't have that and are still suffering, it is your life's purpose to heal others. Keep open to the gifts the universe gives you. With love. Thank you.

—JUDY CARTER, COMEDIAN, MOTIVATIONAL SPEAKER, AND AUTHOR

This book by Guy Giard is not only well written, but also a very useful reference that promotes hope in the therapeutic process of integrating the trauma experienced by victims of assault suffering from Post Traumatic Stress Disorder (PTSD). This book can also be an interesting read for therapists treating victims of aggression.

—MARJOLAINE GOSSELIN, PHD, RETIRED PSYCHOLOGIST

5,0 on 5 stars Such an inspiring book. This book by Guy Giard is quite unique and such a delight to read. It exposes raw emotions and it is written in such a beautiful way but without leaving the complex agony of going through such hardship. I can really relate to some of his emotions and I applaud him for writing this book.

I highly recommend this book as it is so deep and so amazing on such different levels of human emotions. Powerful words for such an incredible story of life not always being what you think it will be... I really loved reading this book. ❤❤❤

—MAUDE D.

The book is very well written, in a fluid style. One always wants to know more, to read the next page. A life full of pitfalls, failures, rejections, abandonments and rebuffs. In spite of all this, the author brings a message of hope to all those who have been flayed by life so that they can reach serenity.

—JEAN-FRANÇOIS D.

I loved your book and devoured it. Not only is it well written, it reads like a gripping detective story. My heart wept as I read about your horrific experiences that cannot help but leave deep scars. Bravo for having the courage and resilience to not only be reborn, but to use those scars for the benefit of others.

—RITA B.

A positive life story that balances the devastation often left by acts of abuse with the redemption or rebirth that the love of others can bring. A life journey that is worth reading and from which one learns beautiful life lessons!

—STEVE H.

What I liked about reading your book was the idea that you wrote about your past and what happened to you, but at the same time you didn't write about it as a victim. You wrote as the person who got through it, as a warrior, a fighter, telling your story and not feeling sorry for yourself. I really liked when you wrote about music, and I was also listening to the music. The music is really important because every time there was an important event there was a music attached to it, and it's funny because I do that in my life too. If I listen to old songs I remember what state I was in when I was listening to that music so I felt like I was really with you in this whole novel, I was really with you the whole time. I think I read it in three days. I came back from work and the first thing on my mind was that I had to finish the book. I really wanted to finish it. And then when you go to do your meditation, I was there, like I was there with you the whole time. So your way of telling things too, we feel like we're really included, like we're really part of your story.

I would definitely recommend this book to people who have challenges so that they realize that you can get through it; that yes you can tell your story but at the same time you are not your story. Even if you were abused in your past, it doesn't mean that you have to be abused today. You can free yourself from that in the process. That's what I see in this book, it's like a story of liberation, a story of healing. It's more a story of healing than of being a victim, and that's why I would recommend it to someone who needs to heal.

—Dominique L.

This is a very interesting book about the life of a child, surviving through all the trials and tribulations of life, growing up this child was able to find the way to joy, empathy, and beauty. A book to read to understand what we can do to not surrender to despair!!!

—Lucie T.

I just finished reading your book, and I wanted to take the time to thank you from the bottom of my heart for sharing your life so openly, with love. The book did a world of good to me, so many passages throughout were very familiar and hit very close to home. You've given me hope, I went through a cornucopia of emotions all week, but a lot of stuff was coming out and staying out!

—Julian L.

Thank you for the joy in this difficult time. I was very tense and nervous at that time. But when you arrived, a miracle happened, I felt light and well, and we could feel the happiness! I am very grateful to you and I am happy that we met. It was a huge relief for me! Especially when you see how your child laughs and rejoices. Thank you Guy! God brought you to us!

—Kseniya R, mother of little Amir in Russia

I want to express my deepest gratitude for believing in me. You have been an excellent friend, teacher, mentor, and a great inspiration for me. You have inspired me to pursue my goals with hard work and dedication. The knowledge you have imparted to me has been a great asset. I truly appreciate and value everything I have learned from you. It will forever remain a major contributor behind my success and achievements. Thank you, once again, for your time, support, and patience.

—GIRI DHARAN, DIRECTOR AND FOUNDER OF
THE THIRD HAND FOUNDATION

We're a small private school for children aged six to twelve, who are either orphans or from disadvantaged backgrounds. Your financial support has enabled us to build a better and more promising future for the school's staff and pupils. It's your extraordinary generosity that enables us to bring big, happy smiles to the faces of our young charges each and every day, and we never would have made it this far without your help.

So I'd like to thank you for being part of our school and for lending your support to the vital cause of giving children from disadvantaged backgrounds a good education. On behalf of our entire staff and all of our pupils, I'd like to thank you from the bottom of my heart and theirs as well.

—FRANCELLINE NAKOULMA, FOUNDER OF SAINT GABRIEL,
A PRIVATE PRIMARY SCHOOL LOCATED IN OUAGADOUGOU, BURKINA FASO

The Alzheimer Society of Montreal had the pleasure of having Guy Giard present a Laughter Yoga workshop. This was an event for caregivers, a luncheon to honor them and allow time for laughter, sharing, and respite. Guy was dynamic, enthusiastic, and instantly captured the attention of our group. Within moments, a group that did not previously have contact with one another were laughing, shaking hands, interacting, and sharing with one another.

—APRIL HAYWARD, DIRECTOR OF PROGRAMS AND SERVICES,
THE ALZHEIMER SOCIETY OF MONTREAL

Contents

PART III - LOVE CLOWN

Foreword

I am so honored to write this foreword to Guy's book, which details his journey to heal from the nightmarish violence he experienced as a child. His remarkable recovery came about by discovering that giving love and fun to others who are suffering can put one's own suffering in perspective. It can also drive one to commit to a life of service to love others and fun.

This happens not through psychiatric analysis and medication, but rather by recovering and discovering one's own powers of love and fun through clowning to ease the suffering of others. Guy first wrote to me in 2013 and shared his pain. I wrote back and invited him on a clown trip to a foreign destination.

Why a clown trip, you ask? Let me give you some background information. I am a physician who has found that fun as a friend and love are the essential tools for being a healthy doctor. In March of 1971, after obtaining my medical degree, I wanted a stress-free practice, aided by being a doctor who never charged money for care. I opened a radical medical clinic with the premise that all the permanent staff would live together in a communal ecovillage. And we'd all make the same salary—$400 a month. The context for healing both practitioner and patient would be a happy, funny, loving, cooperative, creative, and thoughtful, all in a creative hospital / home setting. We operated this experimental hospital in our communal home from 1971 to 1983 and learned the great healing context of those six qualities.

However, during that time, because we were unable to raise funds to keep the hospital going, I realized we would have to go public and use fame as a fundraiser. So we closed the hospital doors, and I became a fundraiser. Unfortunately, within a year, I started to feel empty from not caring for patients. So in 1985, I started taking groups of people (from ages three to ninety-two) to foreign countries to bring love as clowns in hospitals, orphanages, nursing homes, prisons, etc. I like to say that clowning is a trick to get a love dose. I have clowned since childhood and knew it had the power to bring joy to both the giver and receiver, but those who joined us on the trips were not required to have any experience as a clown to participate.

Before meeting Guy, I had taken thousands of people from fifty countries on at least 150 trips. Many of them had previously corresponded with me, so I often knew their stories. For those who were troubled, I suggested that they come on a clown trip and reconnect with their loving, playful self. For many, this opened up doors that not only stopped their suffering, but made them into playful, cuddle buddies. I've had a large paper mail correspondence for 35 years and would get letters from people (many) who said that the clown trips transformed their suffering. In due time, Guy would become one of my clowning buddies.

When I heard that six thousand members of the armed forces kill themselves each year due to a lack of help from the medical profession, I decided to take some veterans on my clown trips. I wanted to make it free for the vets, so I tried for seven years to raise the $30,000 needed to take ten vets (and staff members) to Guatemala for a one-week clowning trip. Finally, that first vet trip to Guatemala took place in 2014, and it stopped their suicidal suffering. We did it again the following year with ten different veterans and the results were the same. We made a film of the trip that really captures their transformation. At the San Jose film festival for the movie's world premiere in 2019 many of the vets were there in clown costumes, happy, and loving.

So, thank you Guy! People like you who experienced profound suffering in the past that needed healing came on a clown trip, stayed in touch, and gave me the confidence to dare to do more trips for wounded warriors. Even as the son of a wounded warrior, I would not have had such confidence without people like Guy sharing their vulnerability. And for those of you reading this, who are suffering, try clowning for love and fun where you live (and with your family) or come on one of our clown trips (sign up for e-newsletter on patchadams.org).

In peace,
Patch Adams
#patch

Preface

Dear friend,

This book is my personal fifty-eight-year-long journey of living through the pain of loneliness, the excitement of daring new life challenges and, ultimately, the joy of finding purpose, love for myself and for humanity.

I wrote it with you, the reader, in mind, retracing my steps to give you hints of how I was able to heal myself from the hurt of childhood sexual abuse. Not only is this my autobiography, it's also a riveting adventure full of passion, art, music, humor, spanning across three continents, written in such a way that you feel as if you're along for the ride on my emotional roller coaster of a life.

Everything you will read in these pages really happened. I've re-created the situations and conversations based on my recollections, correspondence, and diaries, but in some cases, I changed certain physical traits, names, and professions in the interest of protecting the privacy of the individuals whose paths I have crossed. However, a few passages may be sensitive and could potentially have a trigger effect for victims of past traumas. I chose to include these to help readers better understand the pains of abuse and the benefits of the healing process; more so, I have done so delicately and with respect.

Lastly, as an added bonus, you can augment your reading experience with the artworks, music compositions, videos, and interviews described in this book, which are available freely online for your viewing pleasure at www.guygiard.com. It's a virtual-reality extravaganza that will allow you to immerse yourself in my healing journey.

I wish such a book existed when I was at the beginning of my healing journey, but it didn't. So I decided to write it myself to be of service to all who feel that there is more to life then what they are living through presently. I'm gently handing my story to you as a caring friend, and as a life coach if it inspires you to undertake your own healing journey yourself, then I will have reached my goal in writing this book. I have discovered love along the way, and I wish you the same.

Have a wonderful journey.

Love,
Guy Giard

PART I

THE FALL

Chapter 1

NO-MAN'S-LAND

The stage was ready, and the cheers of fans exploded like fireworks. The stuffy, hot bar was crammed from the entrance to the front row.

"Five minutes, you guys. Get ready," the stagehand warned.

I peered through the door across the dimly lit bar and saw my dad and my brother Marc drinking beers. They were squeezed at a table near the front, but this wasn't my dad's type of hangout. I knew he'd rather be in a church pew watching me sing Mozart's Requiem or Vivaldi's Gloria.

Not my brother, though. He was in his element. Back when we were teens, he'd given himself the moniker "the Great Rock and Roll Fan" on the airwaves when he'd called into radio station CHOM. Around that same time, he'd come to me with a new album saying, "Hey, man. The Stones are awesome! You gotta listen to 'Jumpin' Jack Flash.' It's a gas!"

When the stagehand gave the sign that it was our turn to take the stage, I heard the MC take the mic. "Welcome to the Piranha Bar!" he shouted, extending the *r*-sound and making it trill. "Is it hot enough for you? Are you ready to rock?" The people in the crowd stomped their feet and screamed.

Staring at the three little steps I needed to walk up to get to the stage, I thought to myself, *Wow! It took more than fifty years to finally reach this staircase—my first live gig as a lead singer.* As I made my way onto the stage, the blinding spotlights, the roar of the crowd, and a wall of heat instantly took me back to a blazing hot alley. It was the summer of '64, and my brothers were on the prowl.

"I am Batman! I am Batman!" shrieked my eight-year-old brother Luc as he tied a blue bath towel around his shoulders. "And I'm gonna kill you, Joker!"

Marc, my other brother who was seven at the time, was portraying Batman's archrival. He nearly escaped Luc's lunge. Marc was never given a choice as to whether he was Two-Face, the Penguin, or the Joker. But he was never, ever Robin, the friendly sidekick.

My nine-year-old older sister, Mimi, was the exact opposite. "Open your mouth and say, 'Ah,'" she instructed four-year-old me. Dressed as a nurse with a white bonnet in her hair, she was so gentle as she tenderly took care of me, her miniature patient in a bathing suit. "Oh, yes. We definitely need to give you some cough syrup."

The sun was unbearably hot as another heat wave hit Montreal. It was high noon on this particular summer day, and there were no trees for us to take refuge under. We only had our dinky blue plastic pool to cool us off. The cicadas chirped in full harmony and everything was going smoothly until Batman and the Joker veered across the yard and attacked us.

"Leave us alone!" Mimi hollered as she fell backward into the pool, splashing water everywhere.

Taking advantage of the situation, Luc and Marc grabbed me and pushed me to the ground. "BWAAAAAAAA!" I cried from the pain of skinning my knees on the rough, pockmarked, scorching asphalt. As crimson blood pearled down my leg, I shrieked even louder. It hurt like crazy, but truth be told, I was more scared of the neighbor's German shepherds barking over the fence at all the commotion.

Our playground was the back alleys of Hochelaga, "the working-class neighborhood" on the east side of Montreal. More precisely, it was the French Canadian–speaking ghetto and was often denigrated as the home to the "white niggers of North America." A great divide persisted between the English-speaking business owners and the factory workers, the result of Europe's ancestral wars between Great Britain and France. This was even more obvious throughout the province of Quebec, where Irish, Italian, and Chinese immigrants were also considered low-class laborers. But in the backyards of Hochelaga, the patriotic flags had long given way to underwear, socks, and blue factory coveralls on the clotheslines.

Hearing me wail, Mom rushed down to see what all the fuss was about. The second my brothers saw her; they released me and ran down the alley laughing. My sister hurried crying home to change out of her wet clothes. My mom kneeled down and said gently, "Now, now, what did they do this time?" Then she opened a bottle of rubbing alcohol and disinfected my wounds.

It burned. "Ouch, Mommy! That hurts!" I exclaimed as I burst into more tears.

"Shush! It'll feel better soon," she muttered in a tired voice. "Mommy's got a lot of work to do, so play nice." She put bandages on my knees, wiped my nose, kissed my forehead, and disappeared back inside, leaving me with my toys on a yellowed patch of parched lawn.

With me left sniffling all alone, our orange tabby cat strutted by to see if I was OK. "Come here, Taffy," I said as I grabbed him by the tail, pressed him to my chest, and petted him vigorously as if my life depended on it.

I'd recently found him in my grandparents big, red barn as I played near the cows and the chickens. "Meeewww, meewww." I'd heard crystalline cries from a tiny being mewling in a prickly haystack. I gently picked him up and thought, *You're gonna be mine.* I named him Taffy after my favorite sweet. "Daddy, can I take him home, pleeeaasee!"

"I love you, Taffy! I love you!" He was my special—and only—friend in our household. As he purred loudly, he brushed his soothing silky-smooth fur against my face. I then placed his front paws around my neck and tapped him hard on the head with my knuckles. Upset, his whole body stiffened as he tried to escape. But I held him even harder as his hard-tensed legs felt as a veritable hug.

Like countless families of the 1950s, we'd moved from a small farming community called Saint-Hyacinthe on the banks of the Yamaska River, a tributary of the Saint Lawrence. The country road to our barns still carried the family name—Giard—to this day. My father, who was born in 1929, came from a long line of a dairy farmers. He had numerous brothers and sisters—twelve in all—and like me, he was the baby of the family. Sadly, though, he lost his mom when he was very young, so his older sisters raised him. Even so, at a very early age, he learned to fend for himself. He grew up pitching hay, working the soil, and milking cows. "Life is about work, very hard work!" he always said.

He once shared a story with me about how he discovered his life's calling. "When I was eight years old, I was riding along with my brother, bouncing on the tractor seat as he tilled the land. We were hard at work under the scorching midday sun. I felt nails poking my sunburned back as sweat poured down my brow, and I thought to myself, *This isn't going to be my life.* Right then and there, I decided to become a doctor!"

His eyes twinkled as he recalled with wistful dismay that his decision meant he had to leave the farm and his family and move to the city. However, that didn't happen until many years later. My older brothers and sister lived their earliest years in Saint-Hyacinthe, but after I came into this world in 1959, we moved to Montreal.

My mother's story hardly fared any better. She was born in 1931, when most families were still caught up in the tidal waves of poverty during the Great Depression. Such was the case for her father, a jack-of-all-trades. With no work and no income, he decided to pack up and move his family out west in search of a better life.

Promises of work fell through, which was followed by even bigger failures, so mother's family was constantly on the move after being evicted over and over again. Grandma sewed their already tattered clothes as they tried their best to fight the bone-chilling winters, but they often went to bed hungry without having eaten for days. When my mother was eight years old, her older brothers were sent overseas when Canada declared war on Germany and World War II erupted. Cold, hungry, and missing their older brothers, the younger children were told to keep quiet because crying and whining wouldn't achieve anything. With no income, no roof, and no food, my mother's family painfully made the journey back to Quebec more impoverished than before.

They settled in Sainte-Rose, a small village to the west of Montreal, about an hour from where my father grew up. My mother's family got by on her father's meager earnings from his jobs as a taxi driver and sawmill worker. But their strife wasn't yet over. On April 1, 1944, screams of "FIRE! FIRE! FIRE!" tore through the quiet night. Jumping out of bed, my mother and her many sisters stumbled outside in their nightgowns. Standing barefoot in the snow, my mother and her family shivered in the cold as they watched their home disappear in a fiery blaze. Once again, they'd lost everything.

In an effort to help out her family, my mother became a nurse at the local hospital, taking care of premature babies. I can only guess that this is how destiny brought my parents together because they never talked about it. I still have a souvenir matchbox with a photo of them on its flap from their honeymoon. My father was in France for his studies, so my mom joined him in Paris for a few days. She radiated happiness in her beautiful white dress, while my father, with his Clark

Gable-esque razor mustache, was the image of elegance. I cherished this image of their love.

I imagine that they met in the corridors of the hospital and started dating. Within a year, they were married. A year later, my sister, Mimi, was born, followed Luc and then Marc. They were two adults and three babies all living in a tiny apartment in Saint-Hyacinthe. Dad was working hard as a medical resident, so Mom struggled to keep them all clothed and fed.

When I was born, my mother almost bled to death. After that, returning home to an already too small apartment became unlivable for the six of us. When my father decided to specialize in neurology, my parents uprooted us from our extended family and moved us to the big city of Montreal. Isolated and missing the support of her sisters and parents, my mother worked to the point of exhaustion. Finally, her sixteen-year-old niece moved in to provide some help, but after three months, she left unexpectedly, leaving my mom to fend for all four of us children yet again. Even so, I never heard my mom complain. Instead, she'd simply say, "The past is the past. There's no point talking about it."

By the time I was six years old, my father was a full-fledged neurologist. My family was moving up in the world, so we left Hochelaga for Outremont, an upscale neighborhood for professionals that offered single-family homes, manicured lawns, and large, gorgeous public parks. Although our surroundings had improved, the few friends I'd made in Hochelaga were left behind. In addition, my parents decided to send me to public school while most kids in our neighborhood attended private schools. I was a stranger in a strange land. Needless to say, I struggled to make friends.

When I was in second grade, my teacher decided that it would be simply hilarious to Italianize my last name. "Hey, Giardini! Come over here," he'd order me in a mocking voice that was a very sly insult, revealing his racist views about working-class Italians. The whole class laughed. It hurt, but I didn't say anything because I didn't know how to stick up for myself. Immobilized with embarrassment, I simply stared at the papers on my desk. During recess, my classmates further humiliated me by calling me Giardini while pelting me with the ball over and over again while playing dodgeball. To avoid their taunts, I exiled myself to the most remote corner of the schoolyard.

Uprooted and raised without grandparents, uncles, aunts, or cousins, no one was there to protect me from the constant assaults of Batman, the Joker, or the bullies at school. I learned from Dad that life was hard work, and Mom taught me that being quiet was the answer to being hurt. Neither country boy nor city dweller, neither working-class nor professional, I was an outsider lost in an arid no-man's-land like the one that was dividing East and West Berlin. Even Taffy, my only true friend, jumped over the wall and escaped—never to be seen again—leaving me alone in my barren desert of solitude.

Chapter 2

MR. CROOKED TEETH

In 1967, Canada celebrated its centennial year. For this occasion, Montreal opened its doors with a world's fair called Expo 67. Schoolchildren were invited to visit, and as part of a class project, I had to do a presentation on my favorite exhibit.

Because the grounds were humongous and the crowd noisy, when we visited the pavilions, we had to hold hands, which I hated. There were ninety pavilions, but we were only able to see a handful of them, including those from Japan, the Netherlands, and Haiti. But the one that got me most excited had a funny name: USSR. Inside a round movie theater, a film showed the craters and deserts of the moon and Venus. *I'm on the moon!*

Shiny metal balls with long antennas—replicas of the Soviet satellites *Sputnik* and *Sputnik 2*—seemed to float overhead. *Sputnik 2*, which carried a dog named Laika, had been launched into space exactly two years before I was born. But what really got my heart pumping was the orange spacesuit of Yuri Gagarin, the first man in space. *I am cosmonaut Yuri Gagarin in my rocket ship, and I've blasted into orbit!* I was so enthralled with the exhibit that I made a cardboard cutout of a

TV with a rolling montage of drawings of him, his spaceship, and the stars for my class presentation.

By this time, I'd already gotten into the habit of cutting through Outremont's magnificent Joyce Park as I walked home from school by myself. The park's impeccably landscaped grounds, majestic oak, maple, and pine trees, and wildly colorful flower beds were like something out of a fairy tale. Nature had always made me feel alive. It was my peaceful oasis away from the abuse I took from the bullies at school and my brothers. I'd spend hours playing alone in the sandbox under the bright sunshine, building sandcastles and using twigs to create complex forests of leaves, pine cones, and acorns with their funny little brown hats.

The soundtrack to my solitary play was rustling leaves and the *thwonk* of tennis balls bouncing on the courts behind the park's administrative building. As much as I loved the sandbox, my favorite was the swings next to it. They desperately needed oiling, but the *creak-creak* sound they made didn't bother me. I'd sit down on the chipped, red-painted wooden plank, push off with my feet, and thrust my legs out as far as I could up toward the sky, higher, higher, higher! When my buttocks finally lifted off the seat, I'd let go of the chains and blast off into space like my hero, Yuri Gagarin. *I'm coming to rescue you, Laika!* Then I'd hit the ground giggling and run back to the swings to do it all over again.

One afternoon while I was happily swinging through the air, a man sitting on a nearby bench called out to me, "You really like this park, don't you? Just about every time I'm here, I see you playing on the swing set." He was the park's groundskeeper. I knew because I'd often seen him near the playground raking leaves while I played by myself. "It must be loads of fun. Why don't you come here and sit next to me for a while?"

Surprised that someone was actually talking to me, I left my squeaky swings and took a seat next to him. Right away, I noticed his scrawny body, bony face, and worn-out jeans. As he lit a cigarette between dirty, tar-stained fingers, I thought, *His teeth are so yellow and crooked that he must hate going to the dentist as much as I do.* Even so, I liked the fact that someone was finally paying attention to me.

"So you like to swing, eh? I like games too," he said as he inched closer to me. I got a whiff of his foul-smelling breath as he leaned over and whispered in a very coy voice, "Do you know what a pedophile is?"

"No," I admitted. But his question felt off to me, like a mildewed piece of bread or funky cheese odor.

I couldn't really hear what he said after that, but I did hear him say he wanted to show me a game in his office. However, when I got up to follow him, I felt sick to my stomach and my head started spinning, so I quickly turned around and ran past the swings all the way home as fast as I could.

I was out of breath by the time I reached the front door, but to my surprise, I no longer felt dizzy or nauseous. However, I was ashamed of having felt sick so I didn't tell anyone about it.

The following morning as I neared the park on my way to school, as soon as I heard the metallic *creak-creak* of the swings, my vision blurred. I felt a strange pressure around my eyes and a weight on my chest. I couldn't breathe. Panicked, I ran to school and vowed never to set foot in the park again.

Friendless, bullied, and deprived of my beloved sandbox and swings, I fell behind in school and needed a home tutor. As my world closed down, so did my eyesight and I had to start wearing glasses. To ease my pain, I filled myself with candy bars and sweets and, as a result, became overweight. "Four eyes" and "Fatso" became my new nicknames at school. But when the loneliness became unbearable, I adopted my dad's work ethic. I mowed neighbors' lawns, raked leaves, washed cars, and eventually took on a paper route.

Most customers on my route had subscriptions, so I just needed to collect their payments door-to-door. After knocking politely, I took their money and made a hole in their card with my puncher. It all went well until one morning the following summer when I walked up the wooden porch of a red brick house. I rang the doorbell and a woman in a blue velvet bathrobe answered.

"Well, hello, young man. What can I do for you?" she slurred as she held a glass with ice cubes that clinked together. Her breath reeked of alcohol as she moved closer to me, letting her bathrobe peek open to reveal her clingy, see-through, pink negligee.

"I'm . . . uh . . . I'm here to collect the money for your newspaper," I managed to blurt out as I avoided looking at her.

"Oh, you must be thirsty, young man. It's sooo hot outside. Why don't you come in for a drink of water?" she purred.

"Just the money please," I insisted, my whole body tensing up as I concentrated on the pom-poms of her fuzzy, pink slippers. When she took a step closer, pulled lightly on my shoulder, and again asked me to come in, I felt as if an icicle had slid down my spine.

"Um . . . if you could just . . . the money," I stammered as I took a step back, trembling in fear.

She finally went inside, got her purse, and handed me the cash. I punched her card without ever looking up and finished my rounds while quivering from my cold sweat.

Weeks later as I walked up to the same house, my heart pounded and my breath quickened. Sweat was beading on my forehead, so I pulled my cap over my eyes and rang the doorbell. This time, the woman was fully clothed, cold, and distant. And, thankfully, she didn't invite me to come inside. *I'm OK,* I thought to myself, relieved. *She'll pay me, and I'll be on my way.* I was able to catch my breath—until I saw a shadow behind her in the hallway. With his stocky body, shirtless, hairy chest, and goatee, he reminded me of a satyr minus the horns. My heart stopped. It was the teacher who'd called me Giardini!

After that, I gave up my paper route just like I had the swings.

The teacher, the lady, the groundskeeper—I can't trust adults, I concluded. *They're all bad people.*

In 1967, Canadians celebrated and Montreal opened its doors to the world. But in my own little universe, cold and heavy metal gates closed with a clang, trapping me further in the black void of loneliness.

Chapter 3

FELIX

By the time I was twelve, I fled from adults, my brothers, and my classmates. I lived with only one purpose: to be invisible. I was constantly reminding myself, *Make no demands, don't express any needs, and avoid conflict at all cost.* I became a yes-man, a good boy. I left home for school without saying goodbye, I stood in corners away from crowds, avoided people approaching me on the sidewalk by crossing the street, and took long detours home. I couldn't speak. I was numb of all feeling except pain. Longing to experience amnesia, I escaped into the imaginary world of my comic books.

DDDRRRIIINNNGGGG, the red school bell rang, announcing it was lunchtime. As a seventh grader, I got into the habit of hiding out in the school's miniscule library during my lunch break. There were only a few shelves of dust-covered books with a small collection of LPs, but I found solace with my heroes: the adventurous news reporter Tintin, who took me around the world, and the hilarious, fuzzy, brown bear cub Petzi, who wore red-and-white polka-dotted overalls and was friends with a penguin and a seal with a corncob pipe. But my favorite was Noddy, a wooden puppet boy who had a spring-loaded head and wore a blue stocking cap with a little bell. He lived in Toyland and was happy all the time. I often imagined myself as Noddy, the good boy whom everybody loved, in his little yellow car.

During one such recess, while I was sitting on the old, gray carpet and driving happily down the road in my pretend car, shivers suddenly went down my spine. I slowly turned to face a man I'd never seen before. He looked back at me with kind eyes, curly, brown hair, a square jaw, a rugged face, and a guitar dangling on his back. His name was printed on the album cover in large, white letters: Felix Leclerc. *Someone is smiling at me!* I thought. I gently picked up the album and pressed it to my chest, feeling a warmth that I'd missed since Taffy's flight.

The librarian was surprised when she checked out the album and placed it in a blue vinyl pouch. "He's a French-Canadian singer, song-writer, and poet. I'm sure you'll like him."

Later that day, I carefully packed my treasure and hid it under my jacket as I made my way home. Alone in the basement, I kept look-ing again and again at Felix's smile, thinking, *I have a friend.* When I listened to the songs, I discovered that his warm, deep voice was as beautiful as his heart. Something new vibrated within me. I lis-tened to one song over and over again—"Le P'tit Bonheur" ("A Little Happiness")—a ballad about how happiness has abandoned him. The last line was about changing sidewalks to avoid pain. *This song is about me! That's what I do every day!* Miraculously, for the first time in my life, I felt that someone understood me.

Still basking in a warm glow, I stashed the record in my bedroom and made my way to the kitchen for an after-school snack. When I entered the room, my two brothers were wrestling on the floor. As I carefully sidestepped them to reach for an apple on the counter, they raised their heads and screamed at me, "What the fuck are you doing here, you little shit?"

I froze. I just wanted to get by. They stopped and stared at me so hard my eyes melted right in their sockets. The sight of fresh prey was tantalizing to them, their inner predator ready to devour me. With crazed eyes and sharp claws, they pounced as I backed away stuttering, "Stop it! Leave me alone!"

I lost my balance, and my hand landed on the hard, cold steel of a butter knife sitting on the dinner table. Without flinching, I flung it out just in front of them as a warning shot. I didn't want to hurt them, but I ached for the years of pain they'd inflicted on me to stop. As the knife loudly clanged and bounced off the floor, they froze. For once, I was fighting back as if Felix had just given me the courage to finally stand up for myself rather than cross the street in fear.

Unfortunately for me, after their initial shock wore off, their appetite for causing pain only grew. By standing up to them, I had just upped their game. "You little fucker! You're gonna die!" they shouted as they lunged at me.

I picked up a chair and threw it in front of them. "STOP! STOP! STOOOOOOOP!!!" I screamed my lungs out.

There was dead silence in the kitchen. No one in our household had ever dared to stand up to them in such a way. Much to my surprise, they backed away. Maybe it was the scream, the chair, or my presence. Whatever it was, it worked because their relentless bullying of me stopped right then and there—forever. I'd tamed the beasts, but sadly, the incident with the chair and knife severed our relationship. They kept going at each other's throats as usual, but I was given a new identity. I was "the Silent Good Boy," the one they ignored, the one they pretended not to see, the one they didn't listen to or talk to. This was the heavy price I had to pay for my freedom. I silently accepted it, but I felt disconnected from my family and more alone than I did before. A few months later, my heart shriveled up even more when my parents got divorced and Dad moved out.

By then, my grades were so poor that my mother opted to send me to College Notre-Dame du Sacré-Coeur, which, at the time, was an all-boy's Catholic school "Authority will be good for your grades," she reasoned. I would be required to wear a tie, a button-down shirt, and a blazer with the school herald on the pocket. Not only wouldn't I know anyone there, but even worse, I had to repeat seventh grade so my classmates would all be younger than me. In addition to my dad being gone and my brothers ignoring me, I was now pulled away from Petzi, Noddy, and Felix. As the Silent Good Boy, I had no say in being exiled on the city bus to an unknown district.

For the next two years, I desperately needed to connect to someone or something, so I turned to comic book superheroes. *Maybe Batman, Superman, or Spiderman will rescue me?* I soon found that I had more in common with the humorous oddballs who'd been rejected by their peers: Plastic Man with his ridiculous red suit and wide, white, ski goggles and the Metal Men, a group of living robots, each with a unique personality. Of all the Metal Men, I related most closely with the self-doubting and insecure Tin Man.

But the outcasts were the best in my mind. I was the Beast of the X-Men, who was hunted by society; the mild-mannered scientist Bruce Banner, who turned into the green monster the Hulk; the Thing the rock man from the Fantastic Four, Swamp Thing and Man-thing no longer human but a living plant monster and Metamorpho, who considered his superpowers a disease and himself a freak. *I'm a freak. I don't belong anywhere.*

During my adolescence, I created a new family with TV sitcoms. Fonzie from *Happy Days*, a rebel in a black leather jacket à la James Dean, was my older, protective brother; Uncle Bill from *Family Affair* was my caring relative; and Uncle Martin from *My Favorite Martian* was my funny brother. I wanted to be successful like gentleman farmer Oliver on *Green Acres*, but instead I was Gilligan, the young, inept, accident-prone first mate of the SS *Minnow* from *Gilligan's Island*. These characters were dependable and always made me laugh. Dinnertime was always TV time because it was the only way to bring peace to our household and provide a brief respite for Mom.

During the nighttime, though, I was attacked with horrific visions. I was Number Six from the British TV series *The Prisoner*, in which a former spy is kidnapped and held hostage in a small village. Dehumanized and kept under constant surveillance, the main character is stripped of his identity and is simply referred to as Number Six. I could relate to him because I was the Silent Good Boy. And when he repeatedly screamed, "I AM NOT A NUMBER! I'M A FREE MAN!" I felt something stir deep inside me.

Even in my nightmares, I was voiceless. Often I was lost inside an old, dark mansion. Suffocating and feeling threatened, I ran for my life. But no matter which way I went, I encountered locked doors. Every corridor led to another part of the maze. Walls moved and closed in on me. I fell through a trap door and emerged, petrified and alone, shivering from fear. *I am Number Six.* Night after night, I woke up thinking, *Is this my home?*

In my nightmares, if I wasn't trapped in a house of horrors, I was homeless and sleeping in a cardboard box that stank of piss. Still worse—and this one terrified me the most, even in daytime—was being stuck in a dark elevator. When the whole thing jerked into a free fall, my head would spin and crash against the cold, metal gray walls as I was tossed about with nothing to hold on to. Then suddenly it would swerve sideways. Left, right, left again, up, and down, like a roller coaster. Nothing made sense. I was utterly helpless as the cabin spiraled out of control, accelerated, and then crashed, exploding into a million pieces and leaving me a crumpled form in a pool of blood. Each time I had this dream, I would awake with a start, trembling in my cold, sweat-soaked sheets.

As if the nightmares weren't bad enough, when the night terrors began, I really dreaded sleep. I didn't dare shut my burning eyes, even if I was totally exhausted. *Don't sleep. Don't sleep.* I slept with a light on and the radio tuned to late-night call-in talk shows. These became my lifeline with reality, a voice with which I could connect.

But long past midnight, the thoughts invaded my mind: *Where do I belong? Where's my home? I have no origin, no reason to live, no hopes of ever finding love.* I felt a wave of lava burned my skin and set my body aflame. *What is life? What is death? What does it mean to exist? What is forever?* I'd leap out of bed in pure agony, doubled over from stomach cramps, sometimes accompanied by diarrhea or vomiting.

During these episodes, I'd switch on every light in my room, frantically run in circles, jump up and down, slam both fists into my mattress, punch myself in the face, and silently shriek inside my head, *I NEED SENSATIONS! I NEED TO FEEL SOMETHING— ANYTHING!* then removing the lampshade I'd stare directly at the light bulb, blinding my retinas as the burning sensation brought me back to reality. After that, the shaking would subside, my stomach would calm down, and I could breathe again. Nobody knew.

One night, after months of these attacks, I heard a diabolical laughter. *That's it, I've gone completely mad!* I thought. But it was coming from the radio. As I listened this insane giggle calmed me. It was "Speak to Me" from Pink Floyd's album *The Dark Side of the Moon.* It was as if a safety valve had just opened *It's my own laughter – the laughter lurking in my void. It's out there in the real world.* I had found a new anchor to reality: music. Reassured, like a wet lump of clay, I plopped onto my mattress and drifted off to asleep.

The next day, I bought *The Dark Side of the Moon* with its black prismatic art on the cover. Next to it in the record bin was Supertramp's *Crime of the Century.* On that cover, disembodied hands grasped prison bars, which reminded me of Number Six in *The Prisoner.* The song "Asylum" really spoke to me. It made me realize that I wasn't the only one afraid to be locked away in a white padded cell.

I soon discovered that music could help me express my fears, my loneliness, and the sadness I felt, so I bought a tape recorder to create my own mixes. The tracks pacified the anxiety I felt from the barrage of assaults my classmates hurled at me and reminded me that I did, in fact, exist.

When everyone was out of the house, I'd hesitantly sit at the piano in our living room. All of my siblings were offered lessons, but I wasn't. As I attempted to play, the gentle high notes and the deep vibration of the low notes soothed me. When I tried to play a chord of two or three notes at the same time, the harmonies were magical and sparked a tiny light in my void. Many notes followed as I improvised, expressing my longing and my solitude. With pen and paper in hand and figuring out the scales by ear I composed at the age of twelve my first pieces of music. Excited, I got my cassette player and recorded them, hoping that, someday, I could my find my voice.

Chapter 4

WHERE THERE'S SMOKE . . .

"Let's get you to the kitchen sink," Mom said as she led me into the room. When I kneeled on a chair in front of the sink, Mom instructed me to lean my head down.

I was fifteen, and I didn't wash my hair. It was curly and oily and all over the place. I hated showers; I only took baths at home. At school, I had to take off my glasses for swim class, but I wouldn't shower in the locker room because the boys would push me and pummel me with their bars of soap. "Ha! Look at his teeny weiner!" Ashamed, I'd turned toward the wall to take off my bathing suit. I hated my body.

At this time in my life, I reeked with body odor because I didn't wash myself and the polyester shirts I wore would get saturated with sweat. I didn't mind the acrid smell; it reminded me that I actually existed. I also didn't brush my teeth and was deadly afraid of the dentist, so I just stopped going.

One time during a school bus trip to New York City, we stopped at a roadside restaurant in the middle of the night, and I bought a glazed chocolate donut with a creamy filling. *This should keep the nightmares away,* I assured myself. But when I bit into the donut, something grinded against my teeth. At first, I thought it was a pebble, but when I spat it out, I saw that it was a yellowish-brown tooth—my tooth. I'd broken a tooth. Paralyzed, I held my breath and waited to feel the inevitable searing pain. But nothing happened. *This doesn't make sense.*

When I returned from the bus trip, my mom took me to the dentist for an emergency appointment. "I can't do anything for him," the dentist sighed. "He has more than thirty cavities. The damage is too severe so I'll refer you to a periodontal surgeon."

My body was slowly rotting away. I had four appointments, one for each quadrant of my mouth. Sitting for hours in the dental chair, I brought my cassette player and headphones and held on for dear life with Electric Light Orchestra's "Can't Get It Out of My Head" playing. With the song's mix of classical instruments, choirs, and rock, I disconnected myself from the procedure.

During my high school years, I dreaded each day. I never knew what sort of abuse I'd receive. It could be anything from the sting of spitballs hurled at me, the pain of being shoved in the hallway, or the anguish brought on by insults and mocking nicknames. For instance, "Hey, chicken! Did you jerk off again today?" I was the butt of everyone's jokes.

I hated being forced to participate in team sports because I was always picked last, if at all. "Ah, we don't want him. You take him!" The only sport I liked was wrestling, which I was pretty good at thanks to the experience I'd gained fending off my brothers' attacks.

"I don't want to go to school anymore!" Tears flowed down my cheeks as I pleaded at my mother's bedside. "I can't. I can't!"

"Talk to your counselor," she answered.

As I sat in the counselor's office, I tried to give some example of the bullying. Raising one eyebrow, he looked at me with disdain and said, "Be a man and fight back! Stand up to those bullies!"

As I left his office and headed down the stairwell to my next class,

I felt a sharp pain in my back. "Hey, you greasy jerk-off chicken, you lost a feather!"

I looked over my shoulder to see Francis, the slick, blond-haired, blue-eyed resident bully, like Malfoy in the Harry Potter series. He was relentless with the verbal assaults and taunts.

But this time, I couldn't take it anymore, so I took my counselor's advice. I stopped, turned around, grabbed Francis by the lapels, and slammed him against the wall. With my eyes burning with rage, my face red-hot, and my ears filled with the pounding of rushing blood, I screamed, "STOP IT! STOP IT!"

When he fought back, I shoved him even more vigorously and shrieked right in his face, "LEAVE ME ALONE YOU FUCKING BASTARD!"

White as a sheet with his mouth open, he gasped for air like a fish out of water. I was trembling, but he was shaking even harder. He became as limp as a rag doll, then he looked down and nodded. For the first time, I felt a lovely warmth inside me and a new serenity as I finally let go of him. *This is what victory feels like!*

As we made our way down the stairs, I apologized to Francis for my use of force. "You know, this wasn't even my idea; it was the counselor's," I admitted with guilt.

Just then, he stopped and stared me down. On his face, I recognized the look my brothers gave me when they were about to attack. In a flash, he slammed me against the wall. It was over. I'd lost again.

Feeling betrayed and shrinking to nothingness, I didn't return to class and left the school. I had no one to turn to. *No one understands what I'm going through.* When I reached the sidewalk, I saw a bus coming. *Maybe if I jump in front of it, the pain will stop.* I took a step off the curb, but the driver honked and I moved back. I was drifting, empty from the bullying, and I couldn't face my mom or my brothers.

Somehow, I ended up downtown in a record shop, browsing frantically for music. Sweaty and my life being sucked away, I felt an urgent need to fill my void, so I reached out for a cassette tape. Its smooth and cold plastic wrapping felt good in my hands and made me feel like I existed. Like a robot, I absentmindedly pocketed it. Suddenly, there was a presence I could hold on to. I walked up and down the aisles, mechanically taking more cassettes. When my pants pockets were full, I bent down and stuck them in my socks. I experienced no feelings—not even pleasure—and when the security guard caught me, I just followed him to his office.

"Empty your pockets," he sternly ordered.

Me being the Silent Good Boy, I obeyed and put five or six cassette tapes on his desk.

When he saw that I wasn't fighting back, he continued politely. "OK, that's fine. Thanks. I don't think we have too much to worry about."

But much to his surprise and chagrin, I leaned over and emptied my socks for a total of a dozen cassettes. "Oh man, that's too much— way too much," he said with a very sad look on his face. "I'm sorry, but I have to call the cops. It's store policy."

Even after hearing that, I still didn't feel anything.

The officers came in full uniform, sat me in the back seat of their car, and then locked me in a cell. Sitting alone on the wooden bench, I looked at the graffiti on the dirty green walls. One read, "Die, you fucker! Die!" *Yes, I wish I did!*

After Mom came and got me, I had to go to court and apologize for my wrongdoings. The judge ordered me to write an essay on why what I'd done was wrong. I thanked him and apologized again. We never spoke about it at home. I was the Silent Good Boy, and that was how I had to remain.

The following weekend, Dad came to pick up me and my brothers for lunch, as he'd been regularly doing since the divorce. He always gave us some pocket money, but this time, he slipped me a couple extra bills. "Go buy yourself some music, son," is all he said, but it still didn't fill the void. After previously following in his footsteps to work hard, I adopted another one of his habits and bought my first pack of cigarettes.

Hidden from view behind the school, the first time I lit up, I collapsed in a violent coughing fit. I could barely breathe and felt like I was going to vomit. But after a few more puffs—presto—all my pain, shame, and the void miraculously disappeared. *It works! It fucking works!*

As a smoker, I was suddenly seen as cool, and the bullying stopped. At lunchtime, I got out my cigarettes and played cards with the other troublemakers. I was living the lifestyle of the school's ruling class. Francis, the staircase bully, was an elite member of this gang. When he saw me light up a cigarette, his eyes opened wide. "You want one?" I offered.

"Yeah, sure," he said. Then he invited me to sit at his table and join in a game of cards with the other bullies. I still wasn't part of the IN crowd, but I was definitively out of the OUT crowd.

At home, I hid my cigarettes to maintain my image. By this time, my brothers had turned our former playroom in the basement into their exclusive den. The deafening beats of Black Sabbath's "Iron Man," Led Zeppelin's "Stairway to Heaven," and King Crimson's "Red" shook the foundation of our home. Clouds of smoke filtered through the closed door, and the smell of weed made its way upstairs. Screams and banging doors ensued as Mom confronted them. Nothing changed as denial and lies were the golden rules of our family. Ignorance is bliss.

I decided to try some myself, thinking that it might cure my emptiness. After buying some from a neighbor, I locked myself in my room, I lit up and my senses went into overdrive. I choked and coughed with such violence that the room spun around. The lights on the ceiling exploded like fireworks as Jimi Hendrix's "Purple Haze" made my eardrums bleed. I lost my balance and stumbled onto the bed as the room spun faster and faster. *Up, up . . . I gotta get up!* I was so dizzy my insides were reaching up my throat. *Oh shit, I'm going to puke!* My vision blurred, my eyes shifted left, left, left. Then I fell on my knees and threw up. I spent the next few hours with my head in the toilet, feeling abandoned and alone. When I tried weed again a few weeks later, the same thing happened, hopeless, I concluded that it wasn't for me.

During this time, my life was an abstraction. My first hint of salvation came when I discovered like-minded souls in the warped, satirical humor of the British TV series *Monty Python's Flying Circus.* Like the show's characters, I could be in one world for a few minutes and then have an exploding penguin interrupt my reality and create a new one.

After that came a European comic strip about Philémon, a young boy who slipped under and over the frames of the pages, literally breaking free of his reality. Fred, the comic strip's creator, used secret portals, mythological creatures, and vintage engravings in his art, much like Terry Gilliam did in *Monty Python.* Inspired, I bought some paper, pencils, and black ink and set out to create my own stories.

Invigorated by this new possibility, I entered an art supply store and bought brushes, paints, and canvas boards. Using flat colors, I painted *Murky Eye,* a surrealist blue-and-white bull's-eye with tentacles surrounded by more tentacles but none of them connecting. And then, fascinated by the vibrations and beauty of color, I created geometric patterns with gradients of colors in *Vibration Tree.*

My body rejected drugs, but art opened my eyes to a new reality.

Chapter 5

THE RETURN OF MR. CROOKED TEETH

At sixteen, the legal age to be employed in Canada, my first official summer job was at an outdoor swimming pool. The summer of 1976 was warm and sunny. The maple trees were filled with an abundance of green leaves, their branches dancing in the gentle breeze. It felt good. Everyone was happy to have a chance to cool down in the water.

I was proud yet nervous about my first paid job because I didn't know how to interact with people. Luckily, all I needed to do was hand them a basket for their clothes, take it back, and give them a token. But more importantly, I didn't have to wear a swimsuit. Still ashamed of my body, I was content to stand behind a counter. The cloakroom where I worked was dark, damp, and smelly, but earning money felt good—until the kids came.

"Hey piggy, give me a basket. It stinks in your pigsty." The ritual was always the same: a group of middle school-age boys came in with only one thing in mind—to make trouble. In addition to their off-color remarks, they twirled their wet towels and whipped them in my direction. Even though they were younger than me, I couldn't defend myself as I feared bullies. I was stuck. I couldn't avoid their beady, predatory eyes, their raucous laughter, and their taunting, high-pitched voices.

Like a pack of hyenas, they encircled me. Then, sensing my weakness, they launched their attacks. I felt their eyes and their foul breath scarring my soul. I was cornered in the cloakroom with no way out. Lucky for me, they eventually got bored and left. But I knew they'd be back the next day or the next week. Feeling powerless, I sank deeper and deeper into the bottomless abyss, that void of emptiness in my soul.

After taking months of abuse, I moved inside to work at the skating rink when the pool closed for the winter. Stinky socks and soggy winter boots lathered with melting slush became my new companions. The hyenas also came in from the cold. This time when they hurled insults, chewing gum wrappers, and other garbage my way, I ignored them. Armed with my cassette player, Supertramp's "School" soothed me with its beautifully haunting harmonica and "Dreamer" helped me slip away to an alternate reality.

During my breaks, I was able to escape my dreary cavern by hopping across the hall to the snack bar. There, I discovered the pleasure of hot dogs served with raw onions and coleslaw. The buns, steamed along the wieners were spongy white substance that squishes in your mouth. A delight!

After a few months, I graduated to become the lone sales clerk at the snack bar. I filled myself to my heart's content with soggy hot dogs and orange julep drinks, a local specialty. I cut onions, changed cola tanks, made coffee, and filled the candy stalls. Because there was no cash register, I also had to handwrite all the sales, then at closing time, I cleaned up and tallied the money. I loved my new responsibilities and enjoyed the smiling customers.

The hyenas came back, but this time I had leverage. If they mistreated me, I could ignore them or deny them service. Once they understood this, we settled into a sort of détente—an unspoken armistice—a cold war peace accord inside the freezing skating rink, which I thought was very fitting.

And then Mr. Crooked Teeth started showing up at the rink. I'd seen him around there before. He was always carrying brooms or buckets, so I assumed he was the rink's janitor. I had no hard feelings toward him because, basically, I had no feelings. He seemed charming and kind when he'd hang around the counter.

My daily routine went smoothly until one night when someone banged on the closed metal curtain surrounding the snack bar after closing time.

"Hey, let me in. I'm really hungry." I recognized Crooked Teeth's voice.

"You can't come in. We're closed," I insisted. I had already cleaned up and was tallying the cash and filling out the deposit sheet.

But the pounding became insistent. "Ah, come on, man. You won't let your ol' pal die of hunger, would ya?" He walked around and jiggled the service door then began beating on it with his fist. "Ah, come on. Just let me in."

Annoyed, I went toward the back door and said, "Look, I'm sorry but—"

Suddenly, he was in my face. He had forced his way in. "I just wanna buy a snack," he grumbled as he reached for a miniature pie, babbling like an idiot.

"You have to get out right now!"

But he ignored me and opened the pie box while cracking jokes and offhand remarks. After taking a bite of the pie, he pushed the rest in my face. "Ah, come on. You know you like it!"

I stepped back, speechless, with pieces of crust and jelly stuck to my face. Without saying a word, I turned to the sink, grabbed a cloth, and wiped my face.

He just laughed, like it was all a big joke. "Wasn't it good for you?" Seeing that I wasn't playing along, he threw a few coins on the floor and left.

Numb with fear, I walked to the back door and made sure it was closed and locked. Then I swept up the mess and returned to my deposit slip. But the numbers no longer added up. *There are four twenty-dollar bills instead of five. I must've miscounted.* I double-checked, recalculated, and sealed the deposit envelope. I folded my apron and took a look around to make sure everything was clean. Satisfied, I lit up a cigarette, hesitated by the door, then turned off the lights. I wanted to scream, but no sound came out. There was just a void—a cold, empty void like the room itself. Darkness.

The following day, I told my boss I didn't want to work there anymore. "I can't handle the kids hassling me," I lied.

"Money is missing from yesterday's sales. The numbers don't add up," was his only response.

"I counted twice and got a different amount each time. The second time, I counted four twenties instead of five, and your friend came in while I was closed." Yes, my boss and Crooked Teeth were friends. I'd often seen them joking together.

My boss smiled slyly as if he knew something. "Well, count better, and don't let the kids bother you."

I left his office and never returned to the rink.

Chapter 6

CASSANDRA

By the time I was out of the hell that was high school, my brothers and sister had already moved out and the family home was sold. At age seventeen, I was living alone with my mom. I tasted freedom when I started a two-year program of fine arts classes at Jean-de-Brébeuf College in the Fall of 1977.

Attending college was an entirely different experience for me. I had inspiring teachers, made colorful, new friends, and, best of all, shared classes with women. Their long flowing hair, handmade tin jewelry, and ankle-length, earth-toned skirts smelling of incense and sandalwood hypnotized me. Everyone there smiled and seemed really happy. For the first time in my life, I experienced a new feeling: peace.

In my first painting class, Claude, our young, frizzy-haired professor, had us set up our easels and stools in a circle. "Welcome to Painting 101," he said. "Painting is about color and expression. Together, we will explore that magical space where you tell a story."

I picked up the brush and was surprised by how thick its beige bristles were. *This looks wonderful,* I thought joyously to myself.

"I want to get to know each of you, so our first theme is open. Just choose a feeling and explore it on the paper," Claude instructed.

My spirit tumbled. This was the first time anyone had ever expressed an interest in my feelings. My whole life, I'd lived in a state of terror, afraid and lonely, and I didn't know how to express any of those feelings. Then a song came to mind: "Un Musicien Parmi Tant d'Autres" by Quebecois group Harmonium, which talks about the need to listen to children. But my child's heart was empty, and in my head, only one simple thought arose: *I have nothing to say.*

With everyone else busily painting, I dipped my brush in black paint and swept a few thick, vertical lines that looked like prison bars down the paper. I left the rest of the sheet empty.

My next class was art history. Bernadette, or "Belle-nadette," as I soon called her, was my teacher. An ex-nun, she was short and stout with salt-and-pepper hair coiffed in a boyish cut, and her voice was soft and warm like a fleece blanket. Her blue eyes sparkled like sapphires, and she made Roman mosaics come alive. She was the beloved aunt I never had.

Later, when she led the nude model class, I confided in her: "I'm not sure I can do this." I had never seen a woman naked.

"You'll do fine," she reassured. "Don't worry!"

As the first model entered the studio, my heart pounced. Dressed in a blue velvet bathrobe, she reminded me of the negligee woman from my childhood paper route. *This is not the same,* I told myself, urging my heart to slow down. As she walked closer to the stage, my mind wandered to the first time I became aware that women were acutely different from men. It happened last summer while I was working at the pool.

I was in the cloakroom, and by this time, the hyenas were under my control. Impressed that I had cigarettes, they asked to bum one. "No way! Now get outta my sight before I tell your parents." I felt a brief respite as the smoke twirled in the air. It seemed like I would have a good summer after all—and then Cassandra showed up.

She sat at the reception desk and was maybe a few years older than me. Her golden locks flowed all the way down her back. Her sky-blue eyes shined as she laughed and giggled with the other girls. I tried to look at her but hid as soon as she looked in my direction. *If only I could speak to her.* Just then, as if on cue, Rod Stewart's gravelly voice on "The First Cut Is the Deepest" echoed on my tape player and unlocked something inside me. My hormones suddenly kicked in like a meteor crashing into the earth.

Before I knew what was happening, she was standing right in front of me. My heart stopped when she spoke. "Hey, Guy, I need a favor. You're bilingual, right?" When I nodded, she continued, "Can you translate this for me?" She handed me the lyrics to the 10cc's song "I'm Not in Love."

I stared blankly at the sheet of paper even though I wanted to look at her. "Uh, yeah, sure." While sitting next to her, I got a whiff of her lavender shampoo. I ached to reach out, caress her luxurious hair, and plunge into the pool of her eyes.

"Um," I stammered, "how 'bout giving me your . . . um . . . number so I can let you know when I'm done translating it. . . . If that's OK with you."

"Sure," she agreed as she wrote it down and handed me the piece of paper.

It was my golden ticket to her heart—I was sure of it. I dialed her number multiple times but always hung up after the first ring. *What am I gonna say? Nobody likes me.* But by the end of the summer, I was desperate, so I let it ring.

"Hi Cassandra, it's Guy from the pool."

"Oh, yes. Hi."

Dumbstruck, I had no idea what to say next.

"Why are you phoning?" Cassandra asked. When I said nothing, she added, "Are you still there?"

I choked on my unspoken words, words of love I yearned to shower her with. Hesitantly, I finally said, "Well, uh, would you like to meet?"

"What do you have in mind?"

I had no idea. Because I'd never witnessed my parents touching or showing any affection toward each other, my only role models came from romantic movies such as *Love Story*. All I could think of was walking in the park, hand in hand, by the moonlight, "I don't. . . . well, we can. . . . like the park . . . ," I mumbled then went silent again.

"Are you still there? OK. Sorry, but I've gotta go now. Bye." And with that, she hung up.

With the receiver in my hand, the sound of the dial tone was the only sign of life left. It was like my heart had been ripped out of my chest. I felt so utterly alone in the world. I looked outside the window. It was an incredibly hot and humid night without even the slightest breeze. *I need a smoke—NOW!* I stepped outside and lit up, but it didn't stop my descent into the pits of pain. *I need to escape!* I jumped on my bike and pedaled as fast as possible to Mont Royal Park—affectionately nicknamed "the Mountain"—the highest point in Montreal. Covered in sweat and out of breath, I reached the lookout where a few cars were parked for the view.

With my heart still pounding inside my chest, I let my bicycle fall to the ground. Then I stepped over the railing at the edge of the precipice, lit a cigarette, and sat down on the cold metal. Tourist were likely marveling at the panoramic view, while I searched in vain for myself in the tapestry of lights and colors. *I don't belong anywhere.* Dangling precariously over the edge, I was a few inches from falling into oblivion.

Is my life really worth living? I began uncurling my fingers from the railing. *Maybe if I let go, I'll be happy—like Yuri Gagarin on my swing.* I got up, let go, and flew through the air. *Free at last! I'm free at last!!*

But only for a second. At the last moment, I grabbed the railing, which made an awful shrill moan and almost came unhinged as I cut myself.

Staring at my bloodied fingers, I thought *Who am I kidding? I'm such a loser that I can't even kill myself.* I lit another cigarette, inhaled deeply, and held the smoke in to blot out yet another day of excruciating pain. But my hormones had other plans and reared their ugly head weeks later.

While lazily relaxing in bed in my warm flannel pajamas, I peered out my bedroom window. The autumn landscape was rich with a multitude of yellows, oranges, and reds, the colors a balm to my heart. A cold breeze wafted into the room as the sparrows outside sang a tune. Suddenly, I felt the urge to pee, and between my legs, I was surprised by a stiffness. My hands found their way between my legs and stayed on the warmth. It felt soothing.

As my fingers slid up and down, I felt a mixture of pain and pleasure. An electric current traveled up my spine, setting my shoulders aflame as my legs squirmed around. My hands accelerated their vigorous caress until a searing wave of velvety fire instantly spread from my navel to the ends of every hair and toe. I let out a moan as my body convulsed with pleasure, the likes of which it had never known, and then gave way to a quiet rest of fulfillment.

To my horror, a gluey milky substance stuck my fingers and torso together. Disgusted, I panicked and frantically wiped my hands. *OFF! OFF! OFF!* Ashamed of myself, I snuck into the bathroom and scrubbed myself with a washcloth as hard as I could. *I've got to get rid of this horrible thing and this repugnant, sour smell of rotting cheese.* I felt dizzy and began retching, so I knelt down at the toilet, but nothing came up.

Back in my room, I hid my soiled pajamas under my bed and pulled the cold sheets over my head, scared and confused. *It must be that THING—sperm, sex. I hate it! I hate you for having this!* I thought as I slapped my body.

But over the next few weeks, my hormones only intensified, and eventually, I had to get over my revulsion. But the shame, guilt, and disgust remained. I despised myself for experiencing pleasure. *I'm dirty and bad, and I'd be better if I cut it off!*

"Is everyone ready?" Belle-nadette's gentle voice brought me back to reality as she invited the nude model—a woman in her forties—to walk up to the podium. "Now place your thumb toward the model, and measure, like so. Everyone try it now."

The model took off her bathrobe and calmly folded it at her feet. Mortified, I hid behind my easel to avoid looking at her. I stared at the other students to see how they were reacting so I could do the same. They held their thumbs toward the model as instructed, then measured and drew marks on their papers. "View the human figure as a whole. Find the one central movement and let it flow on your paper," Belle-nadette added.

I must do something, but I don't know. I don't know. My heart raced. *I have to at least try.* So I dared to look up and saw her. She was standing just a few steps away from me, posed with both her arms raised in the air as if she were in a dancing ballerina pose. I glanced at her breasts and her dark nipples then moved my gaze down her belly to her mysterious, black pubic hair. I was paralyzed. *I can't draw this!*

Belle-nadette tiptoed over and looked at my snow-white sheet. When she gently put her hand on my shoulder, I felt her kindness and her warmth relaxed me. She whispered, "Just let go, Guy. You're doing great!" It was the first positive thing any teacher had ever told me.

I took a deep breath, picked up the charcoal, and drew the first line of my new life. I still remember that Queen's love anthem "Somebody to Love" was blasting from an adjacent studio. On that day, as I stopped hiding behind my easel, I dared to make a wish: *Please find me somebody to love.*

Chapter 7

CATHERINE

Each morning, as soon as I stepped off the bus on my way to campus, I lit up a cigarette to numb my shyness. I enjoyed getting to know my new classmates, but I just didn't know how to behave. *They'd hate me if they knew how disgusting I am.*

I soon got into a routine of stopping by the cafeteria on my way to class and getting a cup of coffee. I never understood why my dad always started his morning with that awful beverage. I hated the smell and didn't dare taste it. But after seeing so many other students drinking it, I decided to give it a shot. *It's not so bad with lots of sugar and milk. It's almost like a bitter hot chocolate,* I convinced myself. It also gave me energy. It was the perfect combination: I smoked to calm my nerves and numb my fears and drank coffee to make me work. *I'm more like Dad than I thought!*

And as a hard worker like my dad, I diligently completed all my assignments and artwork. Claude taught us sfumato—Leonardo da Vinci's shading technique—and the abstract gestural explosions of Jackson Pollock. But the artist whose work inspired me the most was Dutch impressionist Vincent van Gogh. Sure, there was the famous story about him cutting off his own ear, but as I gushed to a classmate, "His work is amazing—so real, so full of bright colors. And the passion in his brushstrokes—they seem to dance off the canvas!" Then I shut up, afraid I had said too much.

But then Claude stumped me. "OK, Guy, van Gogh did many self-portraits, so now it's your turn."

Shit, I panicked. *I can't do this. They'll see me for who I really am!* I excused myself to go to the bathroom, but instead, I stepped outside for a cigarette. *I have to do this,* I told myself. *It's why I'm here.* With my nerves calmed, I rejoined the class. Everyone was already sketching on their boards. I thought about the geometrical paintings I'd done prior to beginning art school and could at least say that they represented who I am. So my first self-portrait was a robot-like figure made with impersonal and flat primary and secondary colors.

Later in the year, that self-portrait came back in the form of a large woodprint. Like a monster he'd been locked away behind bars with a "NO POSTING" sign. Even in sculpture, he showed up two feet tall (60 cm) and standing straight as a soldier in armor. But when we were asked to create a full body figure, I sculpted a thick, green, muscular figure with a missing arm. He was crouching down and trying to get up with his head bowed. I was this sad, defeated Hulk.

Even though I did get along with my classmates, I worked alone in a corner of the room even when they invited me out to the local pub, La Maisonée. When I did take them up on the offer, I'd sit at the end of the table and chain-smoke, not knowing how to chat. I'd order the cheapest draft beer they had, thinking, *I'm not worth the money.* And if I did loosen up and have more than three drinks, I'd inevitably throw up in the bathroom. Too shy to leave, I'd wait around until everyone else left or simply disappear without saying goodbye. The next day, I'd invariably suffer from a throbbing headache and my mouth would taste as if I'd been chewing cigarette butts. *My body has zero tolerance for drugs, and I can barely stomach alcohol.*

I was absolutely clueless when it came to interacting with women. Males had bullied me in the past, so in a way, I knew how to be around them—as a victim. I ached for connection, but I was guilt-ridden by my own sexuality. Love and sex were so totally foreign to me that I often became enamored of my female classmates without ever even having a conversation with them. I dreamed of embracing them, gazing into their eyes, and having their smiles envelop my body. But I never imagined having sex with them. My love was ethereal and limitless, and each infatuation crushed my soul.

I wrote this poem on December 27, 1978:

One night
There was this boy
Alone in his room.
He was still
With no friends,
No love,
Just heartbroken.
He was there
Feeling low
Feeling down.
Where could he go?
He didn't know.
He was there,
Sitting at his desk,
Writing to himself
'Cause it was the only way
He could talk with somebody else.
He came to this world alone,
And maybe
He would leave, still alone.
The phone rang

But it was not for him,
Still not for him.
He is waiting,
Waiting for love,
For somebody to understand,
For someone who'll understand him.
His heart is heavy.
His heart is crying.
But there's nobody to hear it.
So he is there, sitting, writing,
Alone, and he is waiting, waiting, waiting.

Catherine—with her freckly face, sandy hair, green eyes, and high cheekbones—was one of my infatuations. Her smile was radiant, and I bathed in her light. *How could I ever be worthy of such a goddess?* On the last day before spring break, knowing that the school year was almost over, I thought to myself, *I'm going to lose her forever.* That day, I sat next to her on a bench outside the art history classroom and summoned up the courage to ask, "So, what are you doing over break?" I couldn't even hear her reply because my heart was thumping like a jackhammer. As I hunched over staring at my shoes, like an unexpected lightning strike, I suddenly heard myself say, "I love you."

Although I heard the words come out of my mouth, I didn't know what they meant. It just happened. My heart stopped, frozen. I couldn't look up.

"That's nice. Thank you," Catherine kindly responded.

Petrified, I was speechless and disappeared within the swirling patterns of the green linoleum floor. After an awkward moment of silence, Catherine leaned over and embraced me with a hug. "Is this what you want?" I went into shock and stopped breathing. I had never been touched before.

I left my body.

Is she still there? I didn't know.

Then, after a while, she gently let go, stood up, and walked away. The tapping of a broomstick on my shoe reminded me that I was still at school. I looked up and saw the janitor. "I have to lock up the building," he said.

I walked home, but home was not safe. It never felt safe. So I left right away and wandered aimlessly through the dark snowy streets of Montreal. Night had fallen, but for hours I walked with no direction, no aim, no desires. I simply felt as if I didn't exist.

As the harsh cold wind stung my face, the name of a classmate popped into my mind. *Louis. I'll walk over to his place.* Why him? I didn't know. I didn't know his address. I didn't even have his phone number. I just knew that he lived far outside town.

I had to cross the huge Jacques Cartier Bridge to get to the other side of the river where Louis lived. High above the water, the bridge shook menacingly as cars sped across at high speeds. After making it safely to the other side, I found a phone booth with a tattered directory and searched for Louis's last name. There was only one listing, so I dialed it. One, two, three rings, then his mother answered. *He's home.* "Hey, Guy! What are you doing over here? Would you like to come over? Can we come and get you?"

Louis and his parents welcomed me in their home and offered me supper as we sat and talked. We drank beer, smoked cigarettes, and listened to French songwriter Jacques Brel. We sang "J'arrive," which is about dying. This song resonated deep inside my core because I felt like I was on my last journey, like I was dying.

Well past midnight, Louis's parents went to bed, but he and I continued listening to music. Around four o'clock in the morning, I felt myself ever so gently returning to my body, and I finally drifted off to sleep.

The morning sun's blinding reflection on the immaculate white snow roused me from my slumber. From my makeshift bed, I broke off the filter of a cigarette and lit up. The first inhalation felt like swallowing razor blades. I coughed out my lungs, waking up Louis. The second puff went down like velvet as I felt the buzz of nicotine calming my nerves. *I'm back.*

Louis prepared some espresso in the kitchen, and I was finally able to open up to him. "It's about Catherine," I confessed.

He just listened without asking questions. When his family joined us, we all pitched in to make breakfast. I didn't know this sort of thing was possible—a family sharing and laughing together. They all drove me back home and gave me big hugs. Little did they know that they had just saved my life. That morning, I wrote a poem called *"Quest to Find the Truth"*:

> *It's only those who know*
> *That will find the way*
> *And only those who despair*
> *That will first disappear.*
> *But I am one of those*
> *Who will find a way*
> *To succeed in their search,*
> *Their quest to find the truth,*
> *To find their beginning,*
> *And understand their end.*

***

During the long and hot summer nights after graduation, I became a night owl. My favorite hangout was Le Funambule, a jazz café in Le Quartier Latin, the heart of Montreal's French Canadian culture. This part of the city had preserved the traditions of France, where you'd hear the *Pssshhhhht* of steamed espresso and taste delectable cream-filled pastries. I delighted in the nutty aroma of a large bowl cup of café au lait and a delicious mille-feuille.

The soft lighting illuminated the black-and-white-framed photos decorating the beige walls, which surrounded about twenty small, square tables with old wooden chairs. The dilapidated oak floor cracked under my feet, but the café played wonderful jazz music. Whenever I arrived on my bicycle around eleven p.m., the place would always be full. I felt safe in the anonymity of strangers. They made no demands of me and had no expectations of interaction.

Within the smoky club, I discovered the fascinating rhythms of the Dave Brubeck Quartet's famous piece "Take Five" and the dazzling, melancholic piano improvisations from Keith Jarrett's album *Köln Concert*. Jazz soothed me as I lit up one cigarette scrutinizing the complex rococo patterns from the smoke. *Is this all I am,* I wondered, *smoke and ashes?*

On one particular lonely Friday night in August I opened my sketchbook and wrote:

> *What is my life*
> *Compared to love?*
> *What is my life*
> *Compared to beauty?*
> *What is my life*
> *Compared to living?*
> *What is my life*
> *If I can't even live it?*

Each word I inscribed was a plank of the raft on which I was stranded, sailing on an endless sea of solitude. And as I kept writing, I discovered a new ally: my journal. My first wave of emotions came as my longing for love threatened to drown me. I revealed my secret dreams of love and wiped away the tears of my disillusions: Cassandra,

Catherine, Sylvie, Dominique, and all the other classmates whom I'd passionately loved from afar over the last two years, each one like a dagger plunged into my heart.

Then a second wave of fervor came as I denounced in my journal all that I hated about society. At nine years old, I watched Neil Armstrong walk on the moon. I was awed by the new reaches of humankind, but even at that young age, I asked my mother, "Why send people to the moon when half the planet is starving?" At twelve years old my stomach churned at the photos of nine-year-old Kim Phuc running nude under America's napalm bombing of Vietnam and Buddhist monk Thich Quang Duc setting himself on fire in the streets of Saigon. *The world is a sick place!*

I couldn't make sense of all of these things. Gandhi and Martin Luther King Jr. practiced nonviolence, yet they were assassinated. I was disgusted with apartheid in South Africa while Nelson Mandela was rotting in jail. I even made a stop apartheid badge that I wore alongside my peace and love pin.

The hippies, with their flower power and free love, where are they today? I wondered. *Where has all the love gone? And why is there so much violence?* I didn't trust adults as a child, but now I *was* an adult. To me, Margaret Thatcher and Ronald Reagan were on the bow of a conservative ship, and the English punk rock band Sex Pistols were pirates, counterattacking with their "God Save the Queen" cannonball. *How can I trust the authorities with all of these atrocities? Do I really belong in this kind of society?*

I paused from my writing and took out the book I'd just finished reading, Robert Heinlein's 1961 novel *Stranger in a Strange Land*. It was the story of Valentine Michael Smith, a man from Mars who brought to Earth a message of universal love. But he didn't use the word *love*; he used *grok*. He defined it as being in sync with another's feelings, whether good or bad; a pure, untainted state of complete empathy.

Yes, that's it! That's exactly how I feel and who I am. I was raised in a no-man's-land, and I always felt like a stranger in a strange land. Now I know why! I want to spread grok like Valentine and bring love to this world!

Those were the last words I wrote as I closed my journal in the early morning hours. It was five a.m., and my empty pack of cigarettes, full ashtray, and dried-up coffee bowls. The joyous chirps of sparrows greeted the day as I stepped out into the fresh morning air. I saddled my bicycle, and pedaled into the emerging pinkness of a new day. I thought about how I'd be starting at Concordia University in a few weeks and wondered if my mission of love could begin there.

Chapter 8

FIRST LOVE

In September 1979, I began a three-year program in studio arts at Concordia University, located on the busy streets of downtown Montreal. The Visual Arts Building—an ancient, converted garage made of concrete—offered four floors of studios, a cafeteria, and an art supply store. Every day, it buzzed with hundreds of students, young and old, from the city's varied cultural backgrounds, as well as foreigners from Europe and the Middle East. Some seemed as quiet as me, the Silent Good Boy, while others proudly showcased their spiky, brightly colored mohawks, tattoos, safety pins piercing their nose and ears, and tattered punk clothing.

Overwhelmed by all this new social input, I brought a portable cassette player with me to class to calm my anxieties. Even better, not only could we smoke during class, but a few teachers allowed us to drink wine. My painting teachers, Bob Murray and Yves Gaucher, encouraged a relaxed mood in their classrooms, where everyone was free to explore their own style, so I enjoyed jazz, cigarettes, and an occasional glass of red wine.

Even though I was writing in my journal quite often, I still felt like

I had nothing to say. The bright colors were painted flat—meaning without shadows or apparent brushstrokes—and the shapes were contoured with big, black lines. My painting of a book looked as if it had jumped right off the page of a comic, so with a flair for humor, I added the word **BOOK** to its cover in bold, black letters.

In drawing class, by this time, I was more comfortable with the nude model, and I dutifully followed the teacher's instructions while experimenting with new techniques, such as collage, and materials, including graphite sticks and black India ink.

But when working in sculpture, as soon as I plunged my hands into the cold, wet, slippery gray clay, my body tingled with joy. I experienced pure delight as it filled me with extreme, guiltless, sensuous pleasures.

At first, I sculpted a one-foot-tall torso inspired by Michelangelo's marble statues. With no arms, legs, or head, it leaned backward and passively sat there. After I learned how to make a cast from it, I coated it with an oil-based, black patina and polished it. I loved the result and the technique! There was no thinking or emotions involved. It was magical, like a restful meditation.

Through art, I experienced a rebirth of sorts. But when I'd started at Concordia, I had dreams of spreading grok throughout the world and experiencing true love, and that hadn't changed. Having just celebrated my twentieth birthday, my first attempt came one late November afternoon after the last class of the day was over. I walked around campus with Sasha instead of keeping to myself in the studio to paint.

With short, black hair and deep, hazelnut-colored eyes, Sasha was simply radiant and her laugh was like a trickle of fresh river water. As we sat on a small couch in the deserted corridor and talked about teachers, art, and music, she switched from revealing her soul to me with searing intensity to giggling hysterically at a moment's notice.

I felt light and excited next to her until, in a moment of silence, our eyes met and came to a rest. A soft wave of warmth embraced me as my hand delicately caressed her hair. She welcomed my touch and nestled in my arms, pressing her cheek against mine. After a moment that felt like an eternity, our faces turned so we were once again eye to eye. Her warm breath intoxicated me, and then the fullness of her lips pressed against mine. My first kiss was infinitely sweet.

But like Cinderella near the stroke of midnight, the incessant ticking of the clock on the wall beckoned us. "I have to catch the bus," she said, breaking the magical moment.

After hastily putting on our coats, I took her hand and we walked to the bus stop as the first snow began to fall. One last kiss, one last embrace, *another* last kiss, *another* last embrace, and then she was gone. I waved goodbye until the bus disappeared. Elated, with the snowflakes falling thick and fast, I imagined Tchaikovsky's "Waltz of the Flowers" and danced as if Sasha were still with me.

In the ensuing weeks, we often came back to our intimate hideout because Sasha lived with her family in the suburbs, so she couldn't meet me in the evenings during the week. But when her parents invited me to join them for Christmas dinner "Pleasure to meet you Guy" her mother warmly greeted me as she welcomed me with open arms. Sasha looked beautiful in her red velvet dress, and I sat together holding hands under the dinner table like a couple of giddy teenagers. That night, my heart shined brighter than the star atop the Christmas tree.

Weeks later when the winter session began, I was shocked when I realized that Sasha wasn't at school. Worried, I called her house. "Oh, hi Guy. Nice to hear from you," her mother said. "Sasha can't come to the phone right now, but I'll tell her that you called."

I phoned again and again, but her parents remained evasive. Finally, they explained, "Sasha had a breakdown, and she's been institutionalized."

When I heard that, it was if my heart had been placed into a vise that was being squeezed tighter and tighter. Luckily, her parents gave me permission to visit her. Sadly, it wasn't the first time I'd visited a mental ward. My brother Marc—the Joker, the whipping boy of my oldest brother, Luc—had also experienced a nervous breakdown. My heart broke to see him alone in his room as I knew all too well the painful feelings of solitude and despair. Still, it didn't prepare me for what happened when I visited Sasha.

As I entered the corridor, a sad array of wandering souls greeted me. In their faded gowns, the patients blended in with the institutional green of the hospital's empty walls. Every so often, moans and the *swoosh-swoosh* of dragging slippers interrupted the silence. Among the patients, I finally caught sight of Sasha.

As I approached her and said, "Hello, my love. It's me, Guy," she stepped back as if she barely recognized me.

"Oh, yes. Hello," she answered curtly in an empty monotone voice. Under heavy medication, a menacing frown replaced her smile as she repeatedly said with agitation, "You know they're coming! Did you see them? I'm sure they're here! They're coming for me!" I tried to reassure her, but she wouldn't reach my gaze. Her stare was cold, blank, and as empty as the bland walls. I reached out for her hand, but she backed away from me again. Tears came to my eyes as the pain in my chest choked me.

My first love melted right then and there, like dirty snow on a soiled winter boot, leaving a puddle of slush on the tile floor of the psychiatric ward. Sasha never came back to school and the snowflakes never waltzed for us again.

Alone in my bedroom, my pillow moist with tears, I had a lump in my throat as all the sadness tried to come out. I turned off the lights, lit a candle, and put on French singer Charles Aznavour's song *La Bohème*. His warm, soft vibrato loosened my pain as he sang about a poor artist in the Montmartre section of Paris. I saw myself in a frigid, empty loft, hungry and longing for love. I opened my journal and poured out my heart:

The Beginning of the End!

Once, so many times ago, there was this boy, man, this living thing searching for himself. He was alone, scared, in a world gone mad. But he didn't want to make his journey alone, so he searched for a mate, which he never found because he never realized that he was a loser from the start. But why is he living, still living, he doesn't understand, and he's going mad, mad because of the world that's devouring, destroying, killing him.

On and on he went, never finding what he was searching for: love. He thought he found it once, but he was fooled by his heart, by the one he would have given himself to. She got lost and never came back. He's such a loser.

Success, success, there was none for him. Everything he has ever attempted has failed—and always will—but why? Why? He has a heart of gold, his thoughts are for others, but nobody listens to him. When will they stop laughing? Friends? Sure, he's got some friends. But real friends? Friends who are there when he needs them? No, he doesn't have those kinds of friends. Friends to share life with? No. Where are they? Is he blind not to see them? Are they around him, but invisible to his eyes? I don't know? But I am this boy.

The world is going round and round, but why do I feel like I'm going the other way, like I'm looking in the wrong direction? I'm so trapped in myself that I'm separated from the world. Is life really what I'm living, or am I engulfed in my dreams? Am I like the dog who's trying to catch its tail, oblivious to the world around it? I feel alone, apart, separated from the world that I live in, but is that my own doing or is it a trap, a clause in the contract of life?

So many questions run through my mind during times of despair like this. Are they real questions? Can answers solve my misery (which is imposed by me)? Why do I care so much about my dear little life? Why do I have to be so selfish? Where are the others in my life? Am I really driving them away? Because of me, ME? Why? Why? If only I could cry, but what good would it do me? Ha! Life can be so miserable, but is that the gamble? Is that . . . "normal"? Ha! Me with my normality! Who's normal? I'm just fucking nuts—a super-egocentric, insane person. But who cares? I'm alone in this dumb world. Right? Right! Wrong! You're all wrong! Life is about sharing. Yeah! Yeah! But by whose fucking standards? Yeah, whose?

Ah, what the fuck! This is all there is to it. Life is to live it, and when the time comes, you die. It's just as simple as that. And that's what this young man's story is all about, life . . . and death.

I fell asleep as the record played repeatedly and the candle eventually burned out.

Back in the sculpture studio, I sought comfort by creating a new miniature clay bust to try out different poses. As I pushed and pulled to straighten it its abdomen ripped open. *This is how I feel.* I couldn't destroy my pain, but I was able to bury it in clay. I was so energized by this first win that I proposed a series of five figures that I'd call *Victory.* Each statue would be two to three feet tall (60 cm to 1 m) and would depict a naked man without genitals rising from defeat to victory. The entire ensemble, which would be about four feet wide (135 cm), would take me the rest of the school year to complete, so I immediately got to work.

The first figure lay on the ground. Defeated, deformed, and in agony, its head was turned to the side in supplication. *This is me,* I realized. The second one was on his knees, leaning back with his arms thrown behind him in desperation. He was pleading and on the verge of losing all hope. From the middle position, the third statue could pull the viewer in either direction: despair or victory. Sitting on his knees with his head tilted downward, he had strong legs and a muscular torso. He symbolized the choice of either standing up or giving up. His indecision paralyzed him.

The last two figures came together as one piece. The fourth man was standing up, with one leg pushing as the other knee was lifting off the ground. His face was daring as it peered from behind the last figure. The final figure stood fully erect, proud and strong, his left leg in front of him, the other behind. He was walking forward and looking up with his arms in the air as if shouting, "VICTORY!" Even without eyes to see, mouths to speak, hands to fight, or arms to push forward, the figures were still able to win their battles.

As with Valentine, my grok was to embody all emotions. On the one hand, like in the movie *Apocalypse Now*, we all have the ability to descend into our own living hell when faced with trauma and violence. On the other hand, like in *Rocky*, we also have the potential to rise up from pain and emerge victorious. *We have the power and freedom to choose.* Unconsciously, the writings of my journal suddenly came alive through my artworks "This is great, Guy! You did good work here!" John Ivor Smith, my sculpture teacher, said in his British accent. His kindness reminded me of Belle-nadette, even though he was twice her size and had huge earthy hands. He was the epitome of a gentle giant.

Later that day, he announced a public art competition that we could all take part in. He smiled and wished us good luck as he pinned the information on the bulletin board. It was for four outside sculptures and would take place in Rembrandt Park, in the Côte Saint-Luc borough, not far from the university.

The flyer said that the new sculptures must fit-in with their surroundings: a series of new apartment blocks. I scoped out the grounds like television detective Columbo investigating a crime scene. The residences were all made of concrete and had long protruding rectangular balconies. I thought of the children playing in the park and the families living in these geometric-shaped homes. *Wouldn't it be great if the kids had the same geometry? They'd perfectly match the buildings!*

And then I remembered the two-foot tall (60 cm) walking figure that I'd made in Brébeuf. *That's perfect!* I submitted a much larger version made of steel-reinforced concrete, and to my delight, it was selected.

I spent the summer like Tony Stark welding my Iron Man encased in a heavy protective metal mask, sweat pouring down my face. At the official unveiling, the sculpture stood strong at nine feet tall and three feet wide and deep (3 m x 1 m x 1 m) with a tiny cubic head atop his wide shoulders and long arms and legs.

I had unwittingly added a sixth figure to my *Victory* series. Like the others, this statue didn't have eyes or a mouth to see and denounce, but he did have strong arms and legs in motion. Because he was unstoppable, I named this statue *The Warrior*. My sculpture was featured in a magazine, and I celebrated the end of my first year of university on a high note, thinking, *I am a professional artist!*

Chapter 9

SEX AND ROCKABILLY

During my second year at Concordia I fell in love with ceramics because my teacher, David Dorrance, was a big proponent of humor, so I daringly broke through my "Silent Guy" persona and welcomed "Funny Guy."

I built a turntable with a melting record called *Daliphone* in honor of Spanish artist Salvador Dali. I re-created the iconic 1950s ice cream sundae in a tall glass with whipped cream and a cherry on top. When you lifted up the ice cream top, it revealed a small village, including a church with a tall spire, hence the whimsical title *Ice Cream Sunday*. Pushing my trompe l'oeil technique to its limit, I shaped a hyper-realistic, two-slice toaster, glazed it with 14-karat gold, and built a socle for it where a little figurine took a bath.

For my first group show in the university's gallery, I got audacious by combining real objects with my ceramic art installations. One example used a real single bed with linens included. Four human-sized clay tools lay beneath the sheets. The title *Ball & Kaolin & Talc & Silica*—all names of types of clay—was a spoof of the film *Bob & Carol*

& Ted & Alice, which was about open relationships. I had as much pleasure with the wordplay as I did creating the art.

I spent hours and hours working—including nights and weekends—with my radio and my smokes to keep me company. I'd lose track of time, leave the studio late on a Friday evening, and be surprised that there were so many people in the streets. Then I'd remember, *Oh, yes. It's Friday night.*

In the first days of December, as if nature was trying to shock me out of my fortress of solitude, a storm pounced on the city by dumping such an avalanche of snow that public transit had to shut down.

"Do you want a lift home?" Nan, a fellow student who often asked me for advice, generously offered when she realized that I was stuck at the school. She was petite, twelve years my senior, and had frizzy, dark hair that went halfway down her back. "Don't worry. I've got snow tires, and I'm in no hurry to get home. Besides, it's the least I can do to thank you for all your help."

Mom was away for the weekend, so when we got to my place, I invited Nan to come up for dinner. When we sat down at the table, the wind whistled and shook the windows as the storm intensified. Her car was already blanketed by a mountain of snow by the time I served coffee and dessert, but she wasn't fazed in the least. Making herself right at home, she turned down the lights and threw some pillows on the floor. "Do you have some music?" she asked.

I chose Andrés Segovia's classical Spanish guitar and lit some sandalwood incense. "My parents didn't want me to go to art school," she explained, "but after being in the workplace for so long, I decided to rediscover myself." At that point, she suddenly turned toward me and began caressing my chest.

What do I do? I panicked. After being starved for years for this kind of touch, I had no idea how to react. I was still a virgin and hated even thinking about sex. I remained motionless, except for my heart, which was speeding like a runaway train. As Nan unzipped my pants, she leaned over and whispered, "Shall we move to your bed?"

I guess I nodded because she took me by the hand and we undressed. In the dim light, I was awed by her body and shivered at the softness of her warm skin. She pushed me down on the bed and took hold of my penis. I was ashamed of its stiffening. She straddled me and inserted my penis between her thighs. *What am I supposed to do?* I wondered. *Should I move? Am I doing this right?*

She moaned as she grabbed my shoulders. I felt her move and dance, her hips going back and forth as she whispered, "Mmm . . . that feels good."

I kept silent as I felt a wave of heat approaching in my groin. I recognized it from my shameful prior experience with masturbation and didn't dare to move. *I can't do this—not to her, not here, not now.* But as if a switch suddenly turned on, a thousand prickly needles traveled throughout my body, and in one moment, a burning sensation shot through my penis as I ejaculated.

I dissolved in an ocean of warmth yet felt drowned in guilt. Still, I appreciated the silent calm that enveloped me and slowly welcomed it. But Nan put a dagger in my groin as she jumped out of bed, hollering, "Watch out for the sheets!" Then she urgently ran off to the bathroom to wash herself. It was just like I always thought *OFF! OFF! OFF! I've got to get rid of this horrible thing, this repugnant sour smell of rotting cheese.*

At this point, I knew for certain that sex is dirty. *Nan is dirty. I'm dirty. She must've known I was bad—a monster and a dirty stain on life.*

Even so, my relationship with Nan became a ritualistic cycle of washing, getting dirty with sex, and washing again. I learned to keep my shameful penis clean and never feel anything—no passion or intimacy. We ate and had sex but had nothing to talk about. I began to think that Heinlein was wrong in *Stranger in a Strange Land*: There was no such thing as grok. We were just two perfect strangers acting like perfect strangers.

My relationship with Nan died within in a few months, confirming what I already knew and thought deep in my soul: *I am bad, shameful, and dirty. I was born alone, and I will die alone. My life is hopeless.*

Working in ceramics started bringing me out of my shell, but I still struggled with drawing. As with my painting, I drew everyday objects, but after getting in touch with a more humorous side of myself with ceramics, a change began to occur. I discovered the vibrant colors of oil pastel and started drawing giant-sized pencils, playing cards, and snacks, extending them far beyond the reaches of the paper as if asking, "How much of an object can I show while still maintaining its identity?" Subconsciously, I was really asking, "How much of myself can I reveal while remaining safe and out of sight?" As I obsessively searched for an answer, my drawings exploded to a gargantuan thirteen feet (4 m) wide.

But rather than in the art studio, the answer came in the form of the campus radio station. Before ever entering Brébeuf College for art school, I envisioned myself studying music production so I could eventually work with bands in a recording studio. But I was scared and thought, *Who am I to do this?* Instead, I hosted a weekly radio show at Brébeuf. At Concordia, many of my classmates had formed rock bands, and I was burning to join them. In my gut, I ached to be on stage and let my fire come out. But I was too shy and didn't dare even talk about it. So I took a spot as a late-night DJ at the university's station, which broadcasted all over town. I shared the air with my new Swedish friend, Nils. Tall and skinny as a twig, he sported a blue, spiky mohawk, safety pins, and a generous smile. He thundered the airwaves with the Dead Kennedys and other punk rock bands, while I interwove ballroom music with 1950s rockabilly and '60s surf songs from the Beach Boys and the Ventures. And then a miracle happened when my two passions merged.

It started with a larger-than-life, head-to-tapping shoes portrait of award-winning ballroom dancer Arthur Murray and his wife. The background was radiant with pink-and-beige wavy stripes. Then, in black-and-white, I drew a humongous face of my hero, singer-song-writer Buddy Holly with his thick-rimmed glasses. His portrait stared back at me as if saying, "OK, Guy. Now that you've drawn me, what about you?"

I rummaged through old photos and found one of me at the tender age of six. *Do I dare put myself out there? What right do I have? I'm no one—a nobody.* But then I thought of *Victory* and *The Warrior* and did the unexpected: a self-portrait.

After weeks of drawing, a younger version of myself was staring back at me in shades of gray a round face on four-by-nine-foot (152 cm x 244 cm) paper, cute as an angel with short hair and a beautiful yet shy smile. And I hung it in the lobby of the art pavilion—for all to see—at my first solo exhibition. *These are my eyes. This is my mouth. There's no doubt about it anymore . . . I exist!*

I EXIST!

Chapter 10

CERBERUS

In the fall of 1981, I entered my third and final year of study at Concordia confident after the success of my drawing exhibition and the ceramic installations, but my soul was brokenhearted and disillusioned.

I kept my mind occupied as vice president of the Fine Arts Students Association and my hard work eventually paid off when I published a series of articles in the magazine *Le céramiste* and was chosen to represent the university at the National Canadian Exhibition at the Muttart Public Art Gallery in Calgary, Alberta. Titled *Scene de Bain* (*Bathroom Scene*) this huge four-by-six-foot (120 cm x 180 cm) floor piece presented a close-up view of a two-tone, blue tile bathroom floor with reflective water droplets and a giant pink bar of soap with suds. The corner of a brown folded looped cotton towel completed the scene. Made entirely of clay, it was so heavy that it took three big crates to ship out west.

Confident in my ability as an artist and wanting to obtain a master's degree in ceramics, I sent applications to graduate schools outside the country. I applied to the University of San Diego in California,

Alfred University in New York, and Cranbrook in Michigan. I even considered going overseas like my dad did, so I started to plan a two-month trip to Europe to search for a school. Finally, I started to work at the university's art supply store to pay for my master's degree.

Although I was still intimidated by small talk, having no idea how to connect with people, I enjoyed being a sales clerk. At the store, I could interact with lots of students, answer technical questions, give advice, and share tips and tricks. For instance, I'd say with a laugh, "Don't buy the expensive acid-free paper now. If you're ever famous, let the museums handle it." I just loved being of service.

I also enjoyed my colleagues, Jean-Claude and Suzie. Jean-Claude, or JC as he liked to be called, was an amazingly kind and relaxed guy with thick, bushy, black eyebrows. He was also in a band—The Paradots—that I secretly ached to join. Suzie was tall, slender, and graceful like a dancer from Russia's Bolshoi Ballet. She had a lovely smile that accentuated her magical dimples, and her long, chestnut brown hair and ivory skin reminded me of angels in Renaissance paintings but also of Modigliani's most ravishing portraits of women. Her simple presence soothed my heart.

With her sweet melodic voice, she loved to sing Barbra Streisand's "People," according to which I should've been the happiest person in the world. But what I found most appealing about Suzie was her humor. Together we reenacted various skits from *Monty Python*, like the dead parrot sketch and the lumberjack song. She cracked me up, and I felt a lightness in my heart just looking at her. An entire year of working side by side went by without her having an inkling about my feelings. But I didn't dare dream of asking her out.

But then she surprised me as we closed the shop on the evening of November 4. "Hey, isn't it your birthday?" she asked. "If you're free, would you like to join me for some borscht."

It was a dream come true, and I accepted right away. We made our way to Café Prague, her favorite Czech restaurant, which was nearby.

As we sat at a tiny table covered with a white embroidered table-cloth and a lit candle, I was engulfed in a sweet cloud of bliss. But then I realized that I was so desperate for love that I'd actually lied to Suzie about being free that evening.

At that precise moment, two other women from my studies at Brébeuf were waiting for me. I secretly had a crush on both of them but had never declared my feelings. Even so, they invited me at their place for a special birthday dinner. I had never received such an invitation and now I was going to stand them up.

"Bon appétit," Suzie smiled as the server arrived with the beet soup. "You can mix in the sour cream like this," she demonstrated.

My entrails churned at the sight of the bloodred soup.

I can't leave Suzie. I don't want to leave this cloud, my dream. But I love my friends. If I leave, I'll lose Suzie. I don't know what to do. I am terrified; I need her love, but I can't stay, but I can't leave. On and on my thoughts vacillated all the way through our meal.

"Thank you, Guy. I had a wonderful evening," she said with a smile as we stepped out of the restaurant. "Here . . . this is for your birthday." Then she leaned over and kissed me sweetly on the lips. It sent my heart fluttering up to Heaven while my soul roasted over red-hot coals in Hell.

The next day, I phoned my friends. Stuttering and ashamed, I made an excuse, "Something came up, and I couldn't get to a phone." That was partially true but also a lie. *I am so worthless!*

Nevertheless, Suzie's sweet kiss gave birth to a second date, then a third, and finally, we were a couple in love. At last, I was sharing my life with someone, going out to dance, staying in to make scones, and laughing together at the movies. I still felt ashamed of my body, but with some incense, wine, and the sensuous music of *Ambient 2: The Plateaux of Mirror* by Harold Budd and Brian Eno, I was able to caress her velvety skin. Even so, as we lay in bed, my arm numbed under her waist or needing to get up to pee I dared not move a muscle because

I was so afraid to wake up from my dream come true. *What if she doesn't like me?*

But a year later in the Summer of 1983, Suzie had left the art supply store and we were planning to move in together. That is, until a violent beast emerged one evening.

As we printed photos in the university's darkroom, we discussed an extremely disturbing documentary we'd seen the previous night. It investigated the murders of prostitutes, underscoring the rapes and the incest many of them had survived as children. Suzie had cried in the cinema, and as we talked about it in the darkroom, I held her tightly and comforted her.

"It's horrible, Guy, just horrible," she mumbled through her tears. "How did you feel about the film?"

Feeling panicked and frightened, I released her from my embrace. "I . . . I . . ." I stammered. *I need to get out of here,* I thought. Shaking and feeling suffocated, I ran from the darkroom.

"Guy, what's wrong? Where are you going?" Suzie demanded.

I remained speechless and feared passing out as I ran into the corridor.

But Suzie kept up the pace. "Wait up, Guy! Talk to me! What's going on?"

I threw open the metal door to the staircase and climbed the steps three at a time. Suzie continued to follow me, so at the next floor, I opened the metal door and slammed it shut with a deafening bang. Through the small window, I saw Suzie reach for the handle. I held on tight and yelled, "You can't come through!"

As she pleaded for me to open the door, that's when the violent beast appeared. I came unhinged and completely lost it. In tears, I violently kicked the door over and over while screaming at the top of my lungs, "GO AWAY, GO AWAY!"

With horror in her eyes, Suzie burst into tears. She gave me one more sorrowful look and begged, "Please, Guy, just let me in. *Please!*"

My eyes burned red, I had claws and growled "GO AWAY, LEAVE ME ALONE."

Suzie's face was contorted with pain, confusion, and disappointment as she finally let go of the door handle crying and walked away. I knew right then and there that it was over . . . we were over.

I collapsed like a rag doll, exhausted, depleted, and in tears as a childhood memory resurfaced. I was maybe ten years old—I'm not really sure. But I know it was before the incident with the kitchen knife that sliced me apart from my brothers because during this memory, I was still their punching bag.

It was a sunny and hot summer day and my parents had rented a cottage near a lake at Saint-Adolphe-d'Howard for our family vacation. I was playing by myself on the front lawn when my brother Marc pushed me to the ground and stole my ball.

"Hey, that's mine!" I complained as I got up and tried to take it back. But my brother hit me again and shoved me into the grass. With his knees pressed against my chest, I could hardly breathe.

"Shut up you fuckin' crybaby! Just give me the damn ball, asshole!"

In that moment, I felt suffocated. Blood rushed to my face, and deep inside my bowels, a mad growl erupted as my red eyes spat fire. "RRRRRRRRRAAAAAAAAAAAAAAAAAAAAAAAAAA!!!!!!"

I pushed and threw him in the air, and he landed on his back with a heavy thud. I was Cerberus, the guardian of the gates of Hell, breaking free from my binding chains. I jumped on top of my brother as my fists rained down.

"Stop! Stop!" he cried.

But I pummeled, I bashed, I screamed until someone pulled us apart. With that, the beast vanished as fast as he'd appeared. I sat down on the ground and trembled, scared of myself. I swore to never again let Cerberus see the light of day. I buried that part of me deep in the catacombs of oblivion and denied him forever. And that's where he stayed—until that day with Suzie.

But I'd only been fooling myself because he'd always been lurking in the shadows, feeding my nights with ghoulish nightmares, trying to convince me to jump in front a bus, or let go of the railing and tumble to my death. *What do you want from me Cerberus?* He had just shredded Suzie's love for me in his jaws. He was the guardian of the gates of Hell and I was Orpheus, who'd seen his beloved Eurydice's face through a small window and then lost her forever.

I cried for weeks as I worked at the art supply store, the mere sight of my boss made me weep. Anything that reminded me of Suzie brought me to tears. I was getting even less sleep than usual, and the radio was no longer enough to help me drift off. Worse, if I heard Joe Cocker's raspy voice singing "You are so beautiful," I broke down, feeling as if I were covered with glass shards.

This went on for months. I simply couldn't let Suzie go, and my health began to decline. My head throbbed with incessant headaches. My stomach was constantly in knots, and I was always queasy and on the verge of vomiting. I dragged myself to school, but my head spun. After running to the bathroom and retching several times, I developed a phobia of throwing up in public. It was the ultimate humiliation: *I'll die of shame.*

The university had two campuses, so a shuttle bus transported students between the two. One day, I anxiously got on the bus, but as soon as I did, my heart began to race and I started sweating bullets. I immediately shouted at the driver, "STOP! STOP! I need to get off—*now!*" I rushed to the front, unable to breathe. When I finally got off the bus, I ran away, humiliated. But that incident made me realize that I had a problem. Right away, I decided to seek the help of a counselor at the university.

Soon, I was meeting regularly with Nancy. She was in her forties with short, black hair and glasses that hung from a chain around her neck. During our sessions, she listened to me intently. "Now listen, Guy, most likely you're suffering from depression with episodic panic attacks as a result of your breakup." She got out a book for us to read together: *The Missing Piece* by Shel Silverstein. "Guy, you're not missing any pieces. On the contrary, you're a whole, complete human being."

No, I'm missing something, I silently protested. *I'm a nothing, and without Suzie, I'm even less than nothing. There's a void inside me. I know because I tried to fill it with music, coffee, cigarettes, and wine. And worse, there's a monster with fiery red eyes after me. Cerberus can come out at any time. I live in constant fear!*

I wish I had the courage to tell Nancy all this, but the Silent Good Boy inside me won out. I felt like she didn't understand anything I was saying, so I politely nodded as I made my way out of her office. Feeling queasy as a result of revealing my broken heart, I took refuge in the university library, just as I had during primary school. However, neither Tintin, Petzi, nor Noddy were of use to me anymore. Instead, I was drawn to the book *Help Yourself: Psychotherapy Through Reason* by Lucien Auger, so I borrowed it.

Back in the ceramics studio, I resorted to my father's edict about hard work and Mom's saying: "The past is the past. There's no point talking about it." Throwing myself into my artwork, I kept myself awake with gallons of coffee and numbed my pain with cigarettes and wine.

I often turned on my cassette player and shared my misery with Alice Cooper, who answered with his song "The Quiet Room." The song, which is about a man who's in a mental institution for trying to commit suicide, made me wonder, *Maybe I could escape all the pain by slitting my wrists.*

Chapter 11

JACK THE KNIFE

George Orwell's dystopian novel *1984* described the state of my life as all my grad school applications had been rejected. Having completed all possible ceramic classes at the university, I lost my studio space and quit my job at the art supply store in the spring of 1984. I felt lost, but then Lynn, an old classmate who was leaving for her parents in Peterborough, Ontario, asked me to stay at her apartment, so it wouldn't sit empty. I appreciated having my own place away from Mom, but I was so lonely and depressed that I felt as empty as the space.

My last hope remained in finding an art school in Europe to further my studies. But first I needed money, so I got a job designing window displays. Every day, I'd disappear into the damp basement of my boss's aunt's house to build eye-catching props for clothing stores, shoe stores, and even sex shops. Between the isolation of working alone and the buzz of the flickering fluorescent bulbs in the basement, I became even more depressed.

In the evenings, I had just enough energy left to eat a healthy dinner of fish sticks, sour cream-flavored potato chips, and beer. *I'm not worth anything, so I don't deserve any better,* I reasoned. During this time, I became a veritable couch potato, and, while watching TV shows, I daydreamed of visiting world-famous museums like the Louvre in Paris. "Here on you right, Leonardo Da Vinci's masterpiece *Mona Lisa,* please notice the sfumato" would say the tour guide as I admired the paintings mysterious smile. Suddenly the phone's jarring ring jolted me from one such fantasy.

"Hey, Guy! It's been a while! How are you?" Lizbeth, one of my ceramics classmates inquired. "Do you wanna join us for the festival of student short films screening at the university?"

I felt shy, but I knew that I needed to stop being a recluse, so I said yes.

As I arrived at the auditorium, Lizbeth introduced me to her friend. "Sophie, this is Guy, a fellow artist from the university."

Sophie had curly, sandy blonde hair and blue eyes that sparkled as she smiled. She wore a smartly fashionable blazer like an accountant, which she was. Our conversations were simple and pleasant, and within a few weeks, we started dating.

Sophie was still living with her parents, so they invited me for barbecues at their suburban home on July 1st for Canada Day. I was welcomed as future son-in-law material and thanked her dad effusively when he handed me an ice-cold beer. "Guy, call me Jack," he said, putting an arm around my shoulders. "I want you to feel at home here."

But between both our jobs, we hardly found time to be together. Sometimes, she came over to my apartment, but she never stayed overnight. So when her parents left for the weekend, I looked forward to our first night together as lovers.

It was a particularly warm and humid night in mid-July with crickets rhythmically chirping a tune. As Sophie and I lounged in the living room with the patio doors opened, a light breeze caressed our nude bodies. We were like two nymphs enjoying an innocent midnight snack of chocolate chip cookies and milk. My whole being quivered with the thrill of real love and the idea that sex might be something beautiful and desirable—something to be enjoyed between two people who truly care about each other. The moment felt perfect and timeless, a pure delight in our lover's nest.

Suddenly, we heard a noise at the front of the house and the door swung open! Realizing that her parents had returned home unexpectedly, Sophie jumped up from the couch and yelled, "Don't come in! Don't come in!"

Concerned, her mother rushed in, saying, "What's wrong?" She screamed when she saw us naked.

Right behind her, Sophie's father menacingly raised his fist, shouting, "I'M GOING TO KILL YOU, YOU FUCKING BASTARD!"

Our clothes were upstairs, so Sophie blocked their path as I managed to squeeze by. "YOU SON OF A BITCH, I'LL KILL YOU!" her dad raged, blocking my way back.

"Stop! Stop!" Sophie, still naked, forced him back.

"We're all adults here," I tried to reason. "Let's talk this out."

"Adults! I'll show you an adult!" Jack's face was crimson and his eyes bulged out as he reached for my throat.

Sophie's mom jumped in front of him and screamed at me, "Get out! Get out NOW!"

I flew down the stairs and escaped from the house, barely dressed. Dogs barked at the commotion, but a serene full moon was the only eyewitness as I jumped over garden gnomes and tripped over shrubs like a hurdler having the worst meet of his life. Somehow, I managed to slip on the rest of my clothes as I ran for my life while remaining in the shadows. Completely out of breath, my heart thumped as I swam in my own sweat from the extreme humidity. *This is insane,* I thought to myself. *Sophie and I are both in our mid-twenties. That scene back there was like a Marx Brothers meets Friday the 13th movie.*

Completely lost in a maze of suburban streets, I slowed down, wiped my brow, and lit a cigarette. I imagined full-color photos of my butchered body on the front page of supermarket tabloids: "LOVERBOY FOUND BRUTALLY MURDERED IN SUBURBIA."

Eventually, I wandered to a main road where a bus was approaching at lightning speed. I threw my arms in the air and hollered "STOP, STOP, STOP!" I thanked the Lord as the bus screeched to a halt, leaving skid marks and a trail of smoke in its wake.

"This is your lucky night, sonny," the bus driver remarked, looking puzzled by my sweat-soaked clothes. "It's my last run and I'm behind schedule, so I wasn't going to stop."

I thanked him profusely. With my knees and feet aching from my sprint through the streets, I collapsed on the first seat I saw. I scanned the dark night and took a deep breath, relieved to see that I'd successfully escaped the wrath of Jack.

The next day, Sophie called. "Dad took a long kitchen knife and went after you in his car. He said he was going to cut your throat like a pig!" she cried. "He came back empty-handed after an hour, so I was relieved, but . . . ," she hesitated, "he slashed my bed. I'm so scared, Guy." Her voice quavered as she sobbed, "My father has forbidden me from seeing you again." Then she hung up.

Horrified, I trembled at the thought of losing my love, at the thought of her father wielding a knife like a madman. Losing Sophie gutted my heart. *What's wrong with me? Why does everything I touch turn to shit?*

I turned on the radio and turned off the light. I had no more tears to cry. As B.B. King's guitar Lucille wailed that "The Thrill Is Gone," I felt like Jack's knife was digging deeper into my open wound. And once again, I wondered, *Am I doomed to remain alone, a prisoner of this barren no-man's land?*

Chapter 12

MACK THE NIGHT

I dug my nails into the armrests. *Duh-dum, duh-dum, duh-dum.* My heart thumped so loudly it was as if it was trying to escape my chest. Between the deafening *sssshhhh* from the air vents and the vibrations from the plane zipping down the tarmac, I imagined that every bolt on the aircraft was falling to the ground as we took off. Surely, my face was as white as a ghost when I reached for my headphones and blasted the Rolling Stones', "You Can't Always Get What You Want." The angelic choir reassured me that going to Europe for two months to tour grad schools was definitely what I needed.

After a painful month of despair after losing Sophie I now experienced hovercrafts, speeding trains, and rocking boats. I went from Switzerland's sunny snow-covered peaks to Greece's pitch-black, bat-filled caverns. I slept in majestic castles, earsplitting church bell towers, and on the frozen floors of trains. I savored exotic foods, danced to colorful folk music, and was surprised to discover that Roy Orbison's "Pretty Woman" transcended all borders. I even made friends at youth hostels. Most importantly, I was inspired by the art I saw everywhere.

In Italy's grand city of Florence, I was introduced to hundreds of masterful paintings, sculptures, churches, and Michelangelo's *David*. In Venice, the gold Byzantine mosaics at St. Mark's Cathedral dazzled me. I devoured the vibrant blues and pinks of Giotto's frescoes in Assisi. In Athens, I broke bread with the caryatids at the Parthenon. And in Paris, I recalled Aznavour's *La Bohème* while savoring an espresso next to Sacré-Coeur in Montmartre. The brilliant colors of the stained-glass windows in the Chartres Cathedral took my breath away. Such glory, such beauty, such a visual feast for my soul! But in Naples as I kneeled and sifted the ground between my fingers, I was awed. *It looks exactly like the color 'Naples Yellow' when it comes out of the paint tube!* Art and life were truly melded into one in Europe.

And I finally came face-to-face with the *Mona Lisa,* which until then, I'd only dreamed of seeing. I returned her smile and set out to find the ceramics collections among the nearly half a million works of art on display at the Louvre.

I travelled to the city of Sevres and Faenza, the city that gave clay its name in French: "Faïence". There the art teachers and potters were amazed by my ceramics. "We've never seen such original works! Are they really made of clay?" When I was offered a teaching position at a ceramics studio in Florence, my mind said, *Just say yes! Your dream is coming true.* My heart raced at the idea, but my stomach was in knots. I was too scared, so I declined, hiding behind my return airline ticket. Saddened, I looked towards the setting sun and vowed to return someday.

After eight weeks of traveling, I had a revelation: *Sleeping in trains, eating in parks, and meeting people—this is who I am.* I drank cold instant coffee, bit into fat red tomatoes as if they were apples, devoured chunks of cheese, and tore into fresh baked baguettes. By this time, my hair flowed over my shoulders. I had never felt such liberty. I had left Montreal on a quest for a school, but instead, I found a new way of life, a simpler existence. *I am free! I'm an explorer! And I love it! How can I ever fit back into Canadian society's mold?*

On October 10, 1984, my last night in Europe, I wrote in my journal from Zurich:

In life, we all have our memories, some good and some not so good. There are those that we can relive, feel again within ourselves, and those of which only an image remains, without words, without sounds. Time erases them, only we keep them alive. Our past, however fabulous, thins out and frays with the passing of years. High times get flattened, holes get filled. You should not live in the past, but you shouldn't let it fade away. I am all that I was.

Back in Canada, Lynn had returned from Peterborough, so I moved back in with my mother. I'd quit my job as a window dresser before I left for Europe, so I went back to work at the university's art supply store, hoping to regain my social life. My heart was filled with possibilities, hope, and a new tool: portraits! *Things are going to be different now!*

Inspired by my love for the portraits of Dutch masters such as Rembrandt, Vermeer and Hals, I decided to do the same in my painting. I was much too shy to ask my friends to pose, so I worked from photos. I started with black-and-white portraits of JC from the store, Vincent Van Gogh from one of his paintings and a life size group of friends from Finland on the famous Rialto bridge in Venice

One day while buying supplies at the store, a young art student named Dougal proposed "Hey Guy, you want to share an apartment?" I was overjoyed because I'd finally be able to set up my own studio. With Christmas coming, I decided to do a portrait as a gift for my dad. I chose a black-and-white photo from his graduation. with his Clark Gable moustache, I added two medical tools, and in the background in golden colors, I included a line graph from a brain scan. He loved it and hung it in his spare room.

I then challenged myself to paint with oil paint as the richness and depth of the colors, the shading and sfumato of its light, it's luscious texture and paste was more than I could resist. *If the masters did it, I must a least give it a try!* I loved the earthy smell and the fine art of mixing paint, oil and turpentine as I dared to attempt a full-color self-portrait. After months of work I finally appeared on canvas wearing burgundy rimmed glasses and a matching sweatshirt. Behind me was a striped wallpaper with blue and green vines, and a reproduction of a ceramic plate I'd seen in Faenza merging my two universes as one. Gone was the gray, six-year-old Guy, and in his place was a mature artist who appeared to say, "Hello, I'm Guy Giard, artist. It's a pleasure to meet you!"

And then something unexpected happened. As I had in Europe, I began exploring downtown Montreal with my camera. But instead of taking snapshots of churches, my lens captured the plight of the homeless, the invisible people of the city. For years, I'd had nightmares of sleeping on the streets, so the city's homeless people felt like kindred spirits. I chose one particular photo to turn into a full-length portrait. It showed a woman wearing a red scarf and a heavy black coat. She seemed lost in the cold as she walked bare-legged down the sidewalk, looking at her sneakers. I titled it *In the Street* and featured it in my *Cowboys and Other Idioms* exhibit with JC from the art supply store. It sold and found a warm place in a collector's home.

Daring to tell more personal stories, I painted a family portrait of my mother with my two brothers. Flanked by my brothers, Mom is sitting on the couch, putting together a jigsaw puzzle on the coffee table. There is no communication as an ominous silence fills the room. The colors in *The Holly Family* were as faded as the love between its subjects.

In July of 1985, I watched the Live Aid concert for famine relief in Ethiopia on television and phoned in to donate. Troubled by so much misery, I felt compelled to use my art to address some socially relevant issues such as war. First, I made a realist painting of soldiers in full uniform. Then I created *Memorial Day*, in which two ghostly army officers stand alongside a row of wreaths lined up for a Remembrance Day ceremony. In my studio, I sang along to Edwin Starr's "War (What Is It Good For?)".

Those two paintings unleashed an avalanche of rebellion within me, causing me to fill my journal with my rage. *I hate this! I hate it all. Why is there no grok in this world?* Suddenly, I had something to say, which shattered the cursed lie I'd been living my whole life that I had nothing to say. In that instant, *Mack the Night* was born.

The large six-by-eight-foot (147 cm x 211 cm) painting, which was inspired by the song "Mack the Knife," depicted a nighttime scene taking place in a dark alley. It had rained, the streets were wet, you imagined the cars honking and the muffled music and voices of an excited crowd. In the shadows, a man kneels under a fire escape. Below him, hidden by a dumpster, a half-naked woman lies unconscious on her back. The man one hand on her breast is about to stab her with a fiery glowing knife when he sees another man standing at the entrance to the alley. This second man passively watches the scene with his hands in his pockets. A little farther to the side, a crowd is lined up to enter a movie theater under the colored neon lights of a marquee, which bounce off the rain-dampened pavement.

"Time is suspended. What is going to happen next?" I posed at the opening of *Cowboys and Other Idioms*. "This is the question the painting evokes. You are an active participant in the artwork, but who do you identify with? The killer? Surely, you are not the victim? You might be further away in the crowd, but no, I am putting you in the shoes of the bystander. You've just come across the scene of an attempted murder. What will you do? It's your choice."

I ached that, as a society, we've witnessed war, murder, rape, starvation, homelessness, and more, but there's no counteraction. Worse, violence has become commercialized—even glorified—in movies, TV shows, and comic books as entertainment. "Did the crowd hear the woman's screams?" I asked the audience. "Did they even care? Or were they all desensitized? The only person who didn't have a say was the victim. What is your say?"

I felt all this violence trampling my heart. I didn't want to be the bystander, doing nothing with my hands in my pockets, yet I modeled him after myself. Feeling frustrated as I listened to U2's "Sunday Bloody Sunday," I had only one question: *Are we at war against humanity?*

Chapter 13

ANGELS TO THE RESCUE

On New Year's Eve 1986, I was twenty-seven and celebrated alone as Dougal had left for the holidays to be with his girl-friend. I cracked open a beer, lit a cigarette, and put ABBA's *Greatest Hits* on the record player. Doug often joked that I had eclectic taste in music, and it was—and still is—true. From jazz to disco to punk to classic, I love it all because each genre expresses a different feeling to me. So whatever I'm going through, whatever mood I'm in, music helps articulate it. "The Winner Takes It All" was great for when I was missing an old girlfriend because it brings tears to my eyes. On the other hand, "Dancing Queen" is such a happy, upbeat song that it always brightens my day.

New Year's Eve was also my time to reflect on what I'd done with my life. I had pretty much given up on relationships, but working at the store did offer me some social contact. But what stuck out like a sore thumb was that it had been two years since I was in Europe. *That trip was amazing!* I recalled. *It had given me the courage to express my inner thoughts in portraits and put them out there in the real world at exhibits.*

I hung all my portraits in my studio and listened to "Unforgettable" from the great Nat king Cole. A melancholic warmth enveloped me. *I wish I could sing like him, he's so loving.* I opened another beer, lit a cigarette and watched the wall of kind eyes looking back at me. *Yes, my friends you're all unforgettable* as tears trickled down. It was way pass midnight and all the fireworks celebrating 1987 had long fizzled out. I raised my glass and wished them happy new year, closed the lights and went to sleep.

The next morning, as I walked into my sun filled studio and saw all my portraits one single thought popped into my mind, *I'm going to Europe.* There it was with perfect clarity—no ifs, ands, or buts about it. *I'd vowed to return, and now's the time to do it!*

After much consideration, I applied for a three-year program at the National Academy of Fine Arts (also known as the Rijksakademie van beeldende kunsten) in Amsterdam. I had been moved by the Dutch masters, and of course, there was Vincent van Gogh! Of all the impressionists, his work made me feel alive—so much intensity, passion, and gusto for life! I recognized in his hypnotizing stare a calling that I knew I had to answer.

I immediately enrolled in a Dutch language class at the embassy in Montreal. By sheer coincidence, the teacher was the father of the most exquisite and enchanting angel I had ever laid eyes upon. Wanda was slender and tall with long, platinum blonde hair and a smile that extended from ear to ear. For years, I'd secretly admired her whenever she came into the art supply store, but I felt she was *way* out of my league, another universe way out of my league, and never even dared to speak to her.

When I told her father where I worked, he said, "Oh, you must know my daughter Wanda then."

My legs almost gave out when I realized that I finally had something to say to her. After that, we started going to the movies and to social gatherings at the embassy, and she became a close friend who taught me all things Dutch. I had found an ally in the pursuit of my dream.

And then, as if the stars had aligned, more exciting coincidences manifested when a second guardian angel came into my life. It all started on June 7, 1987. I was lazily lounging in bed on that Sunday morning when Doug called out to me from the kitchen. "Hey, Guy, did you see the paper? There's a Dutch exhibition opening this afternoon."

A thrilling shiver went up my spine. "No . . . how did I miss that?" I jumped out of bed and read the ad: "Out of Holland: Recent Works by Dutch Artists." I felt uneasy at social events and even worse at openings, but I realized that I'd better go to this one. I showered, shaved, quickly dressed, and then put the newspaper in a white plastic bag I'd brought from work. In big, bright red letters the bag had the logo for Talens, a Dutch paint company. I jumped on my bike and sped through a series of underground tunnels toward the museum.

Once I arrived, my night classes paid off as I was delighted to understand some of the conversations. I desperately wanted to meet the artists, but that simple thought made me break into a sweat because I was too shy to introduce myself. After an hour of walking back and forth, I found a place in the corner to sit down. Discouraged and ashamed of my lack of courage, I stared at the floor. *Why do I always end up alone in crowds?*

And then something magical happened: someone noticed my bag and commented to his friends: "Kijk hier, is het niet grappig, Talens." (Look, isn't that funny, Talens.)

Raising my head, I spontaneously replied in Dutch: "Ya, een Talens zaak." (Yes, it's a Talens bag.)

Flabbergasted at my use of his language, eyes wide open he gave me a big smile and extended his hand, "Hi, I'm Emo." He was tall and slim with short, curly, blond hair and kind eyes. "Why are you learning Dutch?"

When I told him of my dream to study at the Rijksakademie in Amsterdam, he lit up, "What a coincidence. . . . That's where I teach!"

I was speechless. Emo and I talked for a while, and when the reception started to wind down, my heart skipped a beat when he invited me to join him and his friends at a restaurant. He wrote down the address and returned to his friends. I waved goodbye and walked toward my bike.

Excited yet terrified, I tried to pedal, but my legs were wobbly. With every fiber of my being, I wanted to join them, but my heart dragged me down into the abyss. *I can't go. I'm worthless. They won't like me. Nobody does. They'll probably hate me.* In desperation, I plunged headlong into the oncoming traffic, barely realizing that I'd risked my life. *If I go fast enough, I won't feel anything.*

I got lost in the maze of tunnels underneath the highway. Bouncing along the cracked asphalt revealing the dirt roads, my wheels jerked, dust filled my lungs, and the bike seat hammered my rear end. Rows of decomposing gray pillars scrolled by like the broken teeth of an old greasy comb. *Faster! Faster!* My heart pounded and threatened to burst. The stench of hundreds of piles of pigeon excrement competed with their fetid rotting feathers and the acrid fumes of beer from the local brewery. I felt nauseous. *I'm going to vomit.*

Just as I emerged from the tunnel, a giant construction truck loudly honked and sped by, throwing gravel at my face. As the sting brought me out of my void, I suddenly recognized the iconic, gargantuan red neon letters from the Five Roses flour factory. I checked the address Emo had given me and made my way there.

I locked my bike a few streets away from the restaurant and dug into my pockets. I only had a few coins, so I felt selfish spending money. From childhood, it had been ingrained into my mind that any amount of money spent on myself was the equivalent of burning it. *I'm worth nothing, not even a penny. I can't go!*

Torn between my desires and my fears, I stood there immobilized.

Out of the corner of my eye, I noticed the blinking orange sign of a fast-food joint. *Cheap comfort food.* I ordered one plain tasteless hot dog and contemplated my dilemma in silence. *Alone, always alone, Should I go? How dare I? How could I? But I've worked so hard, and it's my dream. But they won't like me; they'll hate me for sure! I'll have to buy something, and I have no right to spend money. I'm so fucking worthless!* And on and on, I felt my life disintegrating. I was dying

HERE LIES THE BIGGEST LOSER OF ALL, THE STAIN OF LIFE I imagined my epitaph saying, as if I already had one foot in the grave. On the verge of bursting into tears, a voice suddenly spoke up. "Do you want to go?"

I turned around hesitantly, but no one was there. The strong yet gently affirmative voice came from inside me. "Do you want to go?" it repeated.

I remained silent while the voice patiently waited for an answer. Like the sand of an hourglass, my imaginary grave filled with earth. And then, with the heel of my foot, I broke the tombstone in half and shouted, "YES, I want to go!"

I burst into tears. After twenty-seven years, the Silent Good Boy broke his vow of silence. *I have a voice!*

I walked to the bank, took out twenty dollars, and made my way to the restaurant to join Emo and his friends.

"Guy! So glad you could join us!" Emo was all smiles "Let me introduce you to my friends." As it turned out, some of Emo's friends also taught at the Rijksakademie.

Filled with anxiety and excitement, I chain-smoked and drank beyond my limit. Laden with bravado from by my liquid courage, I invited Emo to view my artworks the next day at the Bonsecours ceramics school as I had been awarded a studio grant.

I brought my most recent oil pastel spatial drawings and posted them alongside my ceramics in the luminous gallery. "This big pink-and-blue eraser, is it also made of clay?" Emo inquired. "It looks like the one I had as a child, that's so cool!"

He enjoyed my colorful drawings also. "Wow, great composition! Thanks for showing me." Duly impressed, he returned to Amsterdam fully endorsing my application.

Months later, as summer neared its end, my mailbox remained as empty as the canvases in my studio. *I guess it was just a dream after all.*

But then a letter from the academy appeared in my mailbox. I felt it between my fingers and thought, *It's too thin; it can't be good news.* I closed the door to my bedroom, dropped it on my nightstand, and stared at it. After a while, I picked it up and meticulously attempted to see through the envelope as if I were a member of the bomb squad disarming a life-threatening booby trap. Blood thrummed in my ears as my heart beat like a wild ensemble of drums.

I delicately tore one side and took out the single sheet of paper. There was only me and this letter in the universe. The drums stopped and the blood receded. Silence. I read it once, twice, and a third time. "Dear Mr. Giard, we are pleased to acknowledge your acceptance in our three-year program at the Rijksakademie van beeldende kunsten."

"Yes, Yes, YESSSSS! I'm in! I got in!"

I screamed, jumped on my bed, and danced around the living room. I couldn't stand still. A torch burned inside me, and I glowed— glowed. Not only was I accepted, I was also awarded a grant.

"I did it! I did it! My dream is coming true and I can finally start my life!"

Hearing the commotion I was making, Doug rushed out of his bedroom, "Hey, dude, what's up?"

"I got in, man! I got in!" I shouted as I waved the letter in the air.

"Of course dude, you did! You're the best!"

I joined him as he sang to the tune of Queen's iconic rock anthem, "We are the Champions" while pointing at me "Guy, *you* are the champion!"

Amsterdam, here I come!

PART II

REVELATIONS

Chapter 14

FREE AS A BIRD

"**W**hat are you doing here? Go away! We don't want you here."

These were the first words I heard as I walked through the train station in Amsterdam the last week of August 1987.

A young man filthy as a scarecrow with straw-like hair and raggedy clothing hunched over me with a fixed gaze as if he were shooing away horrid black crows. After the challenges of a long flight, a train trip, and the haze of jet lag, I wasn't going to let anything darken my mood as I began my new life.

I'm here to study art, and it's going to be great, I reminded myself. With a smile, I kept walking. *Nothing is going to stop me!*

As I exited the iron gates of Centraal Station, I was awestruck. Giant barges moved slowly through the tree-lined quays while seagulls, ducks, and pigeons frolicked overhead. *Amsterdam is really beautiful!*

Clang-clang! Dring-dring! "Out of the way!" My admiration was abruptly interrupted when I had to leap out of the way of a huge iron monster. I learned quickly to avoid the oncoming trams that wiggled around town like centipedes as well as the hordes of cyclists who zigzagged through traffic at breakneck speeds. It was quite a dangerous combination! They certainly weren't all daredevils, but this was their turf, and it seemed like these tall, slender, blond, and blue-eyed folks came out of the womb equipped with wheels! Luckily, the youth hostel was just a few blocks away.

After checking in, I dropped off my oversized backpack and set out to explore my home for the next three years. The first thing that caught my eye was the workmen: Knee deep in the sidewalk? No tar, concrete nor gravel, but under the cobblestone covered streets was a golden beach! I could make out thousand white thumb sized seashells. Yes, a lot of the 'Nether' lands were reclaimed from the North Sea, and as Jacques Brel sang it was a flat land! With the clouds hugging the pointy rooftops, you could sense that the North Sea was just a few minutes away. I found myself in a romantic cityscape with so-named *bruin-cafés* on almost every street corner. Sitting on the terrace of one such place, I had my first taste of *koffie-verkeerd,* which consists of half coffee and half warm milk.

I meandered over to Rembrandtplein Square in the central part of town and admired a life-size bronze statue of the Dutch artist. *How amazing is it that seven years ago my* Warrior *statue was erected in Rembrandt Park? Maybe that was a sign.*

My stomach growled as I suddenly caught a whiff of an amazing and mysterious aroma. My nose led to a small stand that proudly advertised "Belgium Vlaamse Fries". *French fries, yummy!* Salivating, I was astounded by the long list of condiments: mayonnaise, ketchup, Dijon hot mustard, bolognaise, curry, garlic, sriracha, and more. I settled for the local classic: "Can I please have a large *patat met knoflook, astublieft.*"

My hands burned as he handed me a red and white checkered paper cornet of golden fries slathered in garlic sauce. Taking one and admiring its perfect long rectangular shape, I dipped it in the thick beige creamy sauce and bit. It crunched as the tender warm fleshy potato taste brought me to Heaven! *Lekker!* (delicious!)

From there, I made my way along the canals, found an old wooden bench, and sat in the shade. I grabbed my sketchbook, opened it to a pristine white page, and chronicled my new home in charcoal. As I witnessed the trees reflected in the water, I understood how their wiry branches could've inspired Piet Mondriaan to invent modern art with a myriad of intertwining boxes.

As I sketched the scenery, an old man with a white beard and a straw hat covering his balding head sat down and commented, "You like drawing, yes?"

I imagined Mondriaan welcoming me, so I politely nodded and plunged back into my canal. The warm August breeze caressed my long bohemian hair as the seagulls happily swam in the aquamarine sky.

Free as a bird, at long last, I'm home.

Chapter 15

STUDIO SECRETS

right and early Monday morning—with butterflies danc-ing in my stomach—I searched for my new school: the Rijksakademie van beeldende kunsten. *What a privilege it is to attend the same revered institution where world-famous Dutch artist Piet Mondriaan learned his craft! I'll be walking the same hallways he ex-plored!* I stood frozen as I gazed at the immense, green doors. Taking a deep breath, I reflected, *I made it! I've finally made it! I'm here!*

I rang the bell, but there was silence on the other side. After ring-ing again, a dull buzz sounded as the door clicked open. "Hallo. Hoe kan ik u helpen?" (Hello. How can I help you?)" A tall, tan, blonde woman dressed with multicolored scarves greeted me in Dutch with an inquisitive smile. "Oh, so that's who you are! We didn't know if you were coming after all! I'm Anna." Over the next three years, she would become like a thoughtful godmother to me, handling letters and calls from home, which were my lifelines. She was also a practical joker with a very warped sense of humor. I never knew if she, or Jan the handy-man, was pulling my leg.

Next I met with Hannah from the drawing department. She was

a slender, angular brunette with dark curly hair. A native of Germany, she had a no-nonsense way about her and got right down to business. She directed me up the creaking, century-old, wooden staircase to her office. "Have a seat, please," she said, pointing to a brown leather chair. "For the next three years, you will work in your studio by yourself. If you desire to meet with your teachers, you must make an appointment through me." She concluded with a brief overview of the school's rules and handed me keys to the main building and my studio. "I'm here if you need anything else. I hope you enjoy your time here."

My studio was located on the top floor of an old, three-story factory named the VANA. The space was a vast open, dusty square with large windows and a well-worn wooden floor. Another student had to cross my space, so I soon drew up plans for a dividing wall as well as a small, secret mezzanine to hide a mattress because I eventually planned to live there. It wasn't technically allowed, but the school turned a blind eye to it as long as I didn't bother anyone. As insecure as I was, it would take months before I even dared to move in.

For days, I traveled back and forth between my studio and the youth hostel, and then I met a fellow student named Charlie. He was American, so I could relax and have a conversation with him without worrying about tongue-twisting translations. After we got to know each other, he offered me a deal: "I need some help at my gallery in the Jordaan, the old Jewish neighborhood. You can sleep there if you help me out."

I gladly left my noisy bunkmates at the hostel and their smelly socks for my own private—albeit tiny—space. *Finally, I can get a good night's sleep,* I thought as I squeezed in between paintings in the small storage room. But I wasn't alone after all. The next morning, I woke up with painfully itchy red bites on my ankles. *Shit! This place has fleas!*

After obtaining a bicycle, a small fridge, and a hot plate for my studio, I was really starting to settle in. Cycling through the city, I chanced upon a language school for foreigners, so I signed up for an evening class. Coincidently, Wanda, the daughter of my Dutch teacher in Montreal, came to Amsterdam for a weeklong visit with her sister. They introduced me to their favorite hangouts and local delicacies, such as Waterlooplein's open-air flea market where we bought pickled herring with freshly cut onions. "Just drop it in your mouth" she said. Even my dad stopped by for a night on his way to a conference in France. He rented a room for both of us at the luxurious Golden Tulip Hotel. It warmed my heart that he'd traveled out of his way and made time to be with me.

A few weeks into the construction of the dividing wall, I met Pieter. He had just finished the academy, and he and his wife had a room to rent. *What a relief! I can finally bid farewell to those pesky fleas.* But their house was on the north shore, so I had to cross the Amstel River by ferry every day which suited me fine as I loved being gently rocked by the waves.

During my morning commute, I would step out on the deck, drink in the warm rays of the sun, and take large gulps of the incredibly fresh air. In the evenings, the dampness of the glacial river chilled me to the bone, but the rhythmic swells of the river were the perfect prelude to a good night's sleep. Out of this came a series of charcoal drawings, including another self-portrait. I was a tired, bleary-eyed man dressed in a long overcoat and shivering in the rainy drizzle under a harsh, glaring light.

It was all perfect living at Pieter's house until I started getting attacked by mosquitoes on a nightly basis. Nights I became the legendary German World War 1 aviator the Red Baron and hunted them down as red splatters of blood on the stucco walls marked my victories. As much as I appreciated Pieter's hospitality, I completed the dividing wall at my studio and installed a small mattress behind a secret wall. I also needed to install an electrical outlet in my sleeping quarters, but without access to the fuse box, the lights blinked on and off as I connected live wires: sparks flew! Still trembling as I didn't turn myself into a roast, I finally moved in at the end of October 1987, a week before my twenty-eighth birthday. *Finally my home!*

The building had an old, rust-stained toilet down the hall from my studio, and back at the main building, there was a shower in the ceramics department. In the evenings after the studios emptied, I'd scurry nervously like a rat for a quick shower. *Run, Forest, run!* Living in hiding had unexpected consequences, though. With no phone and no doorbell for visitors, isolation started to weigh heavily on me. So when I found a record player at the Waterlooplein market I felt like Aladdin whose genie granted him a wish. I was so excited to have music back in my life.

At Concerto, a shop that sold new and used books and records, I reunited with my childhood comic book friend Petzi and found a core piece of my voice: Supertramp's "School". Its haunting harmonica solo expressed my longing for connection. I also discovered Joni Mitchell's *Blue* album and listened over and over to the track "California." Her tender voice expressed a longing for home. *I don't have a home,* I thought as tears streamed down my cheeks. *I never did. I'm alone, always alone.*

I also bought myself a shortwave radio and found a friend in British-American writer and broadcaster Alistair Cooke. I began listening religiously to his soothing voice and poetic political musings on *Letter from America.* And if I was lucky and could minutely tune the dial like a safecracker, I could hear a staticky broadcast of the news from Radio Canada International. The French Canadian accents of the broadcasters comforted my lonely heart

Determined to break out of my social isolation, I posted flyers all over the school, inviting people to my birthday party in my studio. I'd never had a party much less organized one myself, so I was surprised when dozens of people showed up and celebrated with drinking, smoking, and animated conversation. I was still extremely shy when it came to talking to people I didn't know, so I stayed close to the record player and played DJ. Nevertheless, it was my first attempt at socializing with my classmates in Amsterdam, and it felt good.

Next morning, as the warm bright morning sunrays filled my studio, I celebrated my new home and birthday with a meal worthy of Monty Python by cooking a delicious serving of canned Spam, Spam, Spam Lovely Spam! I lit up a candle on a scrumptious double-chocolate cupcake, closed my eyes and made a wish. *My wish has come true, I am here in Amsterdam!*

But, by far, the best birthday present came the evening after my party. It was opening night in the Aula, the school's art gallery, and as I walked around the exhibition space I discovered hidden in the back room a gleaming grand piano. I ran my fingers across the majestic black lid as I sat on the small bench and started to play my childhood compositions. The breezy and capricious songs created a mood that transported me into my own private dream world. I didn't feel so alone anymore.

After that, I frequently visited the gallery to play the piano day and night. But soon, I began to worry about my art production. Hannah, in her wisdom, told me not to think about it. "If that's what's happening, then let it happen," she advised.

And she was right. The music answered my aching need for connection, and before long, my inspiration came back—however, in a completely different direction, much to the surprise of my professors. Like Don Quixote de la Mancha I started hopping on my bicycle with my sketchbook in hand to hunt down windmills and churches. Petzi showed up in paintings and oil pastels navigating the canals and admiring *Almond Blossom* at the Van Gogh Museum. Even Taffy's ghost appeared in charcoal drawings as he jumped out of boats and windows and lay on the cobblestones. Finally, I drew my beloved kitty sitting calm and serene on a stool listening to me play the piano.

One time, as if by magic, an actual black cat wandered in from the garden as I tickled the ivories in the back room of the gallery. He leaned on my ankles and purred a love song that warmed my heart. *He hears my voice. It's finally coming true. I wonder if others will hear it too.*

Chapter 16

ALL THAT JAZZ

In 1987, Amsterdam was recognized as the Cultural Capital of Europe—not just for the visual arts but also for dance, theater, and music. I attended the Sweelinck Musiek conservatory for many free classical concerts and the outdoor stage of the lush Vondelpark for some pop and reggae bands. On Queen's day the city became an open-air concert hall, with homegrown crooners such as André Hazes in the Jordaan. Beer in hand, people dressed in orange sang and danced to their favorite instrument: the accordion.

In the evenings, I often explored Leidseplein Square, one of the busiest centers for nightlife, which was packed with restaurants and clubs. The colorful marquee of a hot spot called the Melkweg (The Milky Way) grabbed my attention. A mixture of restaurant, art galleries and concert hall it made me think of JC and the Paradots, but I was still too shy to go in.

But finally, after weeks of hesitation, I dared through the front door. Cheb Khaled, one of the key figures of the Algerian Raï movement, was performing. The air was stifling as the stage lights produced colorful flowers on the dense smoke. The crowd was ecstatic, jumping to the call of the fast-paced mixture of folk music, modern instruments and enthusiastic Arabian ululations. I tunneled my way right into the middle of the dance floor, where a bottle of hard liquor was being passed around. I joined in and swallowed a burning swig. I never felt so alive as I joined out a loud their "LULULULULULU!"

Another time when I was exploring the dark side alleys of the Leidseplein, a humongous, golden, one-story-high saxophone caught my eye in front of the Café Alto. The jazz bar was like a long and narrow shoebox, with a counter squeezed on one side and a singular row of tables on the other. As I pushed my way through the club, which was filled to the brim with noisy patrons and clouds of cigarette smoke, I was awed by the photos of jazz greats like Miles Davis, Dizzy Gillespie, Chet Baker, and John Coltrane. *They all played here!*

When I finally nudged my way to the back of the room, a trio of musicians was performing on a stage about the size of a postage stamp. It was just large enough for a double bass, a piano, and drums. The band members flew through scales and chord changes like a speeding train, derailing all my expectations by switching harmonies in feverish improvisation. *Klein'tje!* as I ordered a small tap beer. I took out my Drum tobacco pouch, rolled a filter less cigarette, and took out my own instruments—my sketchbook and charcoal sticks. Dreaming of joining them on stage, I felt I was now part of the band as I drew them.

When I wasn't soaking up Amsterdam's nightlife, I found inspiration in the gorgeous nature oasis of Vondelpark with its bicycle paths, ponds and grazing cows, sheep and goats. My favorite place in the park was the "Filmmuseum's Café"; the most magical outdoor terrace in Amsterdam: I ordered *Een Koffie Verkerd astublieft* from the bar, rolled a cigarette, lit up and enjoy the "Speculaas" spice cookie served with the coffee. Like a Buddha I sat for hours under a magnificent elm tree as cyclist whizzed by. Further away ducks quacked in the pond right beside a generous beautiful weeping tree.

I often sat under the streetlights well past midnight. I loved the quietness, the breeze, and the passing people. It became my favorite spot to write in my journal, which was like a trusted friend that I chatted with day and night. My journal didn't judge me, but the more I revealed my struggles, the fiercer the battle raged right in front of my eyes. *I should, but I'm afraid. I have to hide because if they really knew me . . .* The pages became the battlefield of my soul and dripped with the red spilled blood of my hopes and fears.

It also became a place to write letters to my friends in Canada. Something unexpected happened during that time. Face-to-face with my friends back home, I never would've had the courage to share my feelings. But suddenly, I discovered that I could more easily express myself by revealing feelings and intimate impressions on paper. Sadly, some good friends didn't write back. But much to my surprise, my brother Marc opened up to me. My dad also sent me some money with a note that said, "Take care of yourself, son. I love you."

The more I wrote in my journal, the more compelled I felt to find solutions to my fears. I spent hours excavating golden nuggets in the psychology section of the American bookstore on Kalverstraat. By reading the works of psychiatrist R. D. Laing, psychologist Paul Watzlawick, and anthropologist Gregory Bateson, I was introduced to the concepts of the double bind theory and the interaction theory within the family. I was finally able to decipher my inner struggles with my family, but most importantly, I acquired a new vocabulary and liberated the Silent Good Boy from the censorship of the Orwellian Newspeak I was raised in. Then with the books of psychiatrist Thomas Szasz who wrote about the myth of mental illness and the manufacture of madness I felt that I was sane after all.

One subject that every author addressed was sexuality. Each book stressed that sex is a positive experience that can help bond loving relationships. Looking at my disastrous track record with romantic relationships, I accepted my fair share of the responsibility because of the feelings of guilt, shame, and worthlessness that had plagued me my entire life. I was burning for—even aching for—love, but I'd never had a loving relationship with my body. I'd even considered cutting my penis off in my youth. *Why should I allow these demons to haunt me when I'm only trying to be myself?*

Taking the bull by the horns, the *warrior* in me knew that the solution wouldn't be found in any books. My inner voice rose in anger and declared, *It's time to face your biggest fear: sex.* So I decided to seek the answers in Amsterdam's red-light district.

Chapter 17

Green Light for the Red Light

As I locked my bike next to the Centraal Station, noisy trams, the rumble of buses, and the ringing of bicycles bells competed with my madly thumping heart. *This is it. I have to go through with it.* In De Wallen, Amsterdam's red-light district, prostitution was legal and also viewed as somewhat of a tourist attraction.

As night fell, I finally dared to make my way through the claustrophobic alleys. I rubbed shoulders with groups of rambunctious teens with beers in hand as well as festive tourists, men and women alike. If I didn't know any better, I would've thought I was outside the local stadium waiting to watch the Ajax Amsterdam play a soccer match.

Some streets had bright lights, but the less frequented ones were more daunting. I let myself float along the current of the crowd as if I were drifting down a river. First came a multitude of sex shops with an uncanny variety of oversized glittering toys: boomerang shaped vibrators, pink, rhinestone-covered handcuffs, and multicolored feather boas. Magazines of muscular men and fleshy women catered to people of all tastes. Some covers displayed people in leather and chains while others exhibited so explicit close-ups of organs that they could be used as medical textbooks. Both disturbed me. *Is this what I want?*

Feeling a weight on my chest, my guilt cut through me like I was being pierced with a scalpel on an operating table—without an anesthetic. Sweat dripped from my brow, *I'd better turn back.* But the crowd was so dense that I ended up wandering deeper into the alleys. Then came the actual red lights. Row after row of glass doors lined the sidewalk, and behind each, young women stood provocatively. They ranged from thinly dressed, androgynous nymphets to bulbous belly dancers wearing lingerie so tight that it disappeared under rolling flesh. Like snakes, they undulated to some inaudible music, trying to hypnotize onlookers into their nests.

I retreated behind a group of giggling husbands and wives. "Well, honey, you *could* try this at home," said a balding man as he pointed to a young Asian girl who licked her thick, ruby red lips and languorously puffed up her breasts. I felt a lump in my throat, but they just laughed. *I couldn't speak even if they asked me a question.* Drowning in shame, all I could do was steal a sideways glance at the windows—and even then, only for a half-second.

As I continued down the alley, a group of teenagers taunted their friend. "Come on, Pete! Open the door!" I quickly surmised that the women weren't allowed to open the doors, so they coyly pointed to the doorknobs. Just then, a loud, victorious cry erupted within the crowd as if the Ajax had just scored a goal. Someone had just opened a door.

As my anxiety grew, pressure accumulated on my chest and I felt suffocated. I wanted to run away, but I urged myself on. *Just a bit more.* When the overcrowded alley gave way to a canal, I sat down near the calm waters and breathed in the fresh air for a peaceful respite. I enjoyed the rustling of the leaves, and the weight seemed to fall off my chest—until I heard the loud calls of a circus barker. "The best live sex show on Earth with real live fucking! Come right in! Just ten gilders!" Sporting a red-and-white striped jacket and a porkpie hat à la Buster

Keaton, his hot pink handlebar mustache intrigued me. "Step right up to the Temple of a Thousand Pleasures, ladies and gentlemen."

I stopped under the arches of this is so-called temple, which was adorned with giant, flashing neon breasts, penises, and pink flamingoes. Pasted on the building's columns were photos of stark-naked men and women in positions only a seasoned acrobat could achieve. My mouth dried up as I remained paralyzed in shock. *Is this supposed to be my world? Is this who I have to be?* I'd reached my limit, and urgently wanted to catapult myself out of there, but a dense crowd had gathered behind me. Desperately searching for an escape, the next business seemed to offer one. It opened to a series of small, individual cabins reminiscent of the video arcade where I'd played Space Invaders in my younger years, defending Earth against the onslaught of aliens. I suppose this familiarity made it less threatening. I gave myself one last push and dove in.

A faded sign inviting visitors to choose a cabin and enjoy themselves hung in the ominously dark and silent hall. Along the corridor, a series of black doors each opened to a tiny cubicle as small as a broom closet. There was only room for one person to sit in front of a small TV embedded into the back wall. *I'll be alone, and it's only a screen. I have to at least try something.*

I tiptoed to the nearest one, entered the dimly lit space, and locked the door. Everything in the room was painted black: the walls, the floor, the ceiling, even the primitive, wooden chair that creaked when I sat down. The stuffy air reminded me of the smell of an old taxi that had transported too many passengers. I noticed another faded sign on the wall that instructed: "Drop in a coin. View ten minutes of video. Three channels to choose from." I was so nervous that when I went to get some change from my pocket, several coins landed on the floor with a clang. After picking them up, I inserted a single coin and waited expectedly. *What's going to happen?* I wondered. I held my breath as time stood still. When the screen suddenly flickered on, it was like a jackhammer hit me.

Right before my eyes, a naked woman was screaming. Her wrists and ankles were shackled to a rusted steel frame, and a metal collar around her neck immobilized her. Men and women wearing black leather masks pricked long metal needles into her breasts, which were swollen and had a bluish tinge from the ropes and chains attached to her nipples. Hot, red wax was being poured on her from her breasts all the way down to her shaved vulva. Behind her, other masked people flogged her with long, snapping whips.

I felt her screams, her burnt flesh, and the putrid air as if my own body was being assaulted. I shook violently, and my stomach folded in upon itself. I felt like I was being choked. I wanted to throw up. *I HAVE TO GET OUT OF HERE!* Barely able to feel my legs, I staggered to my feet, knocked my head on the wall, then bumped my knee opening the door. I stumbled through the corridor and scrambled toward the exit. I plowed through the huddled masses of gawkers on the street like a crazed linebacker. I fled the red-light district as fast as I could, but the nightmarish images followed me. I finally sat on a bench near the train station and tried to roll a cigarette but the tobacco shook to the ground as I trembled. After a third attempt, I succeeded, lit up and inhaled deeply hoping it would all turn to smoke.

No, no, no! That's not what I'm looking for! I ache for an affectionate love full of passion and tenderness. I felt like a knife was piercing my stomach as the disturbing images returned. *Why do I feel shame and guilt because of my simple desire for hugs and caresses? It's totally insane!*

Gazing at the tram's tracks, I viewed them as my life's path. *I've come all this way. I've applied to the school, crossed the ocean, and confronted my deepest fears. Why do I hate myself? I have so much love to give, and I deserve to receive it in return, don't I?*

The ear-piercing bells of a tram answered my question by ramming through my wall of doubts. *Thank you, tram. You're right. I do deserve it!*

In my mind, I took all my self-loathing, shame, and guilt, crushed them into a ball, and hurled the ball toward the dark alleys I'd just escaped.

These belong to you red light, I don't need them anymore. My desire is for a sweet and tender kind of love, and now, I have the green light to go find it.

I rode my bike home feeling like a weight had been lifted off my chest. And I thought to myself, *A new day is dawning!*

Chapter 18

VINCENT

During my first year at school in Amsterdam, most *buitland-ers,* or foreigners, seemed to gravitate toward each other. I figured it was because we'd dared to cross oceans just to live our passion.

Olav was one such foreigner, and he became one of my best friends. Tall with wild, dark, curly hair, he looked like a yeti. He also had the robustness of the Norwegian fjords whose banks he climbed in his wall sculptures. He perpetually had a serious frown on his face and could have a critical temperament one minute then suddenly erupt in booming laughter the next. I never tired of hearing his deep, cavernous voice echo his favorite phrase, "Oh, I feel so bad. I drank too much last night!" To sober up, he'd cover his gums with *snus,* a Scandinavian chewing tobacco, which he claimed was laced with powdered glass for better absorption, then he'd disappear for an invigorating walk.

I soon discovered that other Scandinavians, including Ingwill from Norway and Pekka from Finland, shared the same down-to-earth directness and honesty. "It is strange to draw cartoon figures," Ingwill commented as she viewed my drawings of Petzi. Similarly, Pekka had the rare ability to verbally deconstruct and reassemble the entire social fabric with incredible grace and sensitivity.

And then there was Eva. Small with black hair and fiery, deep-set eyes. If you took all the creative arts and placed them on a potter's wheel, turned them into a shapely, prehistoric goddess, glazed her with an explosive Catalan temper, and served her up with a gourmet meal, red wine, and candles, you'd get a bombshell named Eva. "Guy, what you say is pure nonsense!" she'd say. "You're such a fool!" Her opinions were passionate—even shrill at times—yet they always sprang from a deep well of love.

These artists became great friends, confidants, and my support system. But unfortunately, Eva was graduating soon and would be returning home. Even worse, the teachers disapproved of Olav's sculptures and he'd been asked to leave. This was only the beginning of more disturbing things to come.

At first, my teachers were quite taken with the originality of my drawings, inspired as they were by my everyday life with Petzi, Taffy, and the jazz musicians. But as my creative process grew even more intense and experimental, their enthusiasm cooled considerably.

One morning I found an old, broken puppet theater in the trash. Fascinated by it, I picked it up and managed to balance it on my bicycle, which wasn't easy since it was about six feet (2 m) long. As I set it up in my studio, the paint was chipping and it was rickety, but it still held together. It was obvious that it was handmade and the sides were recycled from a baby's crib. I could feel the father's love in creating it. *What kind of loving stories did this daddy create for his children? Could I bring those memories back to life?*

For my first exhibition in the Aula, *Le petit théâtre* (*The Puppeteer's Theater*), I installed the puppet theater in a wooden playpen—which was also rescued from the trash—and surrounded it with a series of intense spotlights as if it were under interrogation. Then I hid a cassette player inside which softly played Dutch street organ music. As I told

Olav, "You only hear it if you come close to it, like a lost childhood memory long forgotten."

Empty, abandoned, and behind bars that both protected and imprisoned it, this small theater seemed very sad. The trickle of music hinted that precious memories were still hidden there unspoiled, and the harsh light suggested an urgent need to pay attention to our lost or long ignored childhood remembrances. This installation was a call for each of us to listen to our inner voice, but to my teachers, it was too much. I was told, "Guy, we see that you are serious, and you work very hard and produce a lot of work. But we don't understand what you are doing, so *you* must be confused. You won't be able to continue the program next year." I was floored.

That's insane! I screamed internally. *I know what I'm doing! All my dreams are coming true now that I'm living here! And now I'm going to lose them. I can't go back to Canada. I'll die there!*

I wanted to answer back, but I couldn't challenge their authority. Because of the incident with the teacher who called me "Giardini" and the school counselor who brushed off my accusations of bullying, I didn't know who to trust. I couldn't sleep. I was scared and felt like I was dying.

Around this time, my American classmate Charlie and his cousin Lloyd had planned a trip to visit some friends in East Berlin. I needed an escape so I asked to join them. As we crossed the German border, armed guards entered our train car and demanded to see our passports. As I studied their holsters, their black leather belts, and their pointed caps, I couldn't help but think: *I didn't do anything!*

Just then, Sasha popped into my mind. "You know they're coming! Did you see them? I'm sure they're here! They're coming for me!" My heart raced as if I was guilty of some heinous crime, but I calmed down when they left our compartment.

After exiting the train station, we walked along the infamous Berlin Wall, which was topped with barbed wire. "Hundreds of people have died trying to cross this death strip over the years," Charlie noted. The sound of barking guard dogs reminded me of my childhood neighbor's German shepherds and the no-man's-land I'd grown up in.

When we arrived at the heavily guarded Checkpoint Charlie, the best-known crossing point to enter East Berlin, a guard asked, "Reisepass bitte." I was puzzled that I had to give my passport a second time. *How strange! It's a country within a country.* As a dozen threatening soldiers in full garb with metal helmets and machine guns surrounded us, I experienced a reality I never could have imagined. I'd seen romanticized World War II movies with Hitler and his tiny mustache and the TV show *Hogan's Heroes*, which was good for a laugh, but having loaded guns pointed at us was no joke! A chill ran down my spine as I thought to myself, *I am Number Six once again.*

As we crossed the border, we entered a world like nothing I'd ever expected. We boarded a streetcar from the 1930s, with no agent on board, only a simple box with a roll of tickets. The traveler paid, teared off a ticket, and controlled his own passage. The streets were gray and silent, and the shop windows were devoid of neon lights and booming music. Getting off the tramway, I walked into a dreary stationery store and purchased a pink notebook so I could document my first impressions of this dismal place.

When we arrived at our destination, peeling paint seemed to be holding the front door together. We entered the building then climbed the musty staircase under a plaster ceiling with chunks missing here and there. After a few knocks, Charlie's friends Antje and Rahman, who, like us, were in their mid-twenties, welcomed us with hugs and smiles to their tiny flat. A sheen of charcoal dust emanated from a nearby hearth and spread across the room. Gray seemed to be the color of their lives

They kindly offered us coffee and snacks. I was touched that despite their drab living conditions, their hearts were full of generosity.

"You know what my biggest dream is? . . . Paris. I'd love to study in

Paris," Antje said with a sparkle in her eyes and a lilt in her voice. Then to prove that she was already studying French, she added, "J'étudie le français vous-savez!"

As we talked, I absorbed the realities that Antje and Rahman faced every day living in East Berlin. "Food is scarce, and there are often long lines outside grocery stores," Rahman described. "So when it's finally your turn, you hope there will still be some food left on the shelves." But worst of all for them was that they weren't allowed to travel to Western Europe. I didn't have any expectations, but soon I saw them with my own eyes. *They literally have a wall keeping them prisoner. Mine is merely made up of fears. I have no Checkpoint Charlie.* My puppet theater hinted at memories of a broken past, but for Antje and Rahman, it was the present that was broken, and they were prisoners.

When we got on the train and headed back to Amsterdam, I collapsed in my seat, physically and emotionally exhausted. *Click-clack, click-clack, click-clack.* I tried to let the rhythmic laments of the steel wheels lull me to sleep, but the light was too bright and the air was too stale. My friends were sleeping, but I was restless as it started to rain, so I turned on my Walkman and wrote in my new pink journal.

April 10, 1988

Berlin, a city torn apart, a symbolic city of politics that destroys all signs of intelligence on Earth. Happy meeting with Antje and Rahman. Talking with these prisoners: listening to them about their country; wanting to know Paris and not being allowed to see it; wanting to know the world and being limited to what you are entitled to. Who owns the planet, an ideology?

I've traveled from one side of the wall to the other: Greece, London, Paris, Canada; no borders, just oceans and distances. Seeing through the gates, the freedom of the other side; seeing the lights of the city; the traffic lights only a few blocks away but farther than the oceans, farther than the poles, farther than the moon and the North Star.

How many of them have invented their rocket to escape? How many of them have dug their own grave to get rid of the limits? Seeing Berlin is like being confronted with the madness of human beings on Earth.

I walk around and see the wall, but understanding the consequences is very different. I was happy to meet Antje and Rahman; I could feel the prison they were in. For me, it is so easy to take a train to Paris. But for them, does this possibility even exist?

When I saw the wall, I had the same feeling I had when I was at the ocean and imagined Europe or America. I couldn't see their shores, but I knew I could get there. Here in East Berlin, I can see the wall, I can feel it, I can live it, but I can't feel the other continents because I cannot go there. They're so close but so much farther than all the oceans.

When Lloyd, the American, left first and we stayed behind in the East, I felt—I experienced—the departure, the death, the hope, and the madness of our hosts' situation: "He goes through the door, but not me. He goes to the other dimension, to the world that I do not see. He lives there, and I remain a prisoner in the city, in life."

Yes, I live what you showed me, but I live my life.

One cannot always be a prisoner.

I closed my journal and mindlessly followed the rain droplets snaking down the window. *How can Antje and Rahman stand to live in a prison?* I wanted to jump on the rooftop and scream at the injustice of their world.

I thought about the Ku Klux Klan, the jailing of Nelson Mandela, and the forcing of Native Americans to live on reservations, and wondered, *Why is there so much hate in this world?* I had no understanding of world politics, but I had crossed Checkpoint Charlie and experienced life on the "other side." *I have just endured the insanity of East Berlin. For a moment, I felt what life is like for Antje and Rahman. How deranged is this world? How can people treat each other this way?* Through my Walkman, the familiar song "Vincent" by Don McLean came on.

Vincent. Vincent van Gogh. He was one of the reasons I applied to study in Amsterdam in the first place. *He fought for his beliefs, and yet, here I am, beaten down, defeated by the academy. Ha, what a joke I am!* All of a sudden, the song's lyrics hit me and made me realize: *Now I understand that Vincent painted his pain while always remaining true to himself.*

I wept silently, even though my body trembled with big sobs. I played the song over and over again until my battery died. As I looked at my ghostly reflection in the window, I saw Vincent's face staring back at me.

"So, Guy, what are you going to do now?" I imagined him saying. Then his encouraging voice added, *"What do you think? Are the teachers really crazy, or are you?"* Patiently, silently, his image awaited my reply as raindrops pelted the window.

Lost in my own no-man's-land between the authority of the teachers and the Silent Good Boy role that my family expected me to play, I was swallowed up in the quicksand of my doubts. But then suddenly, my inner *Warrior* showed up, extended his sculptural arm, and pulled me out.

I'm not crazy! I know what I'm doing. They're crazy! With that thought, I felt light, I felt free, I felt beautiful. And the walls of their authority and my family's role crumbled. I had spoken my own truth!

Vincent smiled and proudly nodded. *"Guy, you got it! Now go get them!"*

Chapter 19

SPARKS OF LIFE

I decided to exhibit all my artworks to explain my evolution as an artist to my teachers, but unfortunately, only one teacher showed up, and that was Emo. Having no support from the faculty in my department, I looked to other departments. However, longtime historical traditions weighed down the mediums of painting, drawing, and sculpture, so my approach to art was considered too contemporary. Thankfully, Klaas Hoek, chairman of the graphics department, was more receptive and invited me to apply there.

But to add insult to injury, since I'd been officially kicked out, I had to reenroll as if I had never been a student at the Rijksakademie at all. After months of nerve-racking insomnia, in the spring of 1988, as the school year drew to a close, I was finally accepted into the graphics program. I was assigned to a new studio and a team of teachers who soon became friends.

My new studio was a tiny, dusty room located in the remotest corner of the top floor of an office building called the Dependance. Sitting next to my studio was an abandoned bathroom, and with the toilet bowl removed there was just enough room for my hot plate and a small fridge. And since it had a small sink and running water, I felt blessed to have a functional kitchen.

I secretly moved my mattress into the building's attic, but it had a skylight, which soon made the room uninhabitable due to the lack of airflow and the scorching sun blazing through. I should've known something was amiss by the countless mice white skeletons on the floor. To escape the oven-like conditions, I moved my mattress to the top of an enclosed staircase. The area was cooler, but because I was hovering over the emptiness, for the first few weeks I was terrified that the floor would cave in under my weight.

My second year of school in Amsterdam starting in fall of 1988 can be described as nothing less than a creative explosion. My work space was about one-twentieth of what it had been the previous year, but my art drastically evolved again. I took up photography and explored in-situ installations. I explained this in a letter that I wrote to Eva, who, by then, was back in Spain. "Installations are the equivalent of set designing for the stage. As opposed to a sculpture with a fixed shape, an in-situ installation literally has to be installed into the space." In my installations, I used elements of everyday life, like furniture to evoke emotions.

In March 1989, I received the awesome news that I was selected to create three installations in an abandoned nineteenth-century military cavalry complex, the Kavallerie Kazerne. With camera in hand, I excitedly explored the empty rooms for ghosts. The horses' stalls had concrete floors covered with gravel, elsewhere office walls were painted in dull gray and desecrated with graffities and nude centerfolds. Because of the desolation of the place, I identified with the young men who'd had to abandon their dreams for military service. *How did they feel and what were their dreams?* I wondered.

For my first installation, I took the *Puppeteer's Theater* out of the playpen and displayed it in a dark, dirty corner as if it were a scared child hiding away at the mercy of the bright spotlights. Trapped and defenseless, there was no escape.

The second work was *Eise's Room*, which I created in honor of eighteenth-century Dutch amateur astronomer Eise Eisinga, who, in 1774, taught himself astronomy, built a planetarium in his home, then showed his neighbors the workings of our solar system.

For this installation, I converted a small office cubicle into a symbolic observatory. I sanded and repainted the walls to pristine off-white, scrapped and brought a shine to the linoleum floor, fixed the small sink in one corner, and dressed the windows with long laced curtains. In the middle of the room I laid a regulation singular army bed with a pillow and heavy wool lined army issued covers. The visitors could lie down on the cot and discover multicolored, concentric circles painted on the ceiling. Each color traced various orbits around the sun to symbolize our solar system. "Where am I in this universe?" I wished the visitor would ask himself. With my life and my art getting further intertwined, I slept on the cot the night before the opening. *This is who I am now,* I told myself. *I survived getting expelled from the program, and now I'm in the right place!*

The third installation, *In Memoriam,* was a whole atmospheric universe in itself: sixty feet long and twelve feet wide in a room with twelve-foot-high ceilings (20 m x 4 m x 4 m), a mezzanine, and supporting posts. The space was pitch-black and the floor was covered with gravel. Visitors' footsteps made an eerie crunching sound that echoed throughout the empty room. A row of floor-to-cciling windows on one side were painted black except for a few broken panes. A draft made the sheer curtains wave in an ethereal way that made the room seem as if it were breathing.

On the other side of the room, concealed in a back corner and hidden under the mezzanine, an old-fashioned oil lamp hanging from the wall emitted a softly flickering flame. As one moved closer, the handwriting on the wall was evident. It read: "Ter herinnering aan de dromen verloren in het gevecht voor eigen identiteit". "In memory of the dreams lost in the fight for one's own identity."

The tiny flame symbolizes our childhood dreams. We may have been forced to grow up and give them up, but in our hearts, they persist. Reminded of the constant hateful fighting between my brothers, the insults, and disrespects toward my mother, I finally recognized the destructive patterns in my family. At an early age, my flame had been extinguished and I'd wanted to kill myself. The urge was so strong that I never considered it abnormal. "Suicide Is Painless," the theme song from the TV series M*A*S*H, was also the soundtrack of my life. *Maybe, just maybe, life can be different now.* This new hope became the inspiration for my first video installation, *I Remember When.*

In the grand hall of the Aula, I drew four large, nine-foot-tall (3 m) wall drawings of smiling faces. The first was my face as a child; the other three were the faces of my adult brothers and sister. In front of the drawings, I placed a television monitor that continuously played a nine-minute video. In it, I shared four childhood memories as if the visitor and I were in the middle of a conversation.

In the video—which was filmed in one take with no editing—I sat in a chair in front of a white wall with only my upper body in the frame. I wore a simple, gray T-shirt and talked directly at the camera. I suddenly sparked to life with a memory, speaking in a highly energetic and joyous tone, and then I became silent, almost absent. After a few seconds, I recalled another memory with enthusiasm then faded off into emptiness again. I did this over and over again. Like a split personality, these two extremes were unaware of each other's presence. All the names of the family members were replaced by the impersonal pronouns *he* and *she.*

As my teachers visited, I asked, "Which of these two extremes constitutes this person's true identity? Is it the exuberant one or the emotionally empty shell? Or none of the above? Or perhaps both?"

Uncertain how to answer, they responded, "Do you mean which one are you?"

I explained for clarity, "In my artwork, I use personal anecdotes, but my intention is not meant to be autobiographical. I wish to touch on the universal, so the viewer can fill in his own stories."

"OK, I get it," Klaas answered. "So it's not about you, right, Guy?"

It thrilled me that he understood. "Yes, that's correct. My installations are meant to be mirrors of the viewer—to make him more aware of himself—not of me. I want my work to raise questions and bring to the surface feelings that the viewer is unaware of or takes for granted."

However, other teachers had an adverse reaction to my work and found me too challenging. "One shouldn't question authority," they remind me.

Taken aback by this, I talked with Maria, one of my new classmates. She and her boyfriend Erwin had this untraditional way of creating artwork as a couple, and they "got" me. "This is typical," she assured me. "You see, Guy, in primary school we learned the old saying, 'In a wheat field, don't be the stalk that sticks out or they'll cut you off!'" she added with a laugh. She had this uncanny gift to be deeply philosophical and introspective then follow it up with a giggle.

When some teachers began avoiding my studio, I started to grow concerned that I would get kicked out again. So I fought back with a special performance installation for the end of the year studio visit. Called *De Boerderij* (*The Farm*), I set up my studio with many of the smaller works I'd produced during the year and prepared a sheet of "instructions" for my visitors. On it, I compared artists to working farm animals and the jury's studio visit as a tour of the stables.

When it was time for the visit, I had my fellow students and teachers wait outside. Some were nervously playing with their papers, others giggled. I sensed the tension as the tables had been turned. After making them wait for a few moments, I opened the door to the dark corridor and let them in one at a time, like cattle entering a slaughterhouse.

As they turned the corner, they were blinded by a flash as Roy, the technical assistant, photographed them. There was some laughter and even some screams, but in the end, everybody enjoyed the performance and my smaller works. But most importantly, my second-year evaluation was a success, and I was allowed to stay for my third and final year.

Chapter 20

THE WALLS CAME CRASHING

With summer vacation in full swing, my inner flame advised me to take care of myself, so I moved my small mattress in the warmth of my well-lighted studio and set out on frequent day trips. I biked for hours along the dykes and windmills to discover the ever-expanding scenic farmlands. The familiar acrid stench of cow manure reminded me of my earliest years in Saint-Hyacinthe. I also enjoyed taking trips to the beaches of Zandvoort aan Zee just west of Amsterdam. I shivered as I plunged my feet in the freezing waters of the North Sea. Relaxing on the yellow sand, my body and soul felt nourished by the rumbling waves and the saline air.

I also drank in the artistic wealth of the museums in Rotterdam, Haarlem, and Groningen. As I admired the intricacies of a golden chalice from the Middle Ages, a beautiful, fair maiden appeared in its metallic reflection. When I turned around, she had vanished, so I figured it must've been my imagination.

But when I entered the paintings gallery, there she was with her silky skin, freckled cheeks, and luxurious hair like spun gold. Our eyes met for a moment, and I felt an instant spark as she gave me a sweet smile. *She's a goddess!* I thought. But I was so shy that I quickly averted my gaze toward the medieval portraits. *Go on, just introduce yourself,* my inner voice urged. I turned in her direction, but she had disappeared once again. As I left the museum, I wondered whether this enchantress was real or had stepped out of one of the paintings.

When school began a few weeks later, my heart skipped a beat as I spotted her in a corridor of the academy. I was even more surprised when she came up and introduced herself to me. "Hi, I'm Erika. I just transferred to the graphics department. It's a pleasure to meet you." This time I didn't look away. She was even more beautiful than I remembered. Her delicate perfume sent tingles throughout my body.

"Welcome. The pleasure's mine." I didn't dare mention our chance meeting at the museum for fear that she would vanish again.

But in the coming weeks, we chatted in the corridors and visited each other's studios. I was enthralled with her thoughts and her soft voice. And her perfume was intoxicating. If she was in another room or down the hall, I knew she was coming because of the amazing scent. When I finally summoned the courage to ask what perfume she was wearing, she said, "I'm not wearing any."

I can only infer that I was so in tune with her pheromones that my body was undulating in waves of passion. Mesmerized by her scent, I drank her in. And then on a Friday afternoon, the day before my birthday, she visited my studio and my internal flame was set ablaze as we connected on a deeper level. We both questioned reality in our art; she worked with mirrors and I photographed the passing of time. "Is life reality or are we just reflections?" she asked with a soft gaze behind her gold-rimmed glasses. "Maybe each of us lives in a fantasy world of our own making?" Then she reached into her backpack and pulled out a small box. "Here, I made these for you. Happy Birthday, Guy!"

Taking the present, I felt a gentle warmth envelop us as our fingers touched. Our eyes locked, and I brought her close to me in a full embrace. Then I stroked her cheek, and we kissed. For two nights and two days, fantasy and reality merged as our bodies became one. *She wants me! Someone really wants me and I don't have to do anything! For the first time, I don't feel dirty or ashamed. I am desired and beautiful and can love freely.*

On Sunday morning, birds chattered by the window. The sun's warm rays caressed our skin as we rested on the embers of our love. *This is pure bliss*, I thought to myself. Then Erika announced, "I have to leave. My husband is coming back tonight, so I have to get home. He's my high school sweetheart, and we're about to celebrate our fifteenth wedding anniversary. You're the only other man I've ever been with."

I interpreted her honesty and integrity—which are my highest values—as compliments: *Why would someone want to be with worthless, shameful me over her husband of fifteen years? It must mean that, at the very least, I'm worth something!* This was the only way I could conceive of someone loving me.

After getting dressed, she pressed her body against mine and whispered, "I'll see you soon." I unlocked the door to my studio and resisted the temptation to follow her.

As the hours dragged on, I lingered in our love's scent. Finally, after several excruciating days, we met we met at a café at Albert Cuyp market for *"Appelgebak met slagroom!"*; apple pie slathered in whipped cream, their specialty.

In Erika's presence, I tingled with excitement. But more importantly, I felt safe—safe enough that a sadness I'd never verbally expressed bubbled to the surface. "I feel so alone!" As a sea of emotions suddenly engulfed me, I trembled and tears poured down my cheeks.

"We can't see each other anymore," was her only reply.

I was speechless.

I heard her words, and my mind justified what she said. *I get it. It makes sense since she's married.* But the walls I'd spent most of my life constructing for protection had just crumbled. It was like a ton of hard, sharp and blood-stained bricks had crushed my soul. My heart, my guts, every cell of my body ached in pain. When she got up and left, I'd never felt more alone in all my life.

At that very moment, four hundred miles to the east, another wall came crashing down. Antje and Rahman launched colorful fireworks as East and West Berlin celebrated the city's reunification. But in a café in Amsterdam, there was no vigil as I silently died, crushed under the debris from my own wall of protection.

As night fell, I dragged myself back to my studio. Cut off from the world without a phone or doorbell, I was truly alone. I chain-smoked, drowned in beers, and wrote to Eva.

November 9, 1989
Dearest Eva,

My life is a mess! How can I keep going? I feel so bad that I need to get drunk. I would kill myself if I had a gun.

What's the point? I'm losing my grip on life more than ever. I've made a big discovery about myself. I'm a very, very, very, very sad and lonely person. I'm losing my grip.

But why? Well, I discovered my loneliness. I mean I finally saw it, admitted it. I am a very sensitive person, and the world scared the shit out of me, but it also scared me out of me. I hid, I built a big wall all around me to hide, to protect myself. But I never saw my prison walls. I didn't know. I never opened up. I grew lonelier and lonelier. Only I existed. I never told girlfriends, family, even friends. I never told anybody.

So, this woman gave herself to me. Now she is gone. Still, she gave herself to me. Totally. I was finally ready, so ready for her, for her love, for her care, for her trust. I removed one brick from the wall, and I told her. And I cried.

The world didn't explode. She didn't laugh. She didn't run away. She still loved me. But then she left.

So now my wall, like in Berlin, is crashing down. All the systems, structures, behaviors, and concepts that had formed my walls are now gone. I mean a man loses his job, or his family, or his love, or whatever held his life together, and he kills himself.

That's where I am. My structure, my fake life, my prison has faded away. So where does this leave me? Alone in bed, and that's bad.

So now I feel more life, but I also feel more pain. My feelings are sharper, they hurt more. Before I was in a general state of not feeling, or feeling through a dense fog. I never felt the sharp edges. But now I do.

When I am with a friend, I am so happy. When I am alone, I am so alone. Life was always abstract for me. And now I don't even have a theatrical structure to hold it together.

But I wonder if I have enough energy not to go over the edge, to lose my grip. This is the feeling I live with. It hasn't become my reality . . . yet.

As I sealed the envelope, I felt as if I'd closed the cover of my coffin. I waited for the pallbearers to come knock at my door. They never came. So I buried myself in work.

Chapter 21

LEAVING HOME

Just before Christmas break, I exhibited two new installations at the Aula. *No Time* was simply a plain white wall with five clocks on it. One was half an hour ahead of the actual time; a second was half an hour behind. Two other clocks were displayed side by side. They were set fifteen minutes apart but in no relation to real time. My thinking was that it was like they were in a race and would never quite meet. The last clock was placed on a podium with only the second hand remaining. *Ticktock, ticktock.* After Erika, I felt my life was out of sync and outside the realm of time itself.

The second installation, *Structured Blues,* was a sixteen-by-nine-foot (5 m x 3 m), navy blue wall with a single bed and an old, wooden work table in front of it. On the wall hung a three-foot-square (3 m x 3 m) tic-tac-toe grid painting with words outlining my theory of the Self inside the squares. Whereas Vincent van Gogh had painted his own colorful bedroom in Arles, mine was a cold, monochromatic blue to illustrate an emotionless mental prison cell. *Who am I? Why am I still living and what is life anyway?*

Maria came into the gallery as I documented the installation. I often imagined her flattening her long, silky, black hair on an ironing board. I asked her to take photos of me lecturing at the table. She laughed and graciously proceeded as I mimed giving a talk on my theory.

"Say, Guy, we never see you anymore. Why don't you come over tonight? Erwin and I are having a few friends over."

My beleaguered soul still ached, but she insisted, so I hesitantly said, "OK. I'll try to make it."

Later that evening, I sat on the sofa, beer in one hand, cigarette in the other. Seconds endlessly turned into minutes, which turned into hours. I had never managed the skill of small talk, and echoes of nearby conversations ping-ponged in my empty mind. Nothing made sense. At one point, for no reason, I turned to my neighbor and casually said in a monotone voice, "If I had a gun, I'd kill myself."

His jaw dropped. "*What?* But Guy, you seem so happy and are smiling all the time!" he stuttered in total disbelief.

At that point, my body just took over and asked for help. I had nothing to gain but it had everything to lose—literally life itself! And my world didn't implode. The person I was talking to didn't laugh or run away. Instead, he scrutinized me with kind eyes and his full attention. "Please, Guy, tell us more."

In that instant, I discovered something new: I had people in my life who cared and listened, who empathized, supported me, and wanted to be present. I was dying under the weight of my crumbled protective wall, but, like a rescue team, they dug out my bloodied broken soul. Over the next few months, I discovered in my classmates Maria, Erwin, Paula, Suzan, Giny, and Rein Jelle an inexhaustible source of loving support.

By the time we all got together to share some roasted lamb, chocolate eggs, and bunny-shaped cookies for Easter, I felt reborn. As we broke bread, a shocking revelation struck me: *The family I'd always longed for is in Amsterdam! Here, I have friends that I love who unconditionally love me in return. They are my Dutch family, and this is my home.* I'd never felt so happy, loved, and fulfilled.

But then another crushing blow hit me. My three-year program was coming to an end, and I faced my worst nightmare: returning to Canada. *Amsterdam is my home! These people are my family! I can't leave! I can't go back! I'll die over there! What do I do?* A fellow foreign student suggested that I apply for a residency visa. I thought it was impossible, but I felt desperate, with no way out. So, despite my fear of the authorities, I sought out an immigration lawyer.

In the spring of 1990, he and I worked together on the necessary authorizations and filled out the requisite paperwork, but I was filled with doubts. *How can I prove my worth when I know I'm worthless? I have no money and have been living illegally like a criminal in my studio for the past three years. I'm terrified of being found out.*

My fears turned into full-blown nightmares with me as Number Six. In the dreams, I saw myself pressing my journals to my chest while I was hounded like a fugitive in a tall wheat field. Dozens of German shepherds gave chase as flashlights blinded me. When they caught up to me, they shredded my journal to pieces with their sharp fangs and then went for my throat! I woke up in a cold sweat, swinging my arms in the air. After weeks of insomnia, I told my lawyer to tear up my application. He looked at me baffled and disappointed. I couldn't tell him or my friends that the real reason for my change of heart was that I was scared. And because of that, my dream of staying with my Dutch family all sank into my abyss.

Resigned, I built a large crate that felt like a coffin and prepared to ship three years of artwork back to Canada. But my nightmares returned. In one, I was wildly searching for my artwork in a creepy, old house. As I ran down the halls, the walls crumbled and dust choked me. *THERE'S NOT ENOUGH ROOM!* I panicked at the thought of leaving my sculptures behind. Then, as I was speeding to the airport in a taxi, I realized that I'd forgotten my passport, so I missed my flight.

In another nightmare, the creepy house burned down with my sculptures in the attic. As I tried to make my way up there to retrieve them, the calcinated beams cracked and the floorboards caved in. I was crushed to death as the whole house collapsed on top of me. I woke up with my stomach in knots, relieved that it was just a dream. Then I cried as reality seeped in: *I have to leave.*

Before sealing the crate, I reflected on all the works I'd produced: the puppet theater, charcoal drawings, clocks, and more. *Maybe I am worthless, but these are beautiful!* With that simple thought, the little spark in my heart suddenly came back to life. *Maybe all is not lost after all. What if I can do the same in Canada? I've exhibited there before, so why not try again?* As a gust of fresh air blew my spark into a full-fledged flame, I decided to meet Maria to tell her my idea.

Over coffee and spice cookies, she responded, "That sounds wonderful, Guy! Would you exhibit the pieces you've created here?"

"Well, I love my site-specific installations like *In Memoriam* at the Kavallerie Kazerne. I also like telling stories with objects like the puppet theater. And then there's my video installation *I Remember When* about my identity within the family."

In a flash, it all came together. "Yes! It'll be about identity—my Canadian family and my Canadian identity. I call it *The Family Show*, and I'll tell stories about Canadian identity through everyday objects. I want the viewer to ponder: 'Who am I, and how much have I been shaped by my family?' What do you think?"

"That does sounds interesting, Guy. But how would it actually work?" Maria always questioned everything. "I mean, what would you actually show in the galleries?"

A geyser of ideas poured out as I visualized myself in the exhibition space. "Well, just imagine, I would arrive in the city where the show takes place at least a month in advance to get a feel for that specific community. Then I'd find tables and chairs and other objects to re-create intimate moments of family life. I could even give talks on family interactions from my notes in my journals." I stopped, took a breath, and stared at Maria before continuing, "I'm jumping into the unknown, and it'll be a blast!"

"You sure seem to know what you're doing, Guy!" Maria laughed.

As soon as I got back to my studio, I got to work writing the description, drawing some sketches, and gathering slides from my latest works. I sent my proposal to galleries across Canada and even asked for a grant. I received several negative replies, but when I opened a letter from Neutral Ground, an artist-run center in Saskatchewan, I screamed in joy!

When my Dutch family invited me for supper shortly before I returned to Canada, I showed them the letters. "Yes! I got it! You see, I wasn't crazy after all! The teachers thought I was confused and kicked me out, but look," I said as I handed Maria a second letter, "I even got a grant!"

"Guy," Maria replied with a stern look, "you may be strange and funny, but we never thought you were crazy!" With that, they all burst out laughing in copious guffaws.

Ready or not, Canada, here I come!

Chapter 22

THE FAMILY SHOW I

"Don't be deceived by the magnificent blue sky because we're in for a real doozy of a snowstorm tonight with a severe freeze warning in effect. So bundle up, folks, or you might find yourself with a bad case of frostbite," the pilot warned with a chuckle. He wasn't kidding, though, because as soon as I stepped out the airport's hall my nose broke off and slid on the icy ground.

I expected to find a dogsled waiting to take me to my hosts' apartment, but all I found was one lonesome cab. "Welcome to Regina! Be sure to watch out for polar bears," the driver quipped as I opened the door. "They're real hungry this time of year." With temperatures reaching an all-time low for January, it seemed that everyone had a weather-related joke at the ready.

My hosts, John and Alicia, were both members of the Neutral Ground gallery, and they'd graciously installed a makeshift bed in a corner of their living room. For the next five weeks, this would be my home. Since returning to Canada, I'd crashed in my mother's basement then on various friends' couches, and now I was resting my weary head on another rolled-out foam mattress.

As night fell, I couldn't sleep because next to my pillow, the apartment's windows banged loudly due to the onslaught of the snowstorm. I turned on a small TV and was horrified by another storm hitting the other side of the globe, the so-called "Desert Storm." Right before my eyes, I watched as US missiles with luminescent green trails rained down on Iraq. *What must it be like for people living in Baghdad? How can this be happening? Is this really our humanity, our human family?* I turned off the news and prayed for the safety of the victims of this insanity.

The next morning, I trudged through knee-high snow to the Salvation Army store. *Let's see what kind of everyday items this rural community offers.* I found long sofas and a lot of wooden furniture, including a large table and several old chairs. There was also a treasure trove of TVs, radios, tape recorders, lamps, and books. It was perfect source material for my local installations. I cataloged all my findings and started to imagine which daily life scenes I'd re-create in the gallery.

After that, I made my way downtown to the Neutral Ground gallery, which was aptly named with its gray wall-to-wall carpet and white walls. With his long beard and unruly, brown curls, Paul, the gallery's curator, looked like a bear emerging from hibernating in his cave. "Ah, there you are Mr. Giard. Please to meet you," he greeted. Then he introduced me to the technical assistant, Julia.

There were no windows in the gallery, which suited me just fine because I could manipulate the lights to create a very intimate "family" atmosphere. After thanking Paul and Julia for their warm welcome, I took out my sketchbook, my list from the thrift store and my sketches from my proposal. Then I drew a floor plan and started to visualize the installations as I scribbled and made some preparatory drawings.

Back and forth, I braved the icy, cold mountains of snow and warmed myself in the gallery to the heart-pounding beats of Technotronic's "Pump Up the Jam." I got the table, chairs, and a bed delivered, and Julia brought me projectors and a screen. Then came the nitty-gritty of tweaking the lighting and sound design. I even reupholstered the chairs. "Every parcel, every light, every small detail has a story to tell, and I need it to be just perfect," I told Paul. "Think of it like Archie Bunker's favorite chair from the American TV sitcom *All in the Family*. It was his throne, and no one else was allowed to sit in it—not even his wife, Edith, and especially not his son-in-law, Meathead! His chair was his persona."

The day before the opening, I was invited at the local radio station for an interview. "This exhibition is about Regina as a community," I explained. "I like to create works of art that allow the viewer to learn about himself and his family relationships."

The show's host was puzzled. "Don't you mean your *own* stories? I mean isn't art supposed to be about the artist's self-expression?"

"That's true," I answered. "But my work is like a mirror. When I look in a mirror, I see myself. But when *you* look in a mirror, who do you see? You see yourself, right? My artwork is like a mirror, and I want you to see yourself in it. That's my passion."

I thanked him and made my way to the gallery, where a local journalist waited for me. The sky was the color of blue topaz that day, but the air was crisp and cool. Even so, the sun was particularly radiant, and I loved the warm rays on my face. As I tuned the dial on my Walkman to the radio station that had just interviewed me, I heard "Coeur de Loup," a bouncy happy song by Philippe Lafontaine. I danced to the beat down the icy sidewalk as all the stress of the monthlong preparations melted away. *Wow! This is amazing! I've done it! The teachers had kicked me out in Amsterdam, and now, I'm opening my first solo exhibit in Canada!* I was ecstatic. I'd never felt so accomplished in my life.

That night, in my journal, I wrote:

Tomorrow, February 7, 1991, is the big day, the day I've been working for all my life, a day I could have only dreamed of before. It feels like a victory, like I don't need to merely survive anymore because I am winning the battle I have fought all my life. The battle of being someone, of existing, of having an identity.

Survival so far meant denying who I was because I was not allowed to be, to express, to be scared or alone. Now, on my own two feet, I rise and I say to myself: "I am."

I break my mother's denial of the past, my father's flight into work, my family's curse of failure. This victory belongs to me, and I'm going to bathe in it and radiate my joy and my pleasure. I may still be alone, but I am all to myself. Tomorrow is my day, and it's the first day of the rest of my life.

"Congratulations, Guy" Paul was all smiles at the opening "Here, try some homemade carrot cupcakes, brownies and oatmeal cookies our members made for tonight." along with red and white wine, local beer, cheese and olives. It was a feast for our guests.

With the event in full swing, the space was submerged in semidarkness and offered five installations, each with its own specific lighting. First was *I Remember When* with each face drawn in pencil lit by a night-light.

Then came *Conversation Piece*, which was about the appearance of communication. Lighted with a single spotlight from above, an old, wooden table was surrounded by six chairs, each with the voice of a different person speaking from a cassette player. All the voices played simultaneously through two huge speakers inappropriately placed face-to-face on the tabletop. From a distance, this conjured up thoughts of harmonious discussions, but as you came closer, all you heard was dissonance. There was no communication, only a cacophony of sounds. The illusion was broken.

"This is exactly how it was in my home," some people told me before proceeding to share their stories. Others had the opposite reaction: "This is not at all like it was in my house. We could talk for hours at dinnertime. But I can see how it might feel in a family that was different than mine. This is horrible!" That was exactly what I wanted to hear: not my story but the viewers becoming more aware of their own. I took pleasure in listening to these accounts.

The third installation, *Memorabilia*, consisted of a row of ten toys lined up on a shelf as if they were in a store. I had selected some of my own childhood toys with the most universal appeal. Each one had a tag with a few typewritten words, such as "He's so polite," "She never causes any problems," and "He's such a good boy." As I'd told the journalist the day before, "I want the viewers to recall about what kinds of labels had been pinned on them as children."

The most personal work in the exhibit was *If Only*, which had been inspired by my unexpected discovery of a carousel of old holiday slides in my mother's basement. They were from Christmas Eve 1961, and the living room was decorated with candy canes, garlands, and snowy cotton balls. In the middle of it all was a glittering Christmas tree full of shiny red ornaments, silver tinsel, and our presents neatly wrapped underneath. My siblings and I gleamed as we ripped the colorful wrapping paper to discover our gifts. From these old slides, I made new ones by photographing close-ups of our blissful, innocent faces.

In the exhibition space, I pointed three slide projectors toward one singular screen, which was encased in darkness. A timer automatically changed the images every three seconds, alternating between three faces, three words, three faces, three words, and so on. The incessant, robotic clicking of the changing slides, the noisy whir of the projector's fans, and the cold, metal shelves contrasted sharply with the happy smiles. The cycle lasted for two minutes after which a poem I'd written was fully completed.

> *If*
> *If only*
> *You had given me the chance*
> *To be myself*

I could have shown you
How much I love you.

Why?
Why were you so afraid
That you would lose me
If you had given me the chance
To be myself?

I didn't think too deeply about who the poem was written for. It might've been about my mother, but it came from my heart. It was as if a voice inside me helped me articulate the words—the voice who told me to go to Amsterdam, the one who opened up about putting a gun to my head. This voice was my ally.

At the other end of the gallery was the last piece: *Going to Bed: To Bed or Not to Bed.* Shrouded in darkness, the space offered a neatly made-up twin bed, a bedside table, and an unlit lamp. The sheets, blanket and pillow were all carefully laid down. Every detail was perfect, except for one: an ominous white light glowing from under the bed frame.

"As children, we're usually afraid of the monsters under the bed," I'd explained to the journalist. "But this time, I reversed the roles: the light is now under the bed, all of reality becomes scary. The monsters aren't hiding there, so where are they? You feel their presence all around you."

"Anyone can be a monster then," the journalist concluded.

"Yes, exactly."

Chapter 23

LI'L BARB

The show opened with good reviews. I even stayed an extra week to give a series of talks at the gallery and the local university.

For my presentation at the university, I prepared a slideshow of my work entitled *Guy Giard: Social Artist*. I covered *Victory* and *The Warrior* along with my paintings of the homeless, the soldiers, and *Mack the Knife*. As I concluded with *In Memoriam* and *I Remember When*, I asked, "What do you think is the role of the artist in society today?"

"To express themselves."

"To bring beauty."

"To reflect on human conditions."

But then one student overtly proclaimed, "Artists are often ahead of their times. They can literally be like a canary in a coal mine, warning us about the threats of capitalism, population control, and manipulation by the mass media."

"These are all great answers," I replied. "You must have great teachers!" They all laughed.

At the gallery, Julia brought her video camera and recorded my talks. The first one, *Myths of Contemporary Art*, focused on the public beliefs of what art should look like and how artists often limit themselves to match those expectations. On the second night, *Interaction Theories* introduced the concepts of the double bind theory and other analyses of family relationships.

I was very anxious because there were no slides to divert the audience's attention. *They're looking at me all the time.* With my hands shaking, I clutched at my notes and perspired under my wool sweater, barely raising my head to look at the audience. I felt relieved when it was over and everyone applauded enthusiastically. "That was great!" Paul said as he shook my hand. "Now I understand how you came up with the idea for the exhibit. Congratulations!

"Oh, by the way, these came for you," he added, handing me a few letters. Three other galleries had just accepted my proposal! Seeing that the fourth letter was from the Netherlands, my heart jumped, thinking it might be from my friends, my Dutch family. However, it was from Eric Hoffmann, a gallery owner in Amsterdam. I'd had some success at a few group shows at his place in the Jordaan neighborhood. He was inviting me to put on a solo exhibit in his gallery this summer. *I'm going back to visit my family and have a show!*

I was so excited that I immediately wrote two letters: one to Eric accepting his offer; the other to Michael and Sylvia, some friends I'd met at Eric's gallery who had invited me to stay at their place anytime. I was so elated by all this great news that I braved the glacial night to chill out at the bar of the luxurious Grand Hôtel Saskatchewan.

Drinking my beer and smoking cigarettes, I blended in with the carpet's field of brown and khaki sunflowers. In the corner of the room, a trio of plaid shirt musicians proclaimed loudly and off-key: "I never promised you a rose garden."

When the band took a much-appreciated break, the twangy complaints were silenced. A woman in a black T-shirt, mug in hand, made her way over to my table. "Hi. May I join you?"

"Sure. Please have a seat. I'm Guy."

She had shiny, long, jet-black hair, a round face, and a plump body, and I soon found out that her name was Michele. "I just arrived in town," she said. "I don't know anyone, and I sure could use some company." Michelle was of First Nations descent but had been adopted and raised out east. She was in town to meet her birth family. Excited by the prospect but a bit nervous, after talking to each other for a while, she invited me to accompany her to their first meeting the next morning. I accepted her offer and told her it would be my honor as I'd always felt a calling toward native cultures, so this seemed like a godsend.

I hadn't any personal experience with the First Nations yet, but was horribly shocked by the stoning of cars last summer: Nicknamed "The Oka Crisis" it had started as a land dispute between Mohawk nationals and Quebecers from the town of Oka a few minutes from Montreal. It made the headlines all the way to Amsterdam. "The people of Kahnawake evacuate their women, children and elders for their safety. Seventy-five cars leave and are met by a furious mob that throws rocks injuring several people!!" *This is insane! How can there be so much hate?* I felt I had received the rocks myself.

We agreed to meet in front of the hotel early the next morning. As I walked back to John and Alicia's place, it didn't feel quite as cold as it had before. *My life is moving in the right direction: first the opening here, then getting offered new shows, the opportunity to return to Amsterdam, and now meeting native folks in their homeland.*

I was so keyed up with anticipation that I couldn't fall asleep. After setting my alarm clock, I admired the constellations through the window and marveled at a shooting star. *I felt alone in Amsterdam, but now, like Little Orphan Annie, all I can think about is tomorrow.*

The next morning, my nose tingled in the arctic air as we made our way to Michele's birth aunt's place. Thousands of thoughts ran through my mind. *What is it like to meet one's family for the first time?* I had just discovered my Dutch family of friends in Amsterdam, yet I felt that I had no place in my own family.

"I can't wait to meet them!" Michele beamed with excitement.

Her aunt opened the door with a welcoming smile. "Michele! So nice to finally meet you face-to-face!" Then she shook my hand and with a welcoming smile said, "I'm Georgina. Welcome to our home!" After the introductions, she brought us into the living room. The apartment was quite bare because they had just moved in. On a wall hung a carpet of a proud buck with majestic antlers, surrounded by his doe and two fawns. On the floor a simple mattress and some boxes and bags lined up against the wall.

"This is Nana Margaret and Papa George, my husband, Ken, and our darling six-year-old daughter, Barbara."

"Hi, everyone! I'm Guy," I said with a wave and a smile. "Pleased to meet you."

Georgina went to the kitchen with little Barbara jumping excitedly behind her, then she came back with a basket of hot cornbread and soft drinks. "Here you go. Don't be shy." I felt at ease right away.

As soon as Michele and I sat on the floor, Barbara ran circles around us. "Catch me if you can!" she giggled while looking at me.

"Calm down, Li'l Barb! Let our guests have a bite to eat," her mother warned.

But Barb's cute button nose enticed me, so I happily granted her wish. I chased her round and round and always "missed her by that much!" as the whole family giggled. Out of breath, she finally let me catch her then proceeded to show me her dolls. Michele's eyes twinkled with delight, and my heart melted as I basked in the warmth of a loving family.

After lunch, I excused myself to go pack, but I assured them that I would stop by before leaving. I wanted to give them something personal and meaningful to show how grateful I was. Among the childhood items I'd brought for *Memorabilia,* I found a necklace that I'd sculpted when I was nine years old. It was inspired by the one that Rahan, a courageous, prehistoric warrior from the French comic book *Pif Gadget,* wore around his neck.

My magical talisman consisted of a flat, round stone with a hole in it and a wooden bear claw that I'd carved. These were tied together with a piece of brown leather. Playing in the sandbox as a child, I felt that the combination of wood, stone, and leather were Mother Nature's protective forces so I always felt safe wearing it.

I was pleased to see that Michele was still with them when I came back. Li'l Barb sprang to the door when she saw me and pulled me in to join the others in the living room. I kneeled down to her and said, "Hi, sweetie. I'm leaving soon, but I brought you a gift."

After I gently placed the necklace over her head, she lifted it up to her face, caressed the wood and stone, then jumped with joy as she held it tightly in her tiny hands. Then she ran around the room joyfully showing everyone and shouting, "Look what I got! Look what I got! It's from Guy. It's a magical necklace to protect me!"

Papa George's face lit up when he saw the necklace. When he put his big, coarse hands on my shoulder and murmured: "Miigwech, Miigwech" thanking me with tears in his eyes, I felt his respect and love. Taking out the camera, we immortalized the moment with a family portrait. It was as if roots had just shot out and grown into the earth. *I have my spiritual family.*

When it was time for me to leave this loving home, I said, "Thank you all for your welcome. Your family is lovely."

"The pleasure was ours, Guy. It was great to meet you, and thanks for the necklace," Georgina answered back. We came together for one last hug, but there was one person missing.

"Hey Li'l Barb, Guy's leaving now," Michele called out.

When Barbara heard that, she rushed into the room and hung on to me with tears streaming down her face. As I lifted her up and squeezed her one last time, I told her, "I'm so grateful to you, my little angel. Wear this talisman always, and I will always be here with you."

When I put her down, she grasped the necklace tightly in her little hand, and ran over to nestle between her parents. As she hugged them, I thought to myself, *There is so much love in this family.*

"Bye little sweetheart," I whispered to Li'l Barb as I waved goodbye. My heart felt a pinch, but a beam of light warmed my face. *Was it the setting sun or did it come from inside me?* I wondered. Although I often felt like a homeless orphan, I now had two additional families: one in Amsterdam and a spiritual one in Canada.

Chapter 24

SAY, IF IT WERE TRUE

"Hey, Guy! It's great to see you. Come on in." Michael looked like a hobbit straight out of Tolkien's *The Lord of the Rings*. He was small and stout with curly brown hair, and he smiled and laughed mischievously all the time.

His wife, Sylvia, poked her head through the doorway, saw my backpack, and was quite surprised. "Guy, how wonderful! Why didn't you tell us you were coming? We were just getting ready for lunch."

They didn't receive my letter! I panicked.

"Hey, girls! Look who's here!" Their two young daughters danced like little elves as they put my bag in the living room and rolled out a yoga mat behind the couch. "Who's ready to eat?"

My stomach growled in anticipation. I could smell the wonderful aroma of a steaming *stamppot*, a typical Dutch dish of mashed potatoes mixed with ham, cheese, and endive.

"Would you like some wine or a beer?" Michael offered. "Help yourself to some bread, butter, and aged gouda.".

Michael and Sylvia welcomed me into their home, and for the next two weeks, we joyfully swapped stories and platefuls of laughter. It was perfect, but I needed a studio space where I could create new works for my upcoming exhibit. Upon hearing of my need, Michael's friends, Wim and Freek, generously offered their attic.

"I used to give private yoga lessons up there, but it's not really supposed to be lived in," Wim said. "But, hey that's fine with us. There's a window, electricity, and you can always join us downstairs whenever you want."

I gladly accepted, hugged Michael and Sylvia's family goodbye, and set off for my new living space.

Just a few streets from the VANA the attic had no telephone or running water, but the window did let in a fair amount of sunlight, and, above all, it was blissfully quiet. I set out for Waterlooplein's market and bought a secondhand hot plate, a radio, and a small, electronic keyboard. Ready to get to work, I made my way to the gallery in the Jordaan district.

"Ah, Monsieur Guy, what a pleasure to see you, please have a seat." Eric, a tall and skinny German in his twenties, always enjoyed calling me ceremoniously by my first name. Like a puppet whose strings had been replaced with rubber bands, his gestures were exaggerated, even comical.

He uncorked a bottle of red wine and began, "So I planned the opening for June 28 . . . in six weeks. What's the title of your show?"

As I looked at the space with its huge white walls and skylight, I thought about my Family Show. A gorgeous, natural light filled the whole space and the wicker-covered floor shimmered like a golden field of wheat. "I'm not sure yet," I confessed. "How much time will I have to set up the exhibit?"

"Well, this show is closing on the twenty-sixth, so you'll have all day on the twenty-seventh and the morning of the twenty-eighth."

As I thought about this, I realized that creating an installation in my tiny attic studio was out of the question. "OK. That's fine," I answered "Let me get back to you about the title in a few days."

Michael had lent me his bicycle, so I rode it to my favorite thinking spot in Amsterdam, the terrace of the film museum in Vondelpark. With a coffee and a spice cookie at the ready, I opened my sketchbook and began jotting down some ideas. But after a few crossed-out drawings, I closed my book and let my mind wander. Between the emerald-green trees, the sunshine, the light breeze, and the quacking ducks, everything seemed so perfect. I was fulfilled and happy, and it felt good.

That's it! The title of my show will be The Pleasure of Happiness. And then I remembered the vibrant objects I'd painted while at Concordia University: the book, bed, umbrella, and green stool. I reopened my sketchbook and drew a dozen colorful stools. *The stool will be my alter ego because nobody pays any attention to it; it's often abandoned, alone in the corner. But not this time. This time, I will dedicate a whole show to it!*

I tried a few compositions with acrylic paint on heavy paper and thought, *This is going to work!* When I announced the title to Eric a few days later, he liked it and said he found it intriguing. It was all settled.

For the next four weeks, working in the attic, I bought bottled water, cans of baked beans and spam as I felt too shy to intrude on my new hosts. I urinated in a jar which I emptied into the gutter just outside my window. And for my bowel movement, I'd squat down over newspapers, folded up neatly and disposed in the public bins. I washed my clothes at the same corner laundry as when I was in the VANA, and enjoyed cool breaks at the local swimming pool.

Evenings I'd often eat out at the local Surinam café. I'd order their specialty, a tasty Gado-Gado consisting of vegetables, fried tofu, eggs smothered in spicy peanut butter sauce! Other nights I would meet with Michael, Sylvia, Maria, Paula, and other members of my Dutch family for a beer. It was the artist's life I'd always dreamed of. Pretty soon I had all my new works ready for the show.

Eric was always the perfect host, and opening night was no exception. He personally greeted the dozens of visitors and introduced them to me. "This is the artist, Monsieur Guy. He's Canadian."

After I shook their hands and thanked them for coming, some would ask me to give them a tour of my paintings. So, with pleasure, I'd lead them around the twenty works on display. "This one is called *Don't Poke Me in the Eye*," I'd announce as I pointed to a stool hidden in what appeared to be an inkblot from a Rorschach test. "And here is *Carriages of Love Can Never Be Found*." It featured a yellow wooden stool on rockers. *The Heart Beats to Its Own Melody* featured a six-legged stool dissolving into the red-hot fire of passion. This was one of two paintings that were sold after the opening.

"You've got an incredible sense of composition and color," one visitor commented, while another praised, "Wow! It's just an ordinary stool. Who would've thought it could be so expressive?"

At the end of the night, Eric gave me a big hug. It was a veritable success for me and his gallery. "Thank you, Monsieur Guy. You've created a wonderful series!"

With the stress of preparing for the show finally over, I took a well-deserved break from my tiny attic by spending a day at one of my favorite beaches at Zandvoort aan Zee. Upon my return, Amphitrite, the goddess of the sea, seemed to have read my mind as I found a place of my own only a few streets from the gallery.

My new dwelling, which was yet another attic, still lacked a phone, but wonder of wonders, it had a sink, a fridge, a toilet in the hallway, and most important of all, a lease. *After four years of living surreptitiously in my studios and sleeping on dozens of couches, I finally have an official home!*

I enjoyed having no fixed obligations and spending hours in Vondelpark reading and writing by the film museum. There I saw the Jane Campion film An Angel at My Table, which follows the true story of Janet Frame who was abused in her youth, alienated and institutionalized and finally saved from a lobotomy by her poetry. I was compelled to see the film four times, and each time, I sobbed uncontrollably. I felt we were kindred spirits who shared the survival spirit of my *Warrior.*

One evening, I was surprised to find the terrace full, so I moved inside where more people were gathered. As the bar became more crowded, I noticed an elegant woman sitting by herself reading a book. Remembering how Michele had had the courage to join me at my table, I dared to do the same. "Hello, would you like some company?"

She smiled and invited me to sit down. Her name was Jos and she was tall and slim and wore her sand-colored hair in short curls. We talked the whole evening, discussing our passion for books and music, especially jazz.

"I love Keith Jarrett's *Köln Concert*!" I exclaimed.

"Chet Baker is the greatest! I love his trumpet playing and his voice is so suave." She answered back with glee.

When the bar closed, we agreed to meet the following evening at Café Alto for some live jazz. She even came to my small attic to hear me play my own compositions on my little keyboard. With its silly drumbeat, my song "Dance" made her giggle. But her eyes glistened when I played my first childhood composition. She came closer and whispered, "You're a very sensitive man."

With sales of my artwork, my own space, and my budding friendship with sophisticated Jos, everything seemed perfect. I felt so peaceful and relaxed that I decided it was time to attend Wim's yoga classes.

"Guy, you finally came! Nice to see you again!" he greeted as I entered the small basement where he taught yoga. "This is my friend, Guy, from Canada. He'll be joining us tonight." The four other students politely nodded and unrolled their mats. Wim started with some simple breathing exercises then led us in various poses. I was awed at his ability to tie his body into knots that would baffle even the most seasoned sailor.

For the next hour, I tried to emulate my childhood comic book hero Plastic Man as best I could. But I failed miserably. By the end of the session, I was exhausted, so I welcomed Wim's instruction to wind down with the lights off and our eyes closed in silent relaxation. His deep baritone voice guided us through alternately tensing and relaxing our muscles. "Take a deep breath, clench your fists, now hold, hold . . . and then let go as you exhale."

After exploring every nook and cranny of my body, I surrendered in a cottony softness and lay in total silence. I was swaddled in pure bliss until an onslaught of terrifying images exploded in my mind: *I'm in danger, someone's attacking me. It's dark. A face with a huge, open mouth lunges at me. I try to scream. I try to fight back. I'm scared. My tiny, chubby hands and legs push against the face. I struggle. I'm on my back—a baby in a crib.*

SMACK! I'm hit with a violent slap! Pain! I don't know where it's coming from; I feel it all over my body. Now everything is gone. I'm alone. The whole world disappears. I've destroyed it. It's my fault. I destroyed the world! It's my fault! I'm bad, and I'm alone. I shriek in tears.

Wim's gentle voice rescued me from my nightmare. "Now start to slowly wiggle your toes and fingers as we come back into our active bodies."

When the class ended, I couldn't get up. Still in shock, my body refused to move. *I . . . I don't know what to make of it. It was so real—all of it. What was it?* I felt raw as if a wound had just been reopened. *Could this really have happened?* I'd never had any memories even remotely like this. When I was finally able to pull myself up from my mat, I rolled it up and thanked Wim for the session.

Why here? Why now? I wondered. *Were these actual memories? There was so much pain, so much fright. I can still feel the slap throughout my body.* For the first time in my life, I was in a good, peaceful, and safe place, but I was haunted by the sight of my chubby, little fingers pushing against the giant face. That night, I wrote in my journal:

July 14, 1991

In yoga, I saw myself at three years old receiving a terrible slap, a big hit from one of my parents. But I couldn't feel where on my body. I feel that when I was three years old, they—Mom and Dad—had a big fight (maybe Mom received the slap?), they shouted and screamed at each other, and I was terribly scared, scared, so scared, like my whole world was falling apart and disappearing. And I screamed and I cried because I was afraid everything was falling apart. I wanted to make it stop, so I screamed harder and then she (Mom) took me out of the playpen in the kitchen and put me alone, crying, in my crib in my bedroom.

I raised my shoulders and cried to myself because I felt like I'd destroyed the world and all that was left was me alone. I dug myself in my shoulders and told myself I would never, never let myself go again because my world would again be destroyed. I killed it. I could never trust again because, at any moment, I could destroy my world by letting go. So I must always be aware, always have structure, always have control. Never trust, never give the control to someone else because, at any moment, I could destroy my world. I am bad. I am wicked. I scream. And that has to be controlled before I destroy my world.

I read and reread what I'd just written, but still I failed to understand. Then I remembered the old family albums I'd found in my mother's basement. Something had bothered me about my childhood photos. In some of them, my youthful, babyish smile had been replaced with a sad frown. As I finally went to bed, Jacques Brel's song "Dites, Si C'était Vrai" ("Say, If It Were True") skipped repeatedly in my mind like a broken record. *What if it wasn't a vision after all?* I wondered. *What if it was an actual memory?*

I never returned to Wim's yoga class, and besides, I had three new *Family Show*s in Canada to prepare for. So, I bought my return ticket, paid my landlady the rest of my rent, and packed up my paintings when the show closed.

"Monsieur Guy, it was an honor—no . . . a real *Pleasure of Happiness* to exhibit your wonderful artwork," Eric remarked with his usual flair.

"The pleasure was all mine," I assured as I gave him a hug and felt a twinge of sadness in my heart.

My last few weeks in Amsterdam flew by like a runaway train as I tried to cram in seeing all my favorite places and friends: Vondelpark, the film museum, Zandvoort aan Zee, Café Alto, and my Dutch family. Maria and Erwin prepared a feast and reunited the gang from the academy who'd rescued me from my inner turmoil. We talked nostalgically about our teachers, Berlin, the secret bedrooms in my studios, and then ended the evening sharing our hopes and dreams. "Guy, we do hope you'll come back to visit," Maria said as I put on my jacket.

"I will," I promised. "You are all my family." Then I hugged each of them one last time. It felt like a hole had opened in my heart, but I had one more person to see on my last night in Amsterdam.

By the time I met up with Jos, night had fallen and she was waiting for me by the lamppost next to the canal. We kissed and held hands as we made our way to my room. She hadn't wanted a relationship because she had just gotten out of a bad one and I was leaving. In essence, we were licking each other's wounds. But even though we'd tried not to, we had fallen deeply in love.

I opened the door to a lone mattress. My oversized backpack, which was filled to the rim, was slouched in the corner. I lit some candles, put on Chet Baker's "Alone Together," and set out a plate of grapes, figs, and, her favorite, white chocolate. Our kisses were sweet as we undressed, caressed, and consummated our love one last time. As we rested in a sweaty embrace, I whispered, "I love you." Then I closed my eyes as her warm breath tickled my neck.

But sleep didn't come. Instead, I got dizzy, hyperventilated, and the room spun as I experienced a spell of vertigo. "Stop it! Stop it!" I cried out to myself, to Jos, to the universe. I wanted off the carousel.

We looked at each other, teary-eyed. There was nothing left to do; our fate was sealed.

At five a.m., we stepped out into the bluish hues of daybreak and made our way to Centraal Station. Pausing at the station's platform, we tried to find comfort in a final embrace, but we both trembled with silent sobs. As I boarded the train, I became Guy, the hero from the 1964 film *The Umbrellas of Cherbourg*. In the movie, Genevieve, Guy's lover (my Jos), sobs with handkerchief in hand and runs after the train. As it leaves the station, she stands alone on the platform then vanishes into the billowing white clouds of smoke from the locomotive as the scene fades to black.

Brokenhearted, in my mind, I saw my own credits rolling as the canal faded from view. Jos, my friends, and the names of my Dutch family members all passed before my eyes as if on a movie screen. Then, as if closing off the latest chapter of my life, I saw the words: THE END.

Chapter 25

FINDING A KEY

With no money and no place to stay, I was relieved to see my dad at the airport. "Hello, son," he greeted. "You had a pleasant flight? I have a sofa bed in my spare room. You can stay there if that's alright with you."

"That's fine, Dad. Thanks." His invitation was more than welcome. When we got back to his place, I was happy to see that the portrait I'd drawn of him still hung on the wall.

Dad spent long hours at the hospital, but when he'd return from work, he'd offer me a beer, turn on the news, and prepare two thick steaks. "With lots of butter, because that's good for you!" Other nights we'd listen to his favorite classical work, Mozart's *Requiem*. "Listen to the Lacrimosa. It means 'weeping.' It's so touching."

But if I talked about my upcoming exhibit, I felt his unease. He disregarded the memories I'd experienced during Wim's yoga class in one fell swoop, saying, "What you don't remember can't affect you!" It was like he'd slapped the whole science of psychology in the face.

I didn't fare any better at family gatherings. Whenever I tried to tell them about my exhibits, I was accused of "bringing our family into the public arena." Amsterdam had changed me, but they were still the same. As always, my one and only role was to play along as the Silent Good Boy and make believe that everything was perfect. Still painfully aware of their dysfunctional abuse, I felt my soul shrivel back into its protective cocoon whenever I was violently criticized. *It's Bateson's double bind in action,* I reminded myself. *I'm damned if I do and damned if I don't. It's hopeless. I have to get out of here as fast as possible!* Not surprisingly, I started to shirk family get-togethers.

Since my second *Family Show* wasn't until November, I had a full two months to prepare, so to earn some money, I took a job as a production assistant at a local cable TV station. My boss was so impressed with my artwork that he asked me to be a guest on the station's culture program "Le riche lieu des arts". With my long, brown hair and round glasses, I discussed my work with Anne-Marie Arcamone while my paintings and installations were shown on-screen. I was finally getting some recognition after being rejected by my family.

I decided to try to find some former classmates to reconnect. Per chance, I met up with one at an art gallery, and magic happened when he introduced me to the curator's sister, who was in town visiting. "Hi, I'm Kathy," she said. "It's a pleasure to meet you. What do you make of this painting?" She pointed to a very expressive wall-sized bird and laughed. "Isn't it funny?"

Kathy was a well-dressed, no-nonsense lawyer with short, sandy-blonde hair and a raspy voice like Janis Joplin. She used the power of the spoken word in defending her clients, but her real passion was writing poetry. I felt a kinship with her as we talked about her poems, journaling, and our travels. She was intrigued by my *Family Show* and wanted to know more, but she had to get back to her hotel because she was leaving the next day. So we arranged to meet early the next morning at magnificent Mount Royal Park in downtown Montreal.

Like Amsterdam's Vondelpark, Mount Royal—affectionately nicknamed "the Mountain"—was my favorite spot in the city. We drank in the fresh autumn air and soaked in the fiery red, orange, and golden leaves. It was a tapestry for the senses.

"Why are you so interested in family dynamics?" Kathy asked.

I averted my gaze from the ground to the deep blue sky then finally peered into her eyes. *Can I trust her—a complete stranger?*

"What's your worst thing in your life?" Before I knew it, I was opening my heart and revealing all the loneliness I'd felt, the painful relationships I'd experienced, and the suicidal thoughts I'd had. It all came out. I even told her about the vision I'd had during the yoga session. As she sat there, silently listening to all my sad stories, I felt her warmth.

"Do you think you were sexually abused?" she gently inquired.

No one had ever asked me that before. Hesitantly, I said that I wasn't sure.

"I just ask because I've read many biographies of authors who were sexually abused as children, and your story seems quite similar."

"Well, that vision of being in my crib definitely felt real, like an actual memory. But I have no idea what it means." Sexual abuse was a term I'd never heard before. "I'd have to ask my mom."

While I walked back to the main road in a contemplative silence, the wind carried my thoughts to the clouds as Kathy left for the airport. *An angel has crossed my path,* I thought, *and now she's returning to the heavens.*

A few days later, I was sitting at my mom's kitchen table while her husband repaired the balcony door. By this time, she was remarried and living in a nondescript row of suburban houses. When my stepdad left for the hardware store to get a part, I asked, "You know the slides I used in *The Family Show*?" She nodded. "Well, while I was going through the old pictures, I noticed that I had this wonderful smile as a baby, but then later, it's gone. Did something happen when I was young?"

There was a moment of silence before she finally said, "Why do you ask?"

"Because I recently had this very strange memory come to me and I don't know what it's all about."

Mom stared out the window then, with a look of resignation, turned back toward me. In a flat, dispassionate tone, the truth unraveled. "When you were about three, my sixteen-year-old niece stayed with us for a couple of months. She helped with the chores, like cooking and giving you boys baths. One morning, I heard a lot of giggling coming from the bathroom, so I went in to see what was so funny. That's when I caught her masturbating you." When she said the word *masturbating,* my shame and guilt wrenched my gut, but she went on.

"I threw the door wide open, yelled, and slapped her. She ran out of the room, but you kept on screaming and crying, so I picked you up, took you to your room, and closed the door. I left you alone while I went back to take care of her. She was gone the next day."

I was floored, utterly speechless. In the twenty-eight years since this incident occurred, no one had ever said a word to me, and they probably never would have if I hadn't asked. *What does this mean?* I wondered. My mom stated it matter-of-factly, without emotion, as if we'd simply purchased a new fridge that year. *I guess it simply isn't important.* Like she always said, "The past is the past. There's no point talking about it."

On the bus heading for home, I suddenly realized it was the same line that saved my life seven years earlier. *What irony! I ran from Jack the Knife as he tried to gut me, and now I've just learned about what my cousin did to me in my own home. Are they connected? Are there consequences? Mom and Dad sure don't think so.* As I tried to wrap my mind around Mom's revelation, I thought with a shudder, *At least I know that memory I had in Wim's yoga class was real.*

Listening to my inner voice, I looked for answers in the self-help section of a bookstore. I could not find any books on men who were sexually abused as children, so I picked up *The Courage to Heal: A Guide for Women Survivors of Child Sexual Abuse* by Ellen Bass and

Laura Davis. Although it was written with women in mind, I figured it could be helpful for any survivor. I bought the book and a coffee, settled into a reading spot, rolled and lit a cigarette. Nervously I coughed at my first inhale spilling burning hot coffee on my lap; my scorched lungs felt good, and bad. The smoke swirled over me as if it were dancing to Keith Jarrett's *Köln Concert,* which was playing on my Walkman. I searched for reassurance with my spice cookie which of course wasn't there.

Journal on the table, pencil next to it, I examined the cover and read the back-jacket text for a third time. *What am I going to find inside? I can't believe Mom finally told me.* As the nicotine buzz took over, I felt numb enough—or perhaps courageous enough—to start reading.

When I opened the book, it was like a bomb went off! *LONELINESS, SELF-HATRED, SHAME, GUILT, SUICIDAL THOUGHTS...* It was like the authors were speaking directly at me with warm and compassionate terms, but the ugly words lashed out like knives slashing my throat, cutting through my heart, and shredding my soul. *This book is about me!* Page after page was an awakening as I discovered words to finally describe my feelings. *You mean there's a name for this and I don't have to live it? I can hardly believe it. All the hurt, all the pain actually has meaning?* At last, my life made sense.

I was grateful that Mom confirmed my abuse as I soon learned that many victims experience blackouts, live in deep denial, or are laughed at for lack of evidence. I now had something concrete to work with. *I'm not crazy after all! Something did happen to me.*

In my journal, I furiously carved notes, copying again and again the words that resonated with me the most: *dirty, shame, fear, suicide, insomnia.* My body shook, but this time it was no longer from pain; it was from the release of tears. *Someone finally understands me, hears me, validates me! This is the happiest day of my life and also the worst day of my life.*

AAAAARRRRRRGGGGGHHHHHHHHHHHHHHHHH!!!

For the first time, a searing flame of anger exploded inside me. *I was justified dammit! I was right! My family, my teachers, society—they all shit on me. Throughout my life, I've felt ugly, stupid, never good enough, always wrong. I've lived in terror, always needing to hide to escape the next hit. Worst of all, I've always felt completely alone—alone with my shameful, dirty sex, wanting to cut off my penis, my heart and my soul shattered over and over again by failed relationships.*

I slammed my fist down on the table, smashing my pencil into a million pieces and startling the other customers around me. They looked at me, but I didn't give a fuck. I felt the need to break something.

I took what was left of the pencil and started writing my story for the first time:

October 13, 1991

FUCK! All these years, I have been repeating the same fucking pattern: finding women who only want to be with me not for who I am but for what they can get from me. You know what my cousin did to me twenty-eight years ago??? She fucking stole my sexuality! You know how it feels to be left behind again and again, to have your heart broken over and over? Because of her, I cried and ached in the night. I always felt I was missing something because she was never there. I BELONGED TO HER!!

I could never experience pleasure for myself. I could never let go. I could never be me because she could always run away with what was left of me. I had to be on my guard all the time, and I couldn't breathe a word because she would abandon me again like the first time. My sexuality wasn't mine; it was hers. I wasn't responsible; I could never do what I wanted. If I was ever attracted to someone, I always had to wait because I had nothing to give anymore. I was destroyed inside.

All these years of feeling empty, out of touch, out of control, suicidal, and never able to give, I had so little left inside. Well the fucker won't get away with it anymore. Today, I'm putting my foot down. No, I'm putting it right in her face like I tried to do so many years ago. Fuck, I was only three years old! I couldn't defend myself. I was fighting her and kicking her, but what could I do against a sixteen-year-old girl?

I was so scared that I died inside. But whatever remained had to go on, so I did. And I forgot—I even forgot to feel empty inside. But then I started to search for her. I was looking for something, and I had no fucking idea what it was! And then when I started having girlfriends, you were not there, so I felt like I was always missing something. You were still using me, you bitch, for revenge or something. But I WAS THREE YEARS OLD! Don't you understand? I DIDN'T HURT YOU? SO WHY THE FUCK DID YOU DESTROY ME????????? The loss and the pain I've experienced because of you, bitch, you had me twenty-eight years ago, and since then, I've always lived scared and felt empty.

We are already alone, did you have to destroy what was left of me? I used to even excuse myself for living! Do you know what it's like to not feel worthy enough to breathe?

Fuck you, woman! I don't want to die anymore! I want to live, I want to be free! I want to experience myself for myself! Damn you! Today I'm back to being three years old, and I'm fucking defending myself! DON'T touch me, you fucking BITCH!!! This is not a body! This is me—Guy, Guy Giard—and I won't let you take anything away from me! I am me! I am a person!

Today, I won't be scared anymore. Nobody—nobody—has the right to take me away from me again! I have regained possession of myself. I'm finally whole again. I'm finally back in my skin, in my feelings. I can take charge and feel again, and I will give and love and grow and cry and feel because I have finally found myself.

Today, I can finally rest; I can finally love, finally be.

Closing my journal, I went back to my father's place, watched the news, and silently ate the thick sirloin steak and beer he served. I figured if he didn't understand the long-lasting impact my cousin's actions had on me since I was three years old, he wasn't going to get it now, either. I thanked him for the nice meal, and as I cleaned up in the kitchen, I said, "I'm off to Windsor in a couple of weeks for my show, Dad."

"That's fine, son. Good night," he replied before disappearing into his room.

I shut off the lights, went to my room, closed the door, and reacquainted with more pieces of myself in *The Courage to Heal.* The book was the key to opening the first door to my freedom.

Chapter 26

THE FAMILY SHOW II AND III

Windsor, Ontario, was half a day's drive from Montreal. The gallery where I'd be exhibiting my work offered its own studio apartment, which suited me just fine. The intimacy of the space made it possible for me to delve deeper into *The Courage to Heal*, which had become the inspiration for the title of my exhibit: *The Family Show II: Family Fil(l)ings*. I chose the word *fillings* as in the lies you've been filled with, and *filings* for the truths left behind. But first, I had to get a sense of the city itself.

As much as Regina was rural, Windsor was a modern urban center with a towering bridge connecting it to Detroit, Michigan. As I visited Windsor's US neighbor, I was shocked to find the downtown core peppered with boarded-up high-rises and abandoned mansions. It seemed that the deep wounds inflicted by the 1967 race riots had left many scars.

After returning to Windsor, I sat on the boardwalk overlooking the Detroit River. Night had fallen and I shivered in the cold as I marveled at the glistening skyline. *Two cities joined by a bridge,* I thought. *Windsor is staring at luminous Detroit like a jealous twin.* Various impressions popped into my mind until one theme became clear: *Yes, that's it! It's about division!* I decided right then that the exhibit, which was set to open a few weeks later, would offer two updated works from Regina as well as two new ones.

Instead of having a twin bed like I did in Regina, I would use two singles with a divide between them. Each bed was covered with a floral-print bedspread and had a brown bedside table, a lamp, and bounded copies of *Reader's Digest*. The beds were placed in a darkened space with white lights emanating from under. With the new title of *Two Beds Are Better than One*, the threatening and ominous glow displayed at the Regina show had been expanded with the coldness of division.

Conversation Piece also transformed from the rural setting in Regina to the smaller family unit of modern cities. Instead of wood, I chose classic 1960s chrome furniture with beige vinyl upholstery. The square kitchen table had a Formica top with a design of dots and lines. It was immaculately set with plates, teacups adorned with flowery decorations and a tall, glass vase with colorful plastic flowers. *It's all too perfect!*

Instead of cassette players, record players on each of the four chairs spun empty under their scratching needles. *Scritch Scritch* The arms tied with metal wire to their stands: it symbolized that everyone had lost their voices and was condemned to remain silent. This represented me. My family's censorship of me weighed heavily on my soul, so the illusion of conversation was replaced with the reality of silence.

A new piece called *Winter Casualty* depicted an abandoned child lying on the gallery floor. The child was wearing a beige snowsuit and gloves and a thick, red-and-blue wool scarf that covered his entire face. In the harsh Canadian winters, young children were so overdressed by doting parents that when they went outside to play, they could barely move. As a result, if they fell on their backs, they'd become prisoners like upside-down turtles. I was that abandoned and suffocating little boy, thinking, *I can't see anything, where is help?*

The most striking installation at this exhibit was *Six Years of Burnt*

Toast: a wall made of pieces of burnt toast. Measuring twelve feet long, three feet high, and twenty inches thick (400 cm x 100 cm x 50 cm), it divided the space in two.

"Guy, what are you planning to do with two hundred loaves of white bread?" the worried gallery director asked me.

"You'll see after I burn them all," I said with a chuckle.

The assistant helped me toast the bread on a grill set up on the patio outside the gallery. We laid down the briskets, lit them and for a full day burned every piece of bread. I carefully wheeled them back in for they broke easily and took two days to pile them up. It was quite a feat considering the pieces of toast only stood under their own weight.

The scent provoked memories that caused visitors to eagerly share their personal stories. One man recalled, "When I was a kid, I tried to prepare breakfast while my parents were still asleep." He started to giggle. "I burned the toast so badly that the kitchen filled with smoke. My dad came running in thinking I'd set the house on fire!" the man roared with laughter.

"That smell," the gallery director and the assistant kept telling me, "it's so powerful! Everyone is talking about it."

"That's the power of the nose. And there's also tension. Imagine what it takes for a person to burn his toast every morning and never learn from his mistake," I explained. "Think about how much denial he has as he carefully piles them up to make a protective wall."

I took a piece of toast, felt its rough texture, studied its charred shades, and wondered what it was trying to tell me. I gently scratched the surface and was surprised by the whiteness of the bread underneath. *I'm like that piece of toast! Underneath my scarred and damaged surface, I've been alive all along!* I left Windsor one step closer in my healing journey.

But once I returned to my father's place, as much as I tried, I couldn't avoid the next family get-together, which was to be held on Christmas Eve when my siblings were planning to come over to Dad's for dinner—without Mom, of course. I had distant memories of my parents being in the same room but none whatsoever of them hugging, kissing, or even smiling at each other. I had just the faintest image of Dad sitting at the round kitchen table for the obligatory Sunday meal, while my brothers went at each other and Mom stood by the stove.

Since the divorce, they only referred to each other as "your mother" or "your father." And so, it became our family tradition to have two birthday parties, two Easter dinners, and celebrate Christmas twice—once with each parent. My heart bled because I never saw them together again, and since there had been no marriages, no christenings and no death in our family this unspoken rule remained unchallenged.

As we sat around Dad's table on Christmas Eve, I casually brought up the subject of my *Family Shows*. But it was the same as usual. "It's just a pack of lies," they accused, "so why don't you just shut up!" It was clear that there was no use discussing my exhibits or the sexual abuse my mother had confirmed.

My brother Marc, the Joker, was the only one who didn't gang up on me. He'd had to deal with his own ghosts while he was in and out of mental wards. I appreciated the letters he and I had exchanged while I was in Amsterdam, and once I returned, we often met for coffee outside the family gatherings. Coincidently, my other brother, Luc, had had his first psychotic episode the weeks after I'd openly talked about abuse.

With my third *Family Show* coming up in Peterborough, Ontario, in February, I kept on studying *The Courage to Heal*. I felt enraged as I recognized time and time again new facets of the hurts I'd experienced all my life. Doubts, fears, insecurity, and insomnia were all maggots eating away at my life. *What can I do,* I pondered, *sweep all my emotions under the rug? No! Life is too short. I can't ignore these feelings. They're too important!* Instead, I took the bull by the horns and made the third show about sexual abuse.

Luckily, the city of Peterborough, Ontario, was only five hours away by train. Most of all, my former classmate Lynn had moved back there. By this time, Lynn was curator of the Artspace gallery. When I shared my childhood experiences with her, tears came to her eyes. When I realized that I could acknowledge her sadness more than mine, I knew I still hadn't connected with my feelings.

Through Lynn, I met Danielle, a fellow artist …and member of the gallery, who I'd be staying with while I was in Peterborough. A short woman in her forties, Danielle was as colorful as her vibrant paintings. Every morning, I awoke to the scent of blueberry pancakes, eggs, and sausages. Her cat, Snowy, with her fluffy white fur, joyfully purred and meowed as she rubbed her big round belly against my legs, begging for a bite of my breakfast. What a treat it was staying at Danielle's place.

The exhibition space was quite peculiar. It had an exposed, red brick wall on one side and the typical, pristine white gallery wall on the other. The third wall, which was opposite the entrance, had an enormous bay window that offered a view of the main avenue. It was like we were basically inside and outside simultaneously. As I sat down on the bland, gray carpet—with coffee and cigarette in hand—and prepared to work, I thought to myself, *What is this room telling me?*

Over the years, with my art I'd learned to trust the process of being still, just letting go and listening. "I'm not waiting for some sort of mystical inspiration," I'd explained to Lynn. "Every portion of the space has a story to tell if you listen carefully." There's something magical about subconsciously processing information.

Quietly, I emptied my mind and let myself get in tune with the "voice" of the space. Five minutes, fifteen minutes, half an hour passed as I took in all the ingredients like a chef: the high ceilings, the brick wall, the immaculate white wall, bringing the outside inside, sexual abuse. And then I saw them: *I'll hang clotheslines like we used to in the back alley of my childhood home, but instead of blue work coveralls, these will be "too perfect," unstained white linen. Yes, that's it! Whitewashing, denial . . . the gallery exposes what has always been denied: Peterborough's stories of abuse!*

The title came to me: *Peterborough on the Line: Clothes to You* as in putting the city "on the line" of danger with stories "close" to them. In my mind's eye, I saw the spotless white clothes floating in the air, like flags out of reach, and four washing machines below them. *How will I get four washing machines up the stairs to the third floor? This is insane! I must do it, but how can I? That's what I want to do, but I don't know how!* I argued back and forth with myself, and after a while, I gave up. *OK, Universe, you want four washing machines, then, so be it!* Resigned, I accepted this challenge and reached out to Lynn and Danielle for help.

While we searched for washing machines, I contacted Peterborough's rape crisis center and presented my project, telling the counselor, "I want this space to be your space to tell the stories that have never been told." He seemed to like the concept, so I added, "This won't be about finger-pointing or being aggressive; I want visitors to be able to under-stand and feel what it's like to have been sexually abused. And I want the survivors to finally have a sense of validation—all in confidentiality, of course."

"That's wonderful, Guy!" he remarked. "I'll send out a call for per-sonal testimonies and will get back to you. Thanks for this very special opportunity." He also agreed to lend me T-shirts with their logo and flyers for the visitors to pick up near the entrance.

We found the washing machines at a local junkyard, and with the help of gallery members, we were able to hoist them up the stairs. I purchased linen at the Salvation Army store, and a couple bags of white garments were donated by members of the community. These items, along with the personal stories I'd collected, really made the installation about Peterborough.

It looked really powerful at the opening. "Above your heads are three long clotheslines with the clothes out of reach as if they are flags on a pole," I explained to the visitors, including the minister of culture.

"The bedsheets, tablecloths, shirts, underwear, everything is perfectly white, too white—the emblems of the 'immaculate family.' It signifies that everything we show the outer world is spotless. But notice the ghostly shadows the items create on the walls. The deeper meaning here is that what is white on the surface can hide something darker."

Below the clotheslines, each of the four installations included a washing machine, a chair, a radio, and a plexiglass covered podium. "I poured Javelle water in the appliances for its acrid smell and to symbolize the whitewashing of the stories," I continued. "And each of the radios are tuned to a different station, which represents that we don't want to hear the truth, so we drown it out with noise.

"The chairs suggest different living environments. This one with old newspapers, crumpled up paper bags, and empty beer bottles is for the families of alcoholics. This chair with pamphlets for the city councilman with well-to-do clothing, blond hair, blue eyes, and sparkling white teeth represents the upper class. This third chair has romance novels for fantasy escapism. And lastly, the blue chair stands for religion. Sadly, abuse takes place across all sections of a community.

"Finally, the four podiums showcase objects that, in their own way, share a personal story of abuse. Two are from your community, one is mine, and the fourth one—the one beside the blue chair—has its radio unplugged. A single sheet of paper rests on the podium with the words: 'This podium is dedicated to the memory of those who have yet to find their voices or are no longer with us.' Sadly, many victims of sexual abuse commit suicide. May they rest in peace." We all paused in silence as those words sunk in. Then I ended my presentation by saying, "Thank you for coming and sharing our stories."

After a warm round of applause, many people shook my hand and offered kind remarks: "Thank you for having the courage to expose the truth. I could never do this." Others shared that they now understood what a friend whom they deeply cared for had experienced. And the minister of culture added, "This is important. You are making a differ-ence. Congratulations."

The week after the opening, I was blessed to lead a workshop for teenagers. "My work is about telling stories," I explained to them. "And for this show, I invited people to tell their stories. So now, I'd like you to do the same." After giving them paper, markers, and crayons, each of them drew a picture about an event in their lives. We hung them on the wall next to the washing machines then had a long discussion. I saw by their smiles that they were proud to claim this space as their own.

The show, along with my lectures and workshops, was well re-ceived and got good reviews in the papers. But I soon had to leave because the final show on this tour was opening in my hometown in just two weeks. As I returned to Danielle's, Snowy greeted me more ardently then ever with incessant meowing as if she were trying to tell me something.

"What's up my little glutton? You want some more pancakes?" She wouldn't leave me alone and insisted that I followed her. "What's wrong, Snowy?" I asked as she led me to my room. As I entered, I heard the faintest crystalline meows coming from my bed. I cautiously raised the bedspread to find a litter of five . . . six . . . seven newborn kittens, their eyes still closed and their tiny pink tongues sticking out in search of Snowy's teats to suckle. A warm glow engulfed me when I brought one minuscule fur ball to my cheek. As I gently stroked its tiny head, I could feel its heart racing. Snowy leaned on my arm, tenderly licked its furry head, and purred like a jackhammer, her vibrating body pulsing into mine.

Snowy wasn't a glutton after all, I realized. *She was pregnant! Taffy had run away from the violence of my family, and now Snowy has chosen me for her family—me! Taffy has forgiven me.* I melted into tears, think-ing, *I'm loved.*

Chapter 27

THE FAMILY SHOW IV

"I've made an appointment for you, Guy," Dad announced as we ate dinner. "The appointment is next week. This therapist was suggested by my colleagues, and he specializes in trauma." Although Dad never took sides at family gatherings and wouldn't discuss it, he also didn't deny the abuse I'd experienced as a child.

"Thanks, Dad. I appreciate it."

After finishing *The Courage to Heal*, I was aflame with urgency. *It's so clear to me now; I need to free myself from the beast.* The last installment of *The Family Show* was going to be the most direct, honest, crude, and confrontational toward my family because I'd decided to address the core of my abuse: incest. *This is my hometown, and my story will be heard.*

I had already visited the gallery space several times, so I just needed to collect the materials for the installation. This time I needed a bed frame, fishing line, fluorescent tube lights, and a crib. I also had the intuition to redraw the four giant faces from *I Remember When*. I wanted to close the loop. When I originally drew the faces, I had no idea that

I'd been a victim of incest, and this was meant to be a conclusion to that chapter of my life.

At my session with the therapist, I readily opened up about my loneliness, my heartbreaks, and my suicidal thoughts. He reassured me that, although painful, these were symptoms of post-traumatic stress disorder (PTSD) resulting from repressed trauma. "You're well on the road to recovery," he kindly assured. "Just be patient with yourself."

I've been patient all my life as the Silent Good Boy. I've had enough! Back in my room, I unleashed my feelings in my journal.

February 28, 1992

My first impression of therapy is that I'm allowed to feel, I'm allowed to hurt, I won't be rejected for feeling bad, and even if I feel or think I'm bad and worthless, there is still a glimmer of hope that things can actually be different. I don't have to carry this pain, this winter cold inside me. Despite my past, I am not alone in this world, there are other people around me, and I don't have to be scared that they are going to destroy my world. When I was young, I thought I destroyed my world, but actually I didn't; it was 'her' who fucking raped me and stole me.

By never opening up, I've accumulated so much pain over the years: first, the pain of my rape and then the loneliness, the abuse, and the hurts of life. I always felt like nobody would listen, nobody cared. I was always alone, so damn alone, and oh so cold.

I took a self-imposed exile of silence because it was not allowed to scream that I was raped. The silence of the dead was more alive than the words that were not to be. Not only was I destroyed emotionally, cut off from myself, but I was further pushed away as I was denied any room for my pain. Silence, denial, and avoidance colored our home, the mother house, the family.

Millions of tears that were never shed have been carried inside, encrusting my soul. Some have dried away, while others created a pool in whose darkness I drowned every night as I turned off the lights. I'd wake up in pain every morning, my shoulders aching from carrying an ocean's weight and the pressure on my chest making it difficult to breathe. I'd look at myself in the mirror and not recognize the person reflected back at me because recognition of my pain might mean a descent within the bottomless pits of despair. I have often felt the pull while standing on the edge, wondering if that would be the day I'd jump from the bridge or walk in front of an oncoming bus. The edges sometime look so fuzzy that I don't know from which side I'm looking anymore.

As I closed my journal, I put these last thoughts to rest and tried to sleep. Lucie Gagnon, the gallery director had phoned earlier to tell me that the space was empty, so I could start setting up in the morning.

Gallery Dare-Dare was situated in the busy core of Montreal's downtown. The space was thirty by thirty feet (9 m x 9 m) with high ceilings and no windows, which was perfect for me. A natural evolution had occurred with my use of light: in the first two shows, the white light of truth emerged mysteriously from under the beds. In Peterborough, the whole room was white—too white—as the truth finally emerged. This time, in Montreal, I plunged the room into the dark recesses of a red light where the secrets resided. I was opening the wound for everyone to see.

I painted one wall black and drew the four huge faces from *I Remember When* with white chalk. Then I constructed the outline of a mattress with curtain rods and weaved in fishing line to support a thin, white bed cover and clear plastic bags blown up to suggest pillows. Miraculously, it held up. Underneath it, I hid a cassette player and two fluorescent tube lights covered with red plastic sheets to give it an ominous feel.

Further away, I placed the white crib, which was lit with a lone night-light attached to its side panel. I hung *The Holly Family* painting on the back wall. Near the entrance, on the floor leaning against the wall, a single sheet of paper was also lit by a night-light. You had to kneel down to read it, like a secret that can only be whispered.

Once everything was in place, I shut off the overhead lights. "That looks very haunting," Lucie commented.

"Yes, let me show you." I led her outside the entrance and took her on a tour through the installation. "The visitor enters into the corridor, which is lit by very bright but cold, fluorescent lights. Then he opens the door into darkness. It takes a few moments for his eyes to adjust to the luminous red hue, which gives the impression that the whole space is on fire. He finds the source of the light: the bed is glowing like a red-hot iron. Then he sees a baby's crib under a small night-light. He can barely see what's inside, a teddy bear maybe. But on the floor, there is definitely something.

"And then he hears the voice of a scared, anxious child calling out over and over again: 'Mama? Papa? Mama? Papa?' But the child is no-where to be seen. He's hiding as he calls for help, but at the same time, he doesn't want to hear the response. The visitor slowly realizes that the voice is coming from under the parents' bed. The bloodred light illuminates through as if it were the entrance to hell itself."

As we made our way to the crib, Lucie asked, "What's that pun-gent smell?"

"I poured some beer, wine, and aftershave into the crib," I replied. Recalling the reactions from my wall of burnt toast, I added, "Memories are strongly associated with the sense of smell."

Inside the crib, a teddy bear and other plush toys sat among the crumpled sheets, which partially concealed a pair of bloodstained un-derpants. On the floor, an empty bottle of baby oil was placed on top a soiled, first Communion dress made of white lace.

"This is awful," Lucie frowned as she looked inside the crib then took a step back.

"Yes, it is. The idea of incest reeks mentally and visually. I don't want to shock people; I just want to share what it feels like."

"And the painting and the giant faces, all of them smiling at this drama. Are they your family?"

"They represent *a* family. The question is: Do they know about it or not? Are they victims, bystanders, or perpetrators?" I responded. "The last clue is down here on the floor." I pointed to the paper leaning on the wall.

Lucie crouched down and read: *"One woman in three is sexually abused before the age of eighteen. One man in six is sexually abused. The aggressors are often men, but sometimes they are women. Eighty-nine percent of the aggressors are family members. The weapon of the aggressors is silence. The family is no longer a safe place. Silence kills. Let's break the silence."*

"I didn't know this," Lucie admitted.

"I didn't know it either until recently. It's crazy how common it is, yet we never hear about it." It pained me to read those facts, but someone had to say it. "Thank you for having me in your gallery."

"You're more than welcome, Guy. I'm sure your exhibit is going to make a difference"

As I sat reflecting on the finished installation, the whole space reminded me of a photography darkroom: the black walls, the red light, the negative white lines of the four faces. *I've subconsciously created a giant darkroom. How fitting that I am bringing the truth of incest into the light like a photograph revealing itself.* When I turned to the bloodred bed, I felt a chill, thinking, *Maybe Cerberus is hiding under?*

When the exhibit opened, I received a very positive review in *Le Devoir,* a renowned newspaper. But what mattered more were the dozens of personal testimonies people shared in the guest book.

"Thank you, Guy, for having the courage to bring the subject of incest to the public's attention." Other testimonials came from survivors themselves. "I was abused by my brothers and never told anyone. Thanks to you, I know I can do it someday."

I felt I had accomplished my mission, but among these, one especially touched me. "Your exhibit is very well done, and I will come back to see it again." It was signed, "Your brother Marc." No one else from my family came. Marc's words gave my broken heart some solace. Even so, I couldn't help but think: *I'm able to express the realities of incest to the citizens of my hometown, but to my own family, I remain an outcast.*

Chapter 28

ON THE OTHER SIDE OF A BRIDGE

Shortly after the exhibit closed in March of 1992, I found a two-room apartment stashed away in an unlit back alley at the end of a parking lot. It was just one street away from the gallery. I was excited to finally move out of my father's place.

From the cracked window of my bedroom, the blinding sunlight bounced off the windshields of parked cars. I slept and woke up to the gag-inducing fumes of exhaust pipes and through the paper-thin walls listened to my neighbor's radio and his conversations. In the evenings, I had a front-row seat to a concert of squealing tires, screaming drunks, and moaning junkies. But it didn't bother me. All I needed was a simple mattress on the floor, a fridge, a stove, running water, a toilet, and a shower. I even had a telephone! I was as giddy as young Jethro from TV sitcom *The Beverly Hillbillies*.

The first thing I did after moving in was create my "love wall": a collage of photos of friends and family in Amsterdam and Regina as well as recent letters and postcards from cities I'd visited in Europe: Antje from Berlin, my friends from Venice and Aznavour's "La Boheme" Place Montmartre in Paris. *Europe's my home away from home, my North*

Star, I'll be back. Joni Mitchell's nostalgic "California" brought tears to my eyes. *I am not there now, but I know that one day I will be.*

My good fortune continued when I landed a summer job as a art guide at the Centre International d'Art Contemporain de Montreal. To work alongside Claude Gosselin, the founder of this yearly international exhibition of contemporary artists, was an honor. Although I was still insecure about my abilities, my passion for art gave me the courage to succeed. I became like Belle-nadette and discovered that I loved to inform and answer visitors' questions. When I began to feel a little more confident, I showed Claude photos from my *Family Shows*. He was impressed, so he asked me to write the tour description for the other guides. I was happy to do so.

During the day, the social interactions of work nourished me, but in the evenings, the isolation weighed on me. I had a phone but no one to call. So, inspired by *The Courage to Heal,* I headed to the bookstore for more reading material. First, because fear ruled my life, I picked up *Feel the Fear and Do It Anyway* by Susan Jeffers. Then *Healing Your Aloneness* by Erika Chopich and Margaret Paul jumped out at me. Next to it was *Inner Bonding,* also by Margaret Paul. These last two introduced me to the concept of the inner child. *Maybe I can reconnect with my scared, little three-year-old self?* I then explored the business section and was surprised by this daring promise of Tony Robbins' book *Unlimited Power.*

As the wounded animal inside me awakened, I became enraged and growled, howled, and pounded the grimy gray carpet in my apartment. *I'm so much more than what my family made me believe. I've had it with all this bullshit! I'm sick of being ashamed of my loneliness and thinking like a passive victim. I have my own personal power! I've had enough!* I went to the art supply store and bought some paints and large sheets of paper. When I got home, I plastered my walls with giant, inspirational quotes painted in bright red, yellow, and blue: I CAN CHANGE MY LIFE! I CAN BECOME THE PERSON I WANT TO BE!

Yet there was something missing. Even though I was gaining personal power, I still longed for personal contact. As I was learning from my reading, shame is a knife that silences truth. My family shamed me into silence; the school bully shamed me into silence; and the incest . . . the incest nearly destroyed me. I also learned that it was important to find an emotional support system where I felt safe opening up and sharing my feelings. Many authors recommended seeking out groups similar to Alcoholics Anonymous (AA).

With some trepidation, I phoned the local rape crisis center. They suggested two support groups: Survivors of Incest Anonymous and Adult Children from Dysfunctional Families Anonymous "There's a meeting tonight," the person on the phone informed me. I was petrified, but I wrote down the address and challenged myself to go, knowing that it would be the next step in moving forward.

At seven thirty, I sat on a park bench outside a church, gazing up at its looming spires. *Why does it need to be in a church basement?* recalling all the unpleasant times I was forced to attend and serve mass as a child. I snubbed out my fourth cigarette in my empty coffee paper cup and thought, *Who am I to be here? What gives me the right?* Fifteen minutes later, the meeting was about to start, so I made my way under the stone arches of the main entrance. Pulling the heavy wooden door, a gush of cold, damp air hit my face, then walked down to the basement, the old stairs creaking with each step.

"Welcome. Is this your first meeting?" a young woman greeted me with a smile. When I nodded, she continued, "You're amongst friends. Here are the introduction documents. Help yourself to coffee and donuts on the table over there. Sit anywhere you like and have a nice meeting."

I thanked her and took a seat in one of the well-worn chairs that had been arranged in a circle. I furtively glanced around and noticed that there were seven of us, both men and women. They were chatting away, even laughing at times. I waited anxiously for the meeting to begin.

"You don't have to share," the facilitator informed us. "You can just sit in silence and listen if that's what you need." The rules were simple: never interrupt, never talk about what someone else says, and keep to your allotted time. "Everything that is said here stays here. We are not here to judge but to accept each other as we are."

On my right, a young lady in black jeans and a T-shirt began angrily complaining about her boyfriend: "The other day he screamed at me again! Why do I let myself be treated this way? My dad threatened my mother all the time. I should know better." She paused, realizing that her fist was clenched. She relaxed and looked up. "Why do I keep getting myself into abusive relationships? I am so damn sick of it!" We nodded in silence.

An older man with a white beard and wearing denim overalls, shared how he feels like he's never good enough. He was constantly criticized as a child and had no one to protect him. "I was left alone to fend for myself. If we spoke up, Dad would get his belt and give us a beating. How can someone be so cruel to beat a child? Fuck!" He stared down at the floor and didn't say another word.

After a few minutes a tall, pale young man with long, stringy black hair broke the silence. "As you can see, I'm still alive this week," he said wryly. But he wasn't joking. He told us that suicide is always on his mind, and he'd already made attempts to take his life but failed each time. Humor and irony seemed to soothe his pain.

Listening to these people, I felt something stir deep inside in my guts. *Their stories are so similar to mine!* I sensed that we were all human and I could trust them, so I dared to speak up. "I feel so lonely and isolated all the time. I don't know what to do. I want human contact, but I feel the need to stay away from my family. I never really knew my grandparents or cousins, and my love relationships have all been disasters." As I paused, my hands jittered from all the coffee I'd had, or perhaps it was my feelings boiling to the surface. While the other group members patiently waited, I felt their warm presence. "Thank you," I finally eked out, holding back my tears. *Thank you, thank you, thank you,* I repeated in my head. *I'm human after all, and it's allowed me to express my feelings to another person.*

Back in my little apartment, I felt less alone and my love wall seemed to have expanded. After taking a hot shower to wash away a day encrusted with too many emotions, I made myself a cup of decaf coffee, lit a candle, and put on Mozart's *Requiem*, which Dad had given me for Christmas. *He's right. The Lacrimosa is beautiful.*

The next morning as I awoke the happy chirps of the birds tweeted their stories, and the rising sun showered my giant banner with an amber glow. I CAN BECOME THE PERSON I WANT TO BE! *The writing is on the wall, but why do I keep mine hidden in a journal?* And then it hit me: *That's it! For my next exhibit, I'm going to literally write my story on the wall. It won't be about family, abuse, or incest; it's going to tell my healing journey so I can help others heal.*

My mind was going a hundred miles an hour. *I've dared to cross so many bridges in my life: the one to Louis's house, crossing the Atlantic to travel to Europe and to study in Amsterdam. These crossings changed my life. Life is about daring to cross bridges when we come to them.*

I opened my sketchbook and started drawing a gallery with a bridge and my quotes and photos on the walls. *This will be a journey of hope for everyone.* I wrote a complete proposal—including the tagline: "On the other side of a bridge, you will discover yourself. You just need to cross it, like I did." Then I sent it to different galleries and requested grants.

I knew I'd need more money for this show, so I looked for a second job. That's how I met Montreal photographer Alain Chagnon. He was looking for intergenerational families of immigrants for his next project, *Clash of Cultures and Generations,* which was about relationships within a family. "When immigrants arrive here, differences between generations widen because children integrate more quickly," he explained. "So I want to show the differences *and* the similarities between three generations." He paused then asked, "Do you think you could find me those families here in Montreal?"

This job was tailor-made for me given my talks on family interaction. It would also take me out of my isolation because I'd be required to contact hundreds of new people. I told him I could and was hired on the spot.

And I loved the work. Whether they were folks from Congo, refugees fresh off the boat from Vietnam, or political exiles from Haiti or Chile, their stories moved me. I saw similarities with the plight of Canada's First Nations, the political refugees and my abuse as all of us had lost friends, families and homes. I decided that my new installation wouldn't just be about me; I would also include the stories of some of these immigrants. *I'll unite those alienated from their homelands, those who had to cross a bridge, so to speak, in search of a new life. Our pain and loneliness are the seeds we'll sow to experience new growth.*

Back in my little hideout, I celebrated when I was awarded a grant from the Canada Council for the Arts and the show was accepted in three galleries. In the coming weeks, I brought dozens of artists together so they could share part of the gallery space to exhibit their own artwork. I also created an eight-evening multicultural festival called "Les soirées du Pont," which brought together poets, musicians, calligraphy artists, mask makers, and more. It was a celebration of our humanity, of everything we share.

To prepare for my part of the exhibition, I selected seventeen photos of myself from the age of three months to thirty-three years, including ones of me as a baby in my crib, a family reunion with dozens of cousins, as an altar boy, a Boy Scout, and me leaning over *Winter Casualty* in Windsor. For each one, I wrote a brief caption describing what I saw, heard, or felt at that age (or imagined I did, in some cases). I wrote each one in English, French, Spanish, and Montagnais, a local First Nations dialect.

Inside the gallery, I also built an exact replica of my first secret bedroom in my studio in Amsterdam. A ladder was provided so visitors could climb up and lie in it to really get a feel for the claustrophobic conditions. Under the mezzanine were four photos of my actual secret living space in Amsterdam with captions describing my fears, anxieties, and the loneliness I felt.

For the festival, I installed chairs in a semicircle in front of the performers, who sang and danced. Despite the success of the evening, when I presented my video, *I Remember When*, I was terrified. I felt so exposed. *They'll see me, my video, my story, me. I don't know if I can do this.*

I chain-smoked and drank way too much beer. Moments before it was my turn, I ran to the bathroom, dropped to my knees, and vomited. *I can't do it!* After a few minutes, I got up, staggered to the sink, and splashed ice-cold water on my face. My stomach was still in knots, and the dark circles under my eyes stood out against my stark white face in the mirror. Then, I caught a glimpse of Vincent Van Gogh next to my reflection. His eyes were filled with compassion as he whispered, "Trust yourself."

"OK, Vincent. You're right. I do deserve better than this." With that, I dried my face, tucked in my shirt, and made my way to the waiting crowd. As I walked to the front, my legs quivered, so I took a deep breath. Standing by the monitor, I closed my eyes for a moment and thought, *I'm not doing this for myself. It's for all those who are suffering in silence.* I took another deep breath, hoping no one would notice my nervousness, then looked at everyone and began my presentation.

"Thanks everyone for coming. Can we really know who we are? That's what this video is about," I said as I pushed the play button. I stood there motionless, revealing my true nature. I nearly fainted, but after nine minutes, I was moved to tears as the audience applauded the real Guy . . . me. *I did it! I am* The Warrior, *and I've just crossed another bridge!*

When I took the exhibit to a gallery in Saint-Jean-sur-Richelieu, a suburb of Montreal, a TV crew interviewed me. Live on TV, *The*

Warrior proudly declared *Victory* for all survivors of abuse. I also offered five workshops on the subject of sexual abuse. My goal was to use my platform to heighten awareness and share the stage with fellow survivors. I had found my voice and wanted to help others express their own.

But what I desired most was to share this voice with someone special. Always being alone in my tiny apartment just wasn't cutting it, I still had the bridge of relationships to cross.

Chapter 29

A Fairy Tale

Downtown Montreal during the summer of '93 was a real furnace. I had to get out of my oven-like apartment, so I made my way to Faubourg Sainte-Catherine, a shopping center with a food court. I loved its huge, enclosed glass terrace with seating overlooking the sidewalk. Sitting under a row of maple trees, the joyful tweets of sparrows filled the cool air-conditioning air with their songs. With my coffee, cigarettes, journal, and books, I watched people walk by as I had in Vondelpark. In the evenings, my social life hadn't improved much. It mostly consisted of attending support groups twice a week, so I still felt so damn alone.

When I wasn't people-watching, I slashed my pen across the pages of my journal like a mad, masked Zorro slicing through my feelings with my sword of awareness: *love, hate, anger, desire, solitude, pleasure, shame, fear, doubts. What are all those feelings? How can I cope with them?* I finally found a first clue in psychiatrist Viktor Frankl's book *Man's Search for Meaning*. A survivor of World War II, he wondered why some prisoners survived Nazi concentration camps regardless of their physical health while others didn't. He believed the difference was that the survivors gave their suffering meaning.

His ideas were in keeping with those of *Help Yourself: Psychotherapy Through Reason* by Lucien Auger, which was based on Dr. Albert Ellis's rational emotive behavior therapy, which, in turn, was in line with the Stoic philosophers of ancient Greece. Epictetus, Seneca, and Marcus Aurelius joined me at my table. *You know, Guy, all external events are beyond your control. Accept whatever happens and be kind and cool brother, peace!* They echoed the famous Serenity Prayer from my support groups.

So, if I give up control, what will I do with my life? I've been so afraid of living that I have no idea who I am or what makes me happy. As I listed my passions, magic happened. Of course, I had my artwork, exhibits, and lectures, but I also enjoyed music, singing, traveling, nature, and stargazing. I'd loved the night sky ever since my childhood fantasies of flying to outer space with Yuri Gagarin and walking on the moon with Neil Armstrong, so I decided to join the planetarium's astronomy club.

A few weeks later, I stood in the dark, empty streets with a dozen other space explorers. The breeze was refreshing as we took turns peering into the club's telescopes. Through the tiny eyepiece, I savored the moon's craters and crevices. I was giddy as a kid. *This is amazing! I can practically feel the gray moondust underfoot.*

"Come look!" a group member called from his perch behind the larger telescope. As I waited, the oohs and aahs sent shivers of expectation down my spine. When it was finally my turn, I peeked through the small lens and saw them with my naked eye: the rings of Saturn. *This isn't a photo or a film. They're real! They are real!* I was transformed, speechless, awed by the beauty of our universe.

I also took courses in Italian and German and enrolled in a self-defense course, vowing to never be a victim again. I also joined a tai chi group for its slow, graceful, and peaceful flow of movements. I even read up on Oriental philosophers like Confucius and Lao Tzu and found serenity in the haiku poems of Matsuo Basho.

Inspired by *The Spirit of Zen* by American philosopher Alan Watts, I built a small altar with pebbles, candles, and incense and practiced zazen meditation. I chose the Bankei Yōtaku's *Unborn* form: sitting on my knees, I'd fix my gaze on a spot on the wall, breathe deeply, and allow my mind to empty. *No more abuse, no more censorship, no more loneliness.* I experienced pure bliss.

However, there was still something missing. The most precious item on my list was my burning desire to sing. The music of Felix Leclerc had saved my life, and playing piano was my first attempt at finding my voice. I'd become a DJ because I was too scared to join a rock band, but now, I was ready.

I auditioned with Martin Dagenais, director of the University of Montreal's Choeur de la Montagne choir. "Don't worry, stand up straight, and just relax, Guy," he repeated. I was as stiff as my *Warrior* statue. "Just repeat the notes as I play them." Although I couldn't read music, I hoped I could sing.

"That's fine. Now let's find your range." He pressed a low bass key then moved to higher and higher pitches. "Great, sounds like you're a baritone, but let's start you as a bass. Welcome to the choir!" he said enthusiastically as he handed me the sheet music to Vivaldi's *Gloria* for the upcoming Christmas concert. I felt glorious myself for this amazing first step. I took a second one with private singing lessons with Louise-Marie Archambault, also from the university. "Let's start with an Italian aria… Caro Mio Ben. It's a love song about a longing heart"

There was one last thing on my list: Mother Nature. I prepared a ham and cheese baguette thick with creamy butter, filled a thermos with chilled red wine and went one day in late June at Le Chalet, a stone building with a huge hall adorned with sculptures of squirrels situated atop Mount Royal. It was a place where tourists flocked to take in a magnificent panoramic view of the city. It happened to be

Quebec's Saint-Jean Baptiste Day, so the square was packed with people, fleur-de-lis flags were everywhere, and fiddlers were leading square dances on the plaza.

Still extremely shy, I bathed in the multitude of international dialects. Whenever I heard Dutch being spoken, my heart skipped a beat. I drank in every syllable like it was nectar. I missed my Dutch family tremendously, so I decided to play the role of the friendly local and struck up conversations by suggesting places to visit and eat. I met people from Germany and Scotland, and then came a petite woman with short, fair hair and freckled cheeks.

"May I sit here?" she politely asked.

"Yes, please do," I smiled back.

She sat down next to me on a bench, took out a guide book, and began to peruse the pages.

"Excuse me," I kindly said as I turned toward her, "are you looking for something to do in Montreal?"

She smiled and turned toward me. "I'm only in town for a few days. I just came to hear the Dalai Lama speak. He was amazing . . . so full of love." Her eyes lit up like scintillating blue topaz. "When he spoke, a wave of compassion swept over the hall and went deep inside me." She placed her hand over her heart. "I was transformed and felt pulled to meditate, so I came here. Oh, by the way, I'm Jeanne. I'm visiting from Paris."

"I'm Guy. I'm from here. Pleased to meet you," I said as I timidly bowed my head.

Jeanne taught humanities at the Sorbonne, so we talked about philosophy, psychology, and the arts; we had so much in common! I was in awe when I realized that we'd been talking for hours. Finally, I asked, "Would you like to taste some of Montreal's ethnic specialties?"

"That would be delightful!" she exclaimed.

As the American robin started its evening song, we took the forest path and made our way to Chinatown. Underneath the glow of the restaurant's red, rice paper lanterns, I proposed, "How about Peking duck and warm sake?"

"Great!" she answered. "That sounds tasty."

Maybe it was the sake, my flushed cheeks, or her blue eyes, but I felt a magnetic pull toward her. After dessert, we cracked open our fortune cookies and had a good laugh. Hers said, "Congratulations! You are on your way!" and mine said, "Nothing is impossible to a willing heart." We wrote our addresses and phone numbers on the back and exchanged them so we could keep in touch when she returned to Paris.

We were the last customers in the restaurant when it closed well passed midnight. As we exited onto the sidewalk, the street was quiet and the moon was high in the star-filled sky. I walked Jeanne back to her hotel, and when we arrived, I held her hand and we kissed goodbye the European way, on both cheeks. Tempted to kiss her on the lips, I hesitated then let her go. "Jeanne, your students are very lucky. You're really special."

"Thank you, Guy. This evening was the perfect gift after the Dalai Lama. You're also very special. Good night." I opened the glass door, and she retrieved her key at the front desk, and disappeared in the elevator.

It was one of the best days I'd ever had. When I got home, I pinned her address on my love wall. Then I meditated and lay down in bed with a huge smile on my face. *Things can only get better.*

Back in le Faubourg I plunged in a second book by Alan Watts: *The Book on the Taboo Against Knowing Who You Are.* His wisdom and humor tickled me as he suggested that as an apple tree made apples, so did the planet Earth made people. We were not born into this world but out of it. *Everyone is an expression of nature* I concluded in my journal. Sunday mornings I joined my Tai Chi group in the park and put into practice Watts' metaphors. *I am the ocean and I am a wave flowing in and out of existence.* My mind became peacefully quiet as with my unborn Zen meditations.

Session over, I stopped by the baker for a warm scrumptious croissant for home. Just smelling its buttery aroma brought waters to my mouth! I prepared my silver moka espresso pot, got out the butter, raspberry jam and I sat down. The phone rang. "Hi Guy! It's Jeanne from Paris. Remember me?"

My heart skipped a beat. How could I possibly forget her?

"You know, I can't stop thinking about you," she confessed. "I really felt a calling to come to Montreal. It's like we were destined to meet."

And so began a series of passionate phone calls and letters. She came back for a weeklong visit at the end of the summer. We dined at Greek, Lebanese, and Polish restaurants and enjoyed making sweet love. As she packed to leave, she floored me by saying, "Guy, come to Paris with me! Marry me!"

My heart jumped! *Paris? Europe? Marry Jeanne?* "Yes, yes! I do! I mean, I will! I mean, I do!" Our eyes locked, and we sealed our vow with a long kiss. Fate had found its way to me and knocked on the door of my tiny two-room apartment. *I'm finally leaving Montréal and crossing a new relationship bridge to Paris. This is magical!*

I started right away with the preparations. I thanked Louise-Marie for my voice lessons, stored my belongings in my mother's basement, shared one last time at my support groups, and went to dinner with my tai chi group. Best of all, Dad came to my first-ever choir concert.

"Your Vivaldi was perfect!" he praised as he gave me a hug, something he rarely did. It brought tears to my eyes.

I flew to Paris, and on Christmas Eve, Jeanne and I exchanged rings and vows at "la Mairie de Paris"'s 18th arrondissement. I was blessed to be surrounded by even more love as Maria, Erwin, and Paula came down from Amsterdam to be my witnesses.

Then came our honeymoon. It felt like a fairy tale as we celebrated on the romantic canals of Venice. My heart literally swayed in the magical gondola. *Life can't possibly get any better than this.*

My new bride had one more gift planned: a weekend workshop on "transpersonal expression." We drove for about an hour through the French countryside until we arrived at a wooden cottage in the middle of a pine forest. The twenty participants lay on yoga mats dispersed across the large, open room. The dim lights, soothing Indian flute music, and incense wafting through the air created a warm and enveloping atmosphere, like a womb.

"Namaste and welcome," a couple dressed in beige lightweight cotton pants and robes greeted. "I'm Jonathan, and this is Julianna. Thank you for coming and sharing yourselves with us. We'll get started shortly."

After an hour of guided meditation and full-body relaxation, I felt as if I were floating directly below the room's ceiling fans. At that point, Jonathan had us sit up on our mats as he explained, "We're going to practice a more dynamic inner-self exploration, so I want you to take long, deep breaths in and out."

As we progressed, ghostly moans eerily filled the space. And then I exploded at the top of my lungs, "AAAAAAAAAAAAAAAARRRR"

Long, hard, limitless, bottomless, topless. I was the scream; howling like a wolf under a full moon. As this primal sound continued to pour out of me, Jonathan rushed in, knelt down beside me, took me in his arms, and whispered, "Let it come. Let it out. Don't hold back." While massaging pressure points on my back, he asked, "What do you see?"

My outcry subsided, and I coughed, gasping for air. "It's night. I'm outside—no, inside a tent. There are other people." My body shuddered as I continued. "I am . . . we are a group of eight-year-old boys, and we're all naked. Some teenagers are pushing us, forcing us. I float like a ghost suspended in mid-air, and I feel nothing. There are smells, colors, tastes—everything seems so real, but I'm an observer. They are, they are . . .

"WWWAAAAAAAAAAAAAAAA!" I shrieked as tears streamed down my face and my body convulsed with deep, guttural sobs. I felt like a knife had sliced me open all the way down my back. When I toppled onto the mat, the visions disappeared.

Jeanne tried to get me up, but the howling wolf had morphed into a lifeless translucent jellyfish. She covered me with a wool blanket and held my hand. I remained immobile until the end of the workshop.

We drove home in silence because I was unable to speak. The darkness of the moonless sky swallowed up the road and me along with it. After a hot shower, Jeanne fell fast asleep, but I couldn't stop wondering: since the vision I'd had during Wim's yoga session in Amsterdam turned out to be true, was this one also true?

I moved to the living room as cats wailed outside the window. I remembered how some photos of me from my *On the Other Side of a Bridge* exhibit had puzzled me because I didn't remember them at all. I took out my documentation and read their captions:

"AT CHURCH":

Every Sunday we go to church. We have to! My brothers, who are only a few years older than me, don't have to go anymore. They're free. Baptism, first Communion—what do these mean? We learn about them in school, and look, I'm even an altar boy. A little bit of red wine here, a few bodies of Christ there. Later, in the church basement, it's the youth mass. They play guitar and I serve soft drinks and donuts. The more things change, the more they stay the same. Why is he smiling at me like that?

Why was I compelled to write that last question? But the most enigmatic of the photos was the one of me proudly wearing a Boy Scout uniform, badges and all. A real trooper! *Me, a Boy Scout?* When I was creating the exhibit, I'd had no memory of that. I'd wondered how that was even possible, so I'd asked my mom.

"Yes, you were a Boy Scout," she clarified. "But after going to summer camp, you decided to quit with no explanation. You never went back after that."

I was a Boy Scout for more than a year and had absolutely no memory of it—none whatsoever! How was that possible? I reread the caption for clues:

"I'M A BOY SCOUT":

Look, I'm a Boy Scout! But I don't remember it. I barely remember anything from my childhood. There are enormous black holes. Who are these men? What summer camp? What happened to me when I was alone and isolated with no escape? My mother recently told me that when I came back from camp, I no longer wanted to be a Boy Scout. And that park groundskeeper . . . what did he want when he asked me: "Do you know what a pedophile is?" I felt bad. I didn't understand, so I ran away.

Was this most recent vision a repressed memory from summer camp? Could I really have forgotten a full year of my life when I was eight? I had so many holes in my childhood, with no friends, no extended family, and Taffy running away. I also had these troubling aversions that made no sense to me. I loved the swings, but the sound of their chains squeaking nearly made me black out. The putrid smell of ripe cheese made me nauseous, and a mere glimpse of a man's spit on the ground gave me the compulsion to lick it. Just that mere thought made my stomach churn.

What could have happened to me?

I put away my papers because there was nothing more I could do at that point. I was married and living in Paris. I had a whole new life ahead of me.

Chapter 30

TEARS ON THE TELEPHONE

Outside our small apartment in lively Montmartre with its fabled Moulin Rouge and Folies Bergère, I was accosted by hookers and transvestites who sometimes pinched my bum. A little farther north, the famous Sacré-Coeur basilica sat near the Place du Tertre where painters set up their easels for tourists. *I can't believe I'm living here. It's just like Aznavour's* La Bohème. *This is my dream came true!*

I taught painting at the local "Centre d'Animation Des Abbesses", and was hired by the Paris City Hall to create a site-specific art installation at L'Espace Cardin with students from the Collège Sainte-Geneviève. On my way to teach, I walked along the renowned Bateau-Lavoir, a former residence for artists such as Gauguin, Picasso, and Brancusi. *I'm literally at the birth place of modern art, history is alive, amazing!*

I rented a tiny studio on Rue des Envierges, in Belleville of the 20th arrondissement. I first painted images of doors in the hopes of prying open a passageway to my missing memories. That didn't work, so I figured my body was trying to protect me. Next, in an attempt to coax my true nature to germinate, I moved on to creating collages of leaves and seeds coated with olive oil. Finally, I channeled my Christian upbringing by fashioning crucifixes out of cardboard boxes. I'd cut them into crosses, mount them on broomsticks, and perform a sweeping motion as if sweeping under the rug memories of my time as an altar boy.

Continuing to pursue my passion for singing, I joined the 18th arrondissement choir at the "Conservatoire Gustave Charpentier". Our choirmaster, Madame Maciocchi also directed at the "Opera Comique de Paris". *What a privilege!* She was demanding and extremely precise as she taught us famous French and Italian choral pieces. "Come on guys, you can do better than this! Watch me and keep to the rhythm, please" But after rehearsals, she often joked with us and joined us for a beer at the local café.

After months of rehearsals, we presented several concerts with the backing of a full orchestra. Dressed in white shirts with black suits with bow tie, I loved our elegance as we performed "L'amour est un oiseau rebelle" from Bizet's "Carmen" at "Les Arènes de Montmartre" and the famous Salle Pleyel. And on June 26, 1994, I felt a deeper purpose when we offered a very special concert to commemorate the fiftieth anniversary of Paris's liberation from German occupation.

Entering the Veterans' 18th arrondissement headquarters, the small low ceiling hall where we performed was filled with surviving relatives still grieving their lost loved ones. Our host—a mustachioed, wrinkled, and aged soldier decked out in full regalia and medals—cleared his throat. "We are here to honor the fathers, husbands, sons, brothers, sisters, mothers, daughters, and wives who gave their lives to protect and liberate us. Let us pray for them." Holding hands, we intoned Verdi's "Chorus of the Hebrew Slaves" followed by "Le Chant des Partisans," which is widely considered the anthem of the French Resistance. As the lyrics about loss and sacrifice resonated, our eyes filled with tears. For those who survived the horrors of war, their pain was finally acknowledged. We were one family healing together.

But with Jeanne, it was quite the opposite. By Easter of 1995, after nearly a year and a half of married life, I felt like I was tiptoeing through a minefield. I had tried to share with her the traumatic memories that had resurfaced, but her reaction was, "Well, that's your problem. Deal with it." If I tried to share my feelings like I had with my support groups back in Montreal, she'd say the same thing. Whereas I was still just discovering my own voice, her tone was harsh. Unable to handle it, I resumed my role as the Silent Good Boy.

Isolated, friendless, when summer arrived and the city began to broil, I decided that I had to do something. Recalling how helpful my support groups had been in Canada, I tried to find something similar. But Jeanne erupted at this idea of public sharing. "Don't go broadcasting your stories for the world to hear! Go see a therapist!" Afraid of any further criticism, I complied.

From the therapist's pocket-size office, I discerned an even smaller courtyard just outside the window. My back sweated as I sat squeezed into a dark brown, leather armchair. The therapist—a stylish, young man with a beard and a slick haircut—had an array of degrees displayed behind him. "What can I do for you, Mr. Giard?" he said as he squinted from behind round glasses.

My pulse accelerated as I described how I ended up in Paris, my marriage, and my memories of abuse. On some level, I felt like I was betraying some family secrets and would be court-martialed for speaking out. The therapist listened intently except for a few times when he said, "Hmm" or "Go on."

Finally, I got to the point. "I feel so much pressure and so many demands from my wife. I tell her my feelings, but she doesn't seem to value them. She just tells me that it's my problem, and I need to deal with it. I don't know what to do!"

Suddenly, the therapist straightened up in his seat, removed his glasses, and opened his eyes wide like an owl preying on a mouse. His response floored me. "Stand up for yourself first and your marriage second!"

Oh no, not again! It was the same advice I'd received thirty years earlier in high school: "Be a man and fight back! Stand up to your bullies!" *Why is this happening to me? Is this really who I am: a doormat to be crapped on?* I needed time to think, to reflect.

Back at home in the sweltering heat, the windows were open but there was no breeze. My thoughts were stifling me, and I felt the walls closing in. At night, the prowling cats painfully roared as if sweaty drunk violinists gutted strings out of their insides. The wailing of a weeping woman added to this dark symphony. *"It's always the same!"* A neighbor joined in: *"Why don't you shut your mouth, you whore, or I'll come shut it for you!"*

This is too much! Please give me some peace! I palmed my ears, and out of this momentary retreat came images of my secret hideouts in Amsterdam. *That's exactly what I need right now! It's only a few hours away by train. I'm going to go see my Dutch family.* Relieved, I could finally close my eyes and escape into my dreams.

"You can't go to Amsterdam!" Jeanne objected. But ultimately, she agreed that some time away would be restful for both of us.

"La Gare du Nord" train station was a noisy vestibule of people scrambling every which way, but I plowed my way through the throngs and reached my train. When I sat down, I noticed a gloomy passenger outside my window, only to realize that it was my own reflection. *I am as immaterial as a ghost.* As the train left the station, it began to drizzle, and it rained the whole way. I stared blankly out the window as the drab-looking landscape whizzed by. Just as we reached Amsterdam, the sun broke through and a magical ray of light shined on Maria, who was waiting for me on the platform.

"Hey Guy, so nice to see you!" Maria's radiant smile instantly dispelled my inner clouds as she grabbed me for a much-needed hug. *The human touch, the human warmth I've so longed for was waiting for me here. I had forgotten how good it feels to be loved!*

Maria and Erwin invited me to stay with them for the week. I told them about my shows in Canada and confided in them my memories of abuse and the difficulties in my relationship with Jeanne. They were shocked and saddened by the whole affair. "How are you taking care of yourself through all this?" Maria asked.

"I don't know," I admitted. "I guess one way is that I'm here."

Erwin poured more wine and offered a toast, "To good friends."

"To good friends," we repeated as our glasses merrily clinked together.

During my stay, I rested on the golden sands of the North Sea, met Jos for coffee in Vondelpark, filled my belly with golden fries with heaps of garlic sauce and tapped my foot to great jazz at Café Alto. I healed my wounds and slept peacefully.

Feeling refreshed and centered, I returned to Paris vowing to take care of my emotional needs as well as Jeanne's. I took a deep breath and suggested, "Let's just take a break. I think some temporary breathing space will do both of us good."

But Jeanne exploded with a threat. "If you leave this apartment, I am filing for divorce!" she screamed, her eyes burning with fire.

Given an ultimatum, I felt as if I'd choked, shriveled up, and died. At that moment, I realized that we were living together, but our hearts were continents apart.

Feeling hopeless and like the flame in my heart had been extinguished, my nighttime panic attacks returned. I was still teaching at the art center, but there was no way I could afford my own apartment. I sought salvation every day at the employment office, aching to find new postings. But there was nothing, and I felt like a noose was tightening around my neck. And then, a small miracle.

Pinned on the bulletin board, under another unappealing offer, was a small, unassuming piece of pink paper that I almost didn't see. It read: "Five-week intensive workshop. Learn techniques to get back into the job market." I didn't know it at the time, but the course was tailor-made for me. After signing up, I held that little treasure close to my heart and practically skipped back to the apartment.

The following Monday, the first day of the workshop, the blue sky seemed brighter, the air purer. The room was barely big enough for everyone who showed up, so twenty of us squeezed like dominos along a long rectangular wooden table. Except for the incessant buzz of the fluorescent lights and the ticktock of the wall clock, the room was silent. Most of us seemed to be in our early thirties, although there were a few older gents. Unsure where to look, we nervously fidgeted and fiddled around in our bags.

Then, as if a spotlight had been turned on an A-list celebrity on the red carpet, in waltzed Daniel. Small, lithe with short, jet-black hair, he was a cross between the White Rabbit from Alice in Wonderland and a TV game show host. He was ecstatic to be there, and it showed.

"Hi everyone! I'm Daniel. Pleased to meet you. You've taken a momentous step by showing up today." After briefly mentioning his theater background, he dropped a bombshell: "I just returned from a workshop in Montreal where I learned the most recent techniques for job-searching."

I almost fell from my chair. This reassuring incarnation of my childhood *Noddy* with his European artistic know-how combined with French Canadian innovation was exactly what I needed.

"Here's what we're going to do. During the first week, we'll define our assets: who are we, what we've done, our qualities, our life goals, and such. In the second week, we'll write our résumés or CVs and presentation cards. During our third week, we'll seek out potential workplaces and learn the technique of cold-calling. After a momentary pause, he continued with a laugh. "Ah, yes . . . the dreaded cold call. Bear in mind, my friends, that acquiring these phone skills is crucial. Be proactive. You are not looking for a job; you are phoning employers to offer them your expertise and asking for an interview! Finally, the last two weeks will be spent going over strategies for returning calls, mastering the interview, and reviewing everything you've learned in this course."

I was in my element during the first two weeks. Writing my résumé came naturally to me because I'd applied for many grants and exhibits over the years. But when I saw the question: "What are you offering?", I realized that I'd never thought about that before. To find the answer, Daniel had us list our best qualities, our dreams, and our accomplishments until a common denominator appeared. This soul-searching exercise revealed a basic objective of my life's purpose: helping people. I was so excited to discover this that I wrote down again and again: "I want to help people." Seeing it in my own handwriting brought a warmth to my body. I'd never had such a clear vision, and it strengthened my resolve to be of service. After that, I felt much better prepared for the cold call challenge.

It was simple enough: pick up the phone, dial the number, ask for the human resources manager, and follow the script. "Hello, my name is Guy Giard. I would like to meet with you to explain the services I can offer." Part of the trick was getting around the "gatekeeper," often a reluctant secretary. Everyone took turns picking up the handset and practicing the lines. When it was my turn, blood raced to my temples, and my heart threatened to jump out of my chest. I became dizzy, my hands were clammy, and sweat trickled down my back. When I tried to speak, I couldn't breathe. I choked. As everyone stared at me in silence, I wanted to run away.

"Well?" Daniel inquired, puzzled.

I remained mute, so he asked again. I opened my mouth to speak, but not a sound came out. I began to shake then finally stuttered, "I . . . I . . . I can't!"

"You can't?" Daniel asked, perplexed. "Why not?"

I stared at the floor, at the phone, back to the floor, but never at

Daniel or any of the other participants. I was too ashamed. "I . . . I just can't," I muttered as tears came to my eyes.

As silence continued to smother the room, Daniel suggested, "OK, everyone. Let's take a break."

Daniel took me into the tiny back room and kindly asked me what was wrong. I froze. I was in crisis. I remembered being at art school and sitting on the bench next to Catherine with her arms around me as she asked, "What do you want?"

But I couldn't answer then, and I couldn't answer now. "I . . . I . . . I can't do it!" I cried as tears rolled down my cheeks. Patiently, Daniel waited. *I can't share my feelings with him. How can I tell him of my shame, my unworthiness, my guilt? Who am I to ask for any consideration? My whole life has revolved around being invisible. That's how I've survived. I'll die if I try to do otherwise.*

Maybe Daniel understood my fears. Maybe he'd even been there himself because he said, "Guy, I know you can do this. Let me help you. Let's try just the two of us." Step by step, with words of encouragement, I felt his confidence and knew that he believed in me. Knowing that, my invisible shell cracked just wide enough for a sliver of self-worth to filter through. I picked up an imaginary phone handset, and after a few failed attempts, I manage to say one word, then a second, and finally, eke out, "Hello, my name is Guy Giard." After a few more minutes of practice, Daniel reconvened the. group but I felt extremely nervous because everyone's eyes were on me.

Hesitantly, I picked up the handset, brought it closer to my ear, took a deep breath, and said, "He . . ." But I couldn't go any further.

Then someone quietly encourage, "Come on, Guy."

So, I tried again. "Hello, my name is Guy Giard." Once these six simple words came out, I felt more at ease, and the rest just flowed out of me.

"Great job, Guy! You did it!" Daniel exclaimed as everyone cheered and applauded.

Once again, tears ran down my cheeks, but this time they were happy tears.

In the following weeks, I phoned more than a hundred employers and landed three interviews at world-famous museums: Le Musée de la Poste, Le Centre National d'Art et de Culture Georges-Pompidou, and the Louvre. What an honor, my passion for art was evident as I felt something I had never experienced before: self-worth. My life was on an upswing, and it got even better when fate stepped in a second time.

Of all the new people I'd encountered at the workshop, the most magical one was Frédérique, a tall and wiry comedian with frizzy dark hair and a smile that beamed from ear to ear! Wearing the typical stripped blue-and-white Breton sweater, one day she mentioned in her musical northern dialect that she was going on tour till the end of Summer and needed someone to stay at her apartment and watch her cat. Of course, I volunteered. It was just too perfect. I was well on my way to a full-time job and my own apartment.

"If you go, I'll file for divorce!" Jeanne angrily reasserted.

But I had no choice; I had to leave for my own sanity. When Jeanne went out of town for a conference, I quickly packed my belongings and moved out, even though a voice in my head was saying, *This is not what I want!* But once I got settled into Frédérique's apartment in Paris's Chinatown section, I had the space I needed to reflect and decide what I really wanted.

I was able to relax with my friendly new roomate Noirot, stroking his short, silky black coat. Each day when I came home, he meowed then settled into a ball, purring on my lap. It was during one such tender moment that the phone rang. It was Jeanne.

In a very calm voice, she declared, "I've started the divorce process. You need to present yourself in three weeks." That's it. No discussion. No argument. She just called to give me the date of the hearing. "Oh, and it's a divorce on the grounds of fault, a simple procedure," she said calmly. "Nothing to worry about. Just be there." Then she hung up.

I just stood there as if in a trance. I felt and heard nothing until the monotonous dial tone brought me back to reality. Once again, I felt like a doormat, and Jeanne had thoroughly wiped her feet on me.

That night, as if fate wanted to mark my downfall in a nightmarish fashion, an electrical storm struck the neighborhood, further adding to my personal apocalypse. Lightning sliced through the inky black sky like a strobe light, and rain pelted the windows so fiercely that I thought they'd shatter into a million pieces. During a particularly loud clap of thunder, Noirot extended his claws and leaped into the air, meowing and hissing like a ferocious demon. His whole body shook in satanic convulsions and came crashing down with a loud bang on the wooden floor. *He's having a heart attack!* I inched myself closer, carefully picked him up and checked his wet belly. *He is still breathing.* We were drenched in sweat as we both descended into the pits of hell.

"Divorce on the grounds of fault. Nothing to worry about." Jeanne's voice echoed in my head. But with an ominous label like that, how could I not worry? *Fault? What fault? I didn't want a divorce. I just needed time to think.*

Frédérique was due back in a few weeks, then I'd be homeless. Remembering my childhood nightmares, I thought, *It's all about to come true. I'm destined to sleep on a piece of cardboard that reeks of dog piss. I'm worthless.*

Once the storm was over, I served Noirot a saucer of milk. He thanked me with a kind purr and a head hug, milk dripping from his whiskers. "What do you think I should do, Noirot?" He raised his head as if wondering who I was speaking to, then went back to his saucer. I patted him on the back and he purred louder. "Daniel, you say? Yes, you're right. He did help me get over my fears." He meowed "Perhaps I should ask for help? You think I could, you think that I'm worth it?" He remained quiet, his way of telling me that it was up to me, and that, after all, he was just a cat.

The next morning, I decided to go to the legal aid office. Dozens of strangers were crammed in the dusty, cream-colored waiting room. The silence weighed heavily, only broken by the wailing of infants. When it was finally my turn, I was directed to the last door down a long corridor.

The room was barely large enough for two chairs and a tiny desk. With sadness permeating the air and bars on the window, the space had the look and feel of a prison cell. A short woman in a pale green suit entered the room, closed the door behind her, and smiled politely as she introduced herself. "Hello, I'm Claudia Barbès. What can I do for you today, Mr. Giard?"

I didn't know what to say. I thought of telling her that I was a doormat, but instead, I hesitantly shared my story: my marriage and impending divorce, my lack of money, and my fear of homelessness. Blanketed in shame, I glanced at her just long enough to see that she was offering me a compassionate smile. When I mentioned the divorce on the grounds of fault, her eyes opened wide. "That's the worst thing she could've done! You have to fight back!"

Her voice almost startled me out of my chair. *But I have no idea how to defend myself, I've never done it.* I thought to myself. I expected the worst and imagined her screaming at me, "*You pathetic fool, you're a loser, a total idiot — you should be ashamed of yourself, and how dare you even breathe the same air as me? Get out of my office — NOW*" smacking me in the back of the head! But she looked at me with kind understanding and made it clear that she intended to help.

"The hearing is only a few weeks away, so we have no time to waste. The first thing we need to do is get you a lawyer. Then we need to get you on welfare, and then . . ." Counting the days on her calendar, she concluded, "I doubt you'll be able to get a lawyer in time, but under the law, you have the right to postpone the hearing until you can be appointed one. It can take up to six months or more."

I couldn't believe my ears. I felt like I was on death row and had received a stay of execution. As the pressure lifted, tears of relief came to my eyes. But I recognized pity in hers. Surely, I was just one of the many sad cases she came across each day.

After signing the paperwork, I wanted to give Ms Barbès a big hug, but I shook her hand instead. As I stepped outside the building, the birds sang and the leaves on the trees seemed brighter than ever. *I am no longer alone, I can breathe again.* When I got back to the apartment, I took Noirot in my arms and covered him with kisses. He looked at me as if he were saying, "See Guy, you can ask for help because you're worth it! You are a wonderful human!"

I picked up the phone and called Jeanne. "I went to the legal aid clinic, and they will be appointing me a lawyer," I calmly shared. "They said the divorce on the grounds of fault wasn't a good idea, so the hearing has been postponed until I'm appointed a lawyer."

I don't know which part of my statement set her off, but she blew up: "YOU DID WHAT?" she screamed. Then she proceeded to hurl insults at me until she violently hung up.

I was shocked at her outburst. I could've been a doormat, but I refused to take it. Instead, I stood up for myself. Noirot jumped on my lap, his warm body vibrating with intense purring telling me *You're not alone, Guy. You'll always be loved.*

I would meet Jeanne only one final time after that—at the divorce proceedings. She would say "Hello" and "Goodbye," but nothing more. Like my mother, she rejected our relationship in one swoop. "The past is the past. There's no point talking about it."

But for now, there was the more pressing matters of preparing for my museum interviews.

Chapter 31

LEGENDS AND GODDESSES

Home to Leonardo da Vinci's *Mona Lisa*, mysterious Egyptian sarcophaguses, and marble statues of Greek gods and goddesses, the Louvre offers the world's most prestigious art collection. In May 1995, during my interview with the head of the education department at the Louvre I was asked to develop a course plan linking classical sculpture to contemporary art. It was a perfect fit for me because as a contemporary installation artist, I'd also mastered the classical techniques of sculpture. I was honored as they hired me to create the workshop.

Right away, I visited the Greek, Etruscan, and Roman antiquities galleries for inspiration. I stopped in awe in front of a massive marble bas-relief entitled *Alexander and Diogenes*. The wall-sized carving depicted a half-naked man living in a large broken jar on the streets of Athens. Before him, Emperor Alexander the Great sat majestically on his horse in all his splendor. "Ask me whatever you want, and I'll give it you," Alexander professed.

"Stand out of my sunlight!" Diogenes answered with one arm

raised. Forefather of the group of philosophers known as the Stoics, he renounced all wealth and the pretenses of authority.

What an amazing story! Diogenes is another antihero like Metamorpho in my comic books. He's not my Noddy alter ego who needs a counselor or therapist to tell him to stand up for himself. He's like my Warrior in full possession of his powers and unashamedly he cries Victory! With the strength of his beliefs, I had found my gold: storytelling.

Part of this project with the education department required me to welcome schoolchildren and introduce them to different narratives from ancient times, after which I encouraged them to invent their own contemporary mythology. One class built a "Tower of Babel" by piling up chairs then used colored construction paper, scissors, and markers to add people and animals to the tower. To conclude, we held an opening where they presented their story and we immortalized their installation with a photo. I tingled all over as it was a resounding success. I loved helping people express themselves through art.

Next came an interview with public program coordinator at "Le Musée de la Poste." "Could you do a review of our education department?" She asked. "It would be my pleasure" And in the following days I met with their staff, read their programs and wrote up my impressions. However, this job and the one with the Louvre was only temporary, and I needed something more permanent.

Thanks to Daniel, I learned to be proactive and kept contact with my work prospects: I called again the secretary at the Beaubourg Museum. This time, instead of the usual flat "You'll have to wait for our call", her voice joyfully rang: "Oh good, I just hung up with someone who quit. I was going to call the next person on my list, but can you start tomorrow?"

"YES! I will be there"

The next day I met up with thousands of cheerful foreign visitors who lined up outside the museum, in the lobby and up the escalators for the retrospective of the amazing Romanian sculptor Constantin

Brâncuși! In addition to my role as guard, I made it my duty to answer all kinds of questions: "Who is this artist? What is cubism? Why is a bicycle wheel nailed to a stool?" I enjoyed extending the conversation beyond our modern art collection and suggested other attractions and restaurants. I met people from all over the world in this role. *Japanese, Chinese, USA, I am hosting the whole planet, travelling around the globe and sleeping home by the end of the day, this is amazing!*

During my breaks, I took in the rich collection and chatted with my new colleagues. There was Tania, a half Polish - Senegalese woman who also worked as a schoolteacher; Patrick, her brother who worked in the audiovisual department; and Chamia, an eloquent Moroccan intellectual whose passion reminded me of my friend Eva. There were dancers, painters, even philosophers—a veritable smorgasbord of creativity. *Should I talk about the divorce, or my art, what should we talk about?*

Unsure of myself, I'd sit alone on the museum's rooftop terrace with my cigarettes, journal and "café crème". I found in author Stephen Covey a new mentor as he advised me to cultivate *The Seven Habits of Highly Effective People* and to take care of *First Things First* as he aptly titled his books. *Yes, I am doing it, but why is my heart always last?*

Friday evenings were the worst because as the city's nightlife came alive, my feelings of solitude weighed heavily on my soul. On June 9, 1995, I wrote in my journal:

> *To get out of my social desert,*
> *Integrate life with friends,*
> *How can I do this, God?*
> *Help me become a friend.*
> *Help me become human!*
> *Help me get out of this straitjacket!*
> *You in your love, your wisdom,*
> *Help me to love,*

To be a good friend.

So when a gallery visitor named Keiko invited me for a coffee, I felt blessed. Keiko, who was in her forties, had elegantly white-powdered cheeks that complemented her exquisite Japanese traits. She was the perfect marriage of Eastern and Western esthetics with her stylish clothing.

As night fell, we made our way to Café Crème, a bistro near the museum. She asked the waiter "May we please sit by the open window" making sure we both bathe in the radiant full moon. Under its light, with her hypnotic gaze and gentle under spoken smile, she whispered: "Look how full, its beauty" Her French accent colored rose petals as Keiko recited the haiku poems of Matsuo Basho, my favorite *"A cotton field that looks like the flowers of a beautiful moon"* and *"The clouds fall, the people rest, the moon shines"* She murmured. "Lean over and feel it". All sounds stopped.

Later, when I walked her toward the subway, I felt the pulse of the moon binding us. But when she asked me to accompany her to her suburban home, I couldn't do it. I mumbled some lame excuse and left her at the station. But I kicked myself all the way home, wondering, *What am I so afraid of and why do I feel always last?*

Weeks later another visitor tried to break me out of my straitjacket. She was admiring Giacometti's *The Nose*, a suspended bronze head with a very long Pinocchio-like nose. I was surveilling the *Féminin-Masculin, le Sexe de l'Art* ("Feminin - Masculin, the Gender of Art") exhibition when she coyly asked, "What do you think the nose is about? It's kind of phallic, isn't it?"

Her name was Marianne, and she was brimming with self-confidence. Elegant and tall, she had long, curly chestnut brown hair that flowed over her shoulders like a waterfall. All of curves, her vibrant flowery robe seemed cut from a Matisse painting: large blue, yellow and pink petals undulated sinuously over her voluptuous body.

"Uh . . . you could say that," I replied. "He was obsessed with reducing the human body to the most basic elements, spending months, if not years, carving away bits and pieces and even exaggerating it like he does here." as I put out my hands measuring his long appendage. She laughed.

"Would you like to go for a cup of coffee?" she proposed with a sparkle in her eyes. "I'm just in town for a conference on the rights of sex workers, so I'd love some company."

"Of course! I get off work in an hour. Let's meet in front of the museum."

She took me to her friend's studio where she was staying. I was awed as we entered a hidden, idyllic alleyway overflowing with ivy. "This is so beautiful" I told her as she found the door and invited me in. Inside, the place was resplendent with velour cushions, gold chalices, intricate Turkish carpets, and the earthy aroma of incense in the air. It seemed like Alibaba's secret treasure trove.

We sat on a large sofa covered with incredibly soft pink and beige pillows and chatted about her presentation on women's rights in Switzerland, where she lived. Her self-assurance and easygoing manner appeased me. When she drew closer, caressed the back of my neck, and gently placed her lips over mine, it sent shivers down my spine. I wasn't sure what to do but trusted her.

Her kisses glided over my face and made their way to my ear where her warm breath sent shock waves throughout my body. She slid one hand under my shirt and unbuttoned her dress with the other. She took my hand and brought it to her breasts, which were spilling over her lacy, beige bra. She moaned when I dared to push my fingers under the lace and gently pinched her hard, erect nipple. She moved her hand down to find the bulge in my pants, and when she squeezed, it sent tingles of pleasure through my groin. She unzipped my pants, pulled them down, and pressed herself against my stiff, burning member. I ran my fingers through her soft long curly hair as her lavender perfume washed over me.

Half-naked, she led me to the bedroom, which was just big enough for a mattress. As we plunged onto the bed, it rippled in all direction. *Whoa!* I thought. *A waterbed!* She was my captain and I was her ship's apprentice as I'd never sailed on one. Jumping on top of me, she unhooked her bra and offered the most beautiful, buxom breasts with wide pink areolas that I'd ever seen. She yanked off my underwear then hers, revealing a rich bouquet of curly dark pubic hair. My skin felt alive and shuddered at the sight of such a beautiful woman.

As our hot skin fused, I licked her silky body, drinking in her scent. Then she magically produced a condom out of thin air and rolled it down as if it were already part of my penis. She shoved me inside her and rode like a locomotive, grunting, grabbing my shoulders, and shouting, "Oh, yes, yes, more, more!" I held on for dear life to her plump breasts like buoys in a sea storm as they bounced up and down in the opposite direction of the waves of the bed. *I'm going to be seasick!* It was all quite comical yet pleasures I'd never known flowed through my whole being.

Suddenly the waves, her breasts, and our hips all synchronized. Our dance accelerated in a mad dash. Our breathing was one as she stood full erect on my groin as she pushed me in even deeper. When I felt her squeezing me inside her, a burning mixture of pleasure and pain enveloped me. Digging her nails into my buttocks, she gave one final thrust. We both screamed as we exploded in a pure carnal orgasm that sent pigeons flying all over Paris.

Falling backward like two ships keeled over after a tsunami, she gently pulled me out of her and tied a knot in the condom. Interlaced in the warm afterglow of our salty lovemaking, her warm breath caressed me like waves on a soft, golden beach. No longer a spineless jellyfish, I felt like a precious piece of coral in her arms.

As we closed the door to the ivy-covered cavern, I felt blessed to have at long last navigated the high seas of sexuality. A Siren had un-leashed an inner-Ulysses that I didn't know I possessed. Marianne had just shown me how to put first things first, and I wrote a poem as we parted ways.

The captain with her magnificently radiant smile
Rang the bell
Raised her anchor
Unfurled her sails and
Sailed on the vast oceans
"Ahoy Sailors, full speed ahead towards a new horizon"

When I returned to Frédérique's place, there was a message from her on the answering machine saying she would be returning in a week. It was time to kick my apartment search into high gear.

Chapter 32

COUNT TOLSTOY

One of my coworkers had a lead on a place I could stay, so I wrote down the address and headed there after work. The apartment was in Montmartre, where I'd lived with Jeanne, but this place was on the other side of the hill in a small district known as Little Russia.

Françoise, a middle-aged woman with brown curly hair answered the door. She looked me up and down, and I must've passed the test because she led me to the second floor. It was sparse—merely a room, a bathroom, and a kitchen—but it was sparkling clean. "I'm divorced and my daughter recently moved out. I live upstairs," Françoise explained. Then we went upstairs and sat down at her dinner table to discuss the details. "I don't like living here alone, so the room is available right away."

"Thank you. This is wonderful." I paid her a month's rent and she handed me the keys. I was grateful that I wouldn't end up homeless.

When Frédérique returned the next day, I was packed and ready to go. "Thank you for everything," I said with a genuine smile. "You've been a lifesaver."

"Likewise Guy" She smiled taking Noirot in her arms "Oh I've missed you" as he purred and licked her hair. I was sad to leave Noirot but excited about my new place.

But by early the next morning, I understood why Françoise no longer felt safe in her back-alley home. It was about five a.m., and the yellowish burn of a hot summer morning was just beginning to dawn. Voices woke me and the pungent smell of cheap lily of the valley perfume overwhelmed my olfactory senses. "Come on! Just do it!" someone grumbled. This was followed by more dribble that I couldn't understand because half of it was drowned in pickled alcohol. When I heard the ruffle of clothes then wet sounds and eerie moans, I glanced through the lace curtains to see a man with his pants down and a woman with her skirt raised. *This is a Toulouse-Lautrec brothel painting in action.*

Pimps and drunks weren't the only problem. I also found used syringes in the gutter. I did my best to watch over my gracious host. I wanted to be there for her since she'd rescued me from living on the streets.

As Fall arrived, some evenings Françoise was kind enough to invite me up for supper. We'd share a bottle of red wine and our stories. Her home was a veritable museum of Russian artifacts: Russian dolls, gold-leafed religious icons, and prints of the wild steppes covered her walls. "You must go there one day sleep in a tribal yurt!" she insisted, her eyes twinkling as if she was still there. I easily imagined her curly, brown hair flowing in the wind as she rode bareback on a muscular, black stallion across the great Slavic expanses.

She was a fine chef, conjuring up many of her culture's fine specialties, including beef stroganoff, borscht, and blini. After the meals, we sat down for Gollandsky cheese, which ironically means "Dutch" and tastes like my favorite cheese from the Netherlands. Then came the chak-chak, balled-up fried flatbread smothered in honey and topped with dried fruits and nuts. *I'm in heaven*

"You sing in choirs? Here, listen to this "spiritual music." She played "Tebe Poem" and other hymns from the Russian Orthodox Church. The deep guttural harmonies resonated through my core. *This is healing for my soul.* Finishing the red wine, she recited Pushkin's poetry. In return, I described my exhibits and my concern for the plight of refugees and First Nations people, to which Françoise surprised me with some history about my own country that I didn't know. "Have you heard about the Doukhobor, a group of Russian refugees in Canada?" When I shook my head, she continued. "They are a sect of pacifist Christians who rejected personal materialism. Sadly, they were persecuted in their homeland for centuries before emigrating to Canada in the late nineteenth century. In fact, author Leo Tolstoy was one of their biggest supporters and financed their resettlement in Canada."

I was shocked. I had never even heard of them.

"Did you know that Tolstoy exchanged letters with Mahatma Gandhi and influenced his philosophy of nonviolence?"

I was dumbfounded. I'd been an ardent admirer of Gandhi since my youth, but I'd never dreamed that his ideas had been shaped by someone else.

"Thank you for such a wonderful evening Françoise, I feel I've been to Russia myself".

She smiled "Well Guy, I wish it for you, it's such an amazing country and the folks are so kind." We hugged and shared the proverbial cheek kisses.

The next day, I went to the bookstore, determined to learn more about Tolstoy. I hadn't read *War and Peace* or any of his other books, but I bought *The Kingdom of God Is Within You*, an acidic analysis of the corruption of the church and the czar. In it, he detailed the nonviolent resistance principles that Christ taught, such as "turn the other cheek," promoted the abolition of violence, even the defensive kind, and urged people to avoid seeking revenge.

But his book was banned, he was put under police surveillance, and the Russian Orthodox Church excommunicated him. *That's insane! I thought. He was encouraging love and peace, and they attacked him.* I voraciously began devouring Tolstoy's writing. According to him, because soldiers were serving the powerful czar and the church, they couldn't be held accountable for the horrible acts they'd committed during war. *If they weren't accountable for their acts, then maybe I'm not to blame for my shame and fear. It was the doing of my abusers. All my life, I've been terrified and on the verge of killing myself. But what if I wasn't responsible?*

And then, oh so gradually, it dawned on me. *All my fears, my thoughts of suicide, and all the years I've spent blaming myself, none of it was my fault! NONE OF IT WAS MY FAULT!* My heart fluttered, and then I remembered that, according to *The Courage to Heal,* guilt was one of the symptoms of post-traumatic stress disorder. Until then, I thought I was to blame for all the trauma I'd experienced, but now I understood that it wasn't my fault. It had never been my fault.

I felt as if a heavy ball and chain had been unshackled from my soul. I'd been a victim for so long and always shouldered the blame. Even though I knew deep inside that all this suffering was wrong, I had no words for it. But now Tolstoy had opened my heart to a new understanding. *Maybe I had been a victim of abuse and neglect, but I had no control over it; I was not to blame. There were even larger forces at hand: politics and religion.*

After living all my life under dark clouds of guilt, suddenly the skies opened up, and a new light of peace, harmony, and serenity shined down on me. Inside my head, the relentless voice of self-judgment disappeared. I wanted to sing, dance, and celebrate my new freedom, so I sought out Madame Maciocchi and my old choir.

"Guy, you're just in time!" She was overjoyed to see me because they had just started rehearsing for a celebration to commemorate UNESCO's fiftieth anniversary at their headquarters. Not only this, but it was also around my birthday! *What a gift of love!*

I had the pleasure to once again put on my full concert attire with matching bowtie along with more than a hundred people singing on stage in addition to a full orchestra. I was moved to tears as we sang the lyrics to Beethoven's "Ode to Joy," particularly the line: "Alle Menschen werden Brüder," which, in English, means "All men become brothers."

Tolstoy was right, there should be no guilt, and we need to forgive because we are all brothers. This is for you, Mimi, Luc, and Marc. I forgive you. I was so honored to be a part of the celebration. After us came Jean-Michel Jarre, who performed with Cheb Khaled, the famous Raï singer I had danced to in the Melkweg in Amsterdam! *This is amazing, what a beautiful a poetic circle that just closed.*

A few days later, I was discussing Tolstoy with a work colleague when she mentioned a unique therapeutic method called Vittoz. "It's all about bringing the mind, body, and spirit together into one cohesive unit. It changed my life."

She seemed so enthusiastic about it that I was compelled to try it as well. After obtaining a list of practitioners, my eye was drawn to one name, Blanche, as in Blanche Neige (Snow White). *Snowy, like my hostess' cat in Peterborough!* She has to be the one, and made an appointment.

My heart was racing as I arrived at the address. I was early—a nervous habit of mine—so I circled the block a few times. I felt light headed when I finally rang the doorbell, I heard, *Bzzzz. KLAK.* Then the massive wooden door eerily opened by itself as if I was in a horror movie.

I stepped over the doorframe and ascended the creaking, spiral staircase that looked like it came straight out of Hitchcock's movie *Vertigo.* At the landing, I noticed a door that was slightly ajar, so I knocked, went inside, took off my shoes, and sat down on a large, white couch. "Do I lie down?" I asked.

No, no she assured, "unless you feel the need for it." Blanche, who was in her mid-fifties, was petite with a roundish figure and short, gray hairstyle "a la garçone" that complemented her gentle face. She reminded me of Belle-nadette, my drawing teacher, with her soft, cottony voice that was like a whisper in the wind.

Everything about the room was comforting: plush carpet, soft beige cushions, white lace curtains over a large window. The sun filtered in and added a heavenly glow to the angelic room. Nothing to excite the senses except tiny colored pots dotting a hanging shelf. My breathe settled and joined the waving motion of the curtains.

As the session got underway, Blanche instructed, "Are you sitting comfortably? Relax with your hands on your legs. Breathe in gently. Don't force anything. Just relax, there's nothing to do. We're here to reconnect mindfully with your body."

After a few moments to relax my body, Blanche continued, "I'd like you to get up and walk slowly around the room, as if you're on a cloud. While you do this, be particularly aware of the soles of your feet." The exercises were extremely gentle yet powerful. Next, I mindfully caressed my arms, then moving up to my face, I explored its bumps and valleys with my fingertips. "No judgment," Blanche advised. "No need to verbalize what you discover. Just use your senses."

I was in a state of pure beingness as I plunged in the stillness of a limitless ocean. A new sensation of peace flowed from within.

My poor, poor body, how much I had hated it! All these years it had been my enemy. *It's your fault I was abused.* I'd think. So many times, I wanted to cut off my penis, "my vile dirty enemy!" And now for the first time I felt every cell in my body releasing and taking a deep breath of fresh air. *I have a home, and it's in me!*

I had been at war my whole life, living in a ravaged field of buried land mines and surrounded by rats dragging rotting veils of shame and disgust. But during my session with Blanche, I signed a truce and came out of the trenches. Sitting on the shore of my previously tumultuous inner sea, I quietly watched the waves cleanse the skeletons from my past. At last, I felt peace.

After thanking Blanche at the end of the session, I slowly made my way down the staircase, feeling every step under my feet, my fingers gently brushing the railing. When I reached the door, night had fallen and a rare dusting of snow covered the sidewalk. *Maybe, we'll have a white Christmas.*

On the way home, I stopped at Sacré-Cœur Basilica and lit candles for Jeanne, my family in Canada and for my dear Taffy. I closed my eyes and prayed for them and for peace to all as echoes of a children's choir filled the church with "He Is Born, the Divine Christ Child."

Chapter 33

NOW OR NEVER?

As the winter of 1995 turned to the spring of 1996, I gave my landlady Françoise notice that I'd be moving out. I was leaving Little Russia for a small room a few streets away from the renown Parisian landmark of the Arc de Triomphe. My time as Françoise's neighbor was great, but after months of working with Blanche, I was ready for my own place. My new space with its monastic simplicity reflected the inner peace I was longing for.

Each day, I walked up and down six flights of stairs on Brunel Street to reach the heavy fireproof metal door of my typical Parisian "Chambre de bonne"; a maid's quarters with running water, a telephone, and electricity tucked directly under the rooftop. The matchbox-sized space could barely fit a single bed, a chest, and a chair with just enough space to pry the door open. The only way to use the small sink was to bow down under the slanted ceiling, which offered the luxury of a skylight. However, during the daytime, the scorching sun produced a waxy smell from the shiny ceramic tile floor, and the nights were so stifling that I kept the door ajar for some soothing fresh air.

The bathroom was located on the landing, and I had to share it with four other neighbors, including a family with children. I couldn't make out what language they spoke, but I understood why they argued so much—I couldn't imagine so many people living in such conditions.

What I didn't understand at first were the "Turkish toilets": basically a hole in the ground "on the sixth floor!". They had all the convenience of a modern system, but much to the dismay of my pants, I quickly learned to diligently move away from the "Niagara Falls" flush!

With no refrigerator or stove, my meals consisted mainly of cans of sardines and fresh produce purchased at the nearby street market: avocados, tomatoes, carrots. These products and the tastiest baguettes in Paris spread with butter, creamy camembert cheese and country ham were more than enough! On weekends, I sat in the warmth of the sun in the lush forest of the Bois de Boulogne. I enjoyed the rustling of the leaves and the melodious chirping of the birds as the ducks and geese quacked and jumped on each other while I tossed pieces of bread. I was enveloped by nature's warm blanket and meditated, eyes closed and hair flowing in the wind, sitting on a bench by the lake. I rediscovered the simple life I had known on my first trip to Europe in 1984, and with this new serenity, food and wine, I felt at home.

I reveled in the varied activities that my new 17th arrondissement offered. I walked up the 284 steps to the observation deck of the Arc de Triomphe and viewed the magnificent Champs-Élysées. I attended openings for artists from my homeland at the Maison du Quebec. I had discovered this cultural center last year when Quebec's vote for independence took place. I added fun by doing a performance of smiles and winks in front of the live TV cameras to surprise my friends and family in Canada.

I also reconnected with my love of music by joining the choir at Saint George's Anglican Church, one of the few English parishes in Paris. It was also host to people from Madagascar community. Fran Horner, our American director, had the gift of bringing together members of many different cultures as I sang with fellow Kenyan chorister

Ann Wambugu. Her ebony dark complexion and refined traits embodied Picasso's intense love for African masks. We sang in English and Malagasy, danced in long, purple-and-orange robes, and clapped to the rhythms of "Rainay any an-danitra": the Lord's Prayer.

As spring blossomed into summer, I joined the hordes of tourists and Parisians exploring the riches of the city and came upon "Les Jardins du Luxembourg" in the 6th arrondissement. The Royals left a rich heritage of luxurious palaces now transformed in richly designed public gardens. With its tree-lined promenades, playgrounds, French and English gardens, and gorgeous flower beds, I had found my new writing oasis.

On my days off work at the museum, I'd make my way to a small café-terrace with typical green cast iron tables and chairs early in the morning. I'd sit at a table near a tree and savor my hot espresso and butter croissant while, nearby, teenagers hit tennis balls, old men played a local lawn bowling game called *pétanque*, and children gleefully kicked a soccer ball. I shared my crumbs with the multitude of prancing little sparrows who merrily tweeted their delight. *Thank you, my little "Piafs" for your happy songs.* With the sun, a gentle breeze, the exquisite view, and the company of joyful strangers, I couldn't help but think, *This is perfect, absolutely perfect!*

I admired the children's spontaneity, innocence, and amazing energy and wondered, *Was I ever an innocent child?* But then I got to thinking about what Tolstoy had written about the soldiers: that they were just following orders from more powerful people. They were victims like I had been.

A young boy's hollering suddenly snapped me out of my train of thought. "Mommy, Mommy! Can we have some ice cream now, please?" I watched as the children, who had just finished their soccer game, returned to their parents. "Sure, come on over," their mom replied. I felt so much warmth just watching them leave hand in hand. Then it hit me: *My family!*

I felt a twinge in my heart: *Mom, Dad, my brothers, my sister—they were all victims as much as I was. Who are they really after all? Before I left for the Netherlands, I had no voice or roots to speak off. I was scared; fighting every day for my survival. I had no room in my heart for myself, much less for them.* I felt a lump in my throat as my eyes welled up with tears.

Maybe I can make room in my life for them now? My heart pounded as I realized: *Here in Paris, for the first time in my life, I'm totally independent. I have a home, a job, and enough money to live. I've made it and could make a fantastic life for myself in Europe. Yet my parents are getting older. If I don't go back now, I might miss the chance to get to know them— really know them—before they pass away. If that happens, I'd feel like this was a turning point, an opportunity where everything could've changed, and I would've squandered it. What should I do?*

I saw a window of opportunity opening and closing. I searched for a sign from Taffy or Vincent, but neither of them appeared to offer advice. I knew it was up to me. It was now or never. In my mind, I heard a cracking sound as my *Warrior* sculpture appeared. A fracture crept right through his center as dust and pieces of debris fell off. The fissure engulfed the entire sculpture until, in a loud bang, it exploded into a thousand pieces.

ITS NOW!

Stepping out of my shell, I felt light and energized because I knew what I needed to do: pack up my life and return home. But not before I made myself a promise. *This time, going back to Canada is my choice. If I ever decide to move across the world again, it will be my choice for my future, and I will have my own job and my own money. I will never, ever again put myself in such a horrible situation where I could end up living on the streets. Never again. I am beautiful, and I am worth it!*

Montreal, here I come!

PART III
LOVE CLOWN

Chapter 34

THE KING OF NEUROLOGY

A nurse rapidly guided me through a labyrinth of underground passages. Pipes snaked across the low ceiling where fluorescent lights flickered, creating eerie shadows on the sickly green walls. The hum of a furnace buzzed in the fetid air. In these dust-covered catacombs, everything looked faded.

"He fell into a coma two days ago, and we don't expect him to come out of it," a nurse had told me over the phone. "He's been moved to palliative care."

Sixteen years had passed since my return to Canada in 1996. During that time, I'd been living in Montréal and teaching in museums. When I got the call, I canceled my workshops and hurried to the hospital.

As I entered the room, a whiff of musty air wriggled up my nostrils. A tiny grilled window with drab green curtains added a melancholic light. In the dark corner, a red light from a piece of hospital equipment blinked on and off. *Beep. Beep. Beep.* On the wall hung a lone child's drawing of a castle. Sitting on the angular folded sheets, the bed gave out a languishing complaint. Everything in the room seemed old, washed out and dull, and in the middle of it all lay my dying father.

"Hi Dad. It's me, Guy," I whispered. *He's a mere shadow of himself.*

Six months earlier, he'd been admitted to the intensive care unit for reasons he'd never talked about. The nurses admired his good humor as his colleagues and old students paraded by to pay homage to the "Good Doctor Giard." Now, he couldn't heal himself. As an outstanding neurologist, department head, and professor, he'd spent sixty years of his life in these same halls. He knew the drill, and he hated it. "Let me have the dignity of dying in my own home!" he'd complained, but his doctors wouldn't allow it.

I lightly stroked his dry, chalky cheek, afraid to break his paper-thin skin. *Where have you gone, Dad? Let me breathe for you.* When I reached out to hold his hand, it was so cold. I tried my best to warm it up then closed my eyes and prayed.

Before I left Paris, I'd written to Marc and told him of my desire to reconnect with my family, but that dream had been shattered. At birthdays and Christmas gatherings, I'd ask about their work and their hobbies. But no sooner would the words leave my mouth than my siblings would abruptly interrupt, making it clear that personal information was not to be shared. "Get me a beer." "Who has the remote?" "Where are the chips?" This was the extent of our discussions—at least when obnoxious behaviors or insults weren't being volleyed back and forth. Nobody asked about my time in Paris or my future plans. *It's as if I never left. They still don't care to hear anything about my life!*

Marc sometimes tried to talk to me—but only in private. On these rare occasions, we'd meet for a cup of coffee and swap stories. Once, he'd hinted that he'd also been abused in his youth. He'd always been aware of it while I had repressed my experiences. I don't know which is worse but he never mentioned it again.

Even though our get-togethers were total failures, I still invited my family members to my exhibits and concerts. They could no longer accuse me of airing personal matters as my new artworks were inspired by Tolstoy and focused on the plight of everyday life people. I built a

European style water filled basin to wash laundry called *Le Lavoir* and presented five afternoons with local musicians from Montreal Southwest working class neighborhoods. In 2002 I constructed an 18-foot-long (5.5 meters) ship-sculpture entitled *Le Voyage de L'Espérance* ("Voyage of the S.S. Hope") on the grassy banks of the Lachine canal. The hull was decorated with paintings from a workshop I gave at the CIVA center for adults living with a physical disability. That same year I presented an installation on slavery in Montréal retelling the forgotten life of a young black slave named Marie-Josèphe Angélique in 1734. I organized concerts and poetry readings in her memory, along with lectures by historian Marcel Trudel and other guest speakers such as from the UNICEF on today's reality of human trafficking and child soldiers.

In 2004, I commemorated the bicentennial anniversary of Haiti's independence with an installation of twelve 10 minutes videos entitled *Angélique 1734 - Haïti 2004: The master's story* also with varied lectures. The videos were later combined as one movie and projected in festivals. The following year I was selected for the 3rd International Manif d'Art, a bi-annual exhibition in Quebec City and created a series of 5 videos on the cynicism inspired by Diogenes.

But during that time, Mom only came to a few events and Marc showed up when no one else was around. I'm proud to say that Dad became one of my biggest fans, and every year, he attended my choir concerts. "Congratulations my son. It was beautiful!" He was a man of few words.

But actually, there was one person who was present at all my exhibits and concerts. The woman who posed as Marie-Josèphe Angélique when I needed a model: Tania, my wife and former coworker whom I'd met at the Beaubourg Museum in Paris. I still remember the first time we met.

One day on a break at work, she smiled and said to me, "Hi, I just started a few weeks ago with the Brancusi retrospective. Are you from Quebec? I recognize your accent. I've always dreamed of going there!" There was a melodic lilt in her voice that was different from the usual Parisian staccato. She was petite with brown eyes, and her short, curly, black hair complemented her amber complexion, as if Serge Gainsbourg had composed his song *Couleur Café* especially for her. When my break time was over, we gave each other kisses on the cheeks like they do in France, and I hoped to see her again.

Over the coming months we met in the museum's hallways and I learned that her father was from Senegal and her grandmother was from Poland. She grew up in Paris but spent most of her summers on a farm in the northern part of France, so she was half city girl and half country girl, and her dad had also been uprooted like mine. From feeding cows to playing with kittens to traveling in the back seat of the family car, we shared many similar stories.

Meanwhile the museum opened the Russian artists Ilya Kabakov's installation *We are living here.* I loved his work as we were kindred spirits, using everyday objects to create a scenic human story as in my *Family Show.* I was fascinated by one of the rooms he created. It was called *The man who flew into space from his apartment.*

In a small cubic room covered with Russian propaganda posters, hung a large tractor seat attached by four giant springs to the upper corners of the space. The ceiling had a gigantic hole, and the floor was littered with broken pieces of plaster and drywall. One could easily guess that the occupant had catapulted himself from the shackles of communism. All my themes were there, escaping abuse, Yuri Gagarin and the tractor seat for my father. Feeling more confident after a few sessions with Blanche, when I saw Tania visiting the gallery, I asked her if she wanted to go for a movie down the Champs-Élysées. She agreed.

As Spring 1996 came around we often strolled through Buttes-Chaumont parc and enjoying the flowers the Jardin des Plantes. One time, during a sudden springtime downpour, we took shelter under a Japanese cherry blossom tree. Just to see her pearly smile, I jumped into a puddle and sang "Singin' in the Rain" then hopped over the low garden fence like Gene Kelly. She laughed as I twirled and tiptoed around. On that day, the first sparks of love ignited in our hearts.

I was worried about telling her about my decision to return to Canada, but instead of driving us apart, it brought us closer, and in the weeks that followed, a gust of wind fanned our spark into a real flame. Walking to the top of the Coulée Verte Renée-Dumont: a former railroad bridge converted into a splendid aerial park, we stopped to admire the view of the Viaduc des Arts. My arm tightened around her waist; she accepted the gentle embrace, moved closer and rested on my shoulders. The minutes passed. Turning slowly, I touched her cheek carefully and leaned in for a first kiss. The sun, the caressing breeze, everything was perfect as we became one.

On the last day of August 1996, as we sat in the last row of a bus zooming like a hurricane toward the airport, I squeezed her in my arms. Tears streamed down her cheeks and her body quivered under rolling sobs. I was her first boyfriend, her first lover, and this was her first separation. "You can come visit when I get settled," I whispered in her ear.

To me, I wasn't leaving her as much as I was reuniting with my family. By the time she came to visit me a couple months later, the absence had transformed our passion into a deeply felt love. Although we were wary of long-distance relationships, we agreed to try out for two months the following summer.

Finally, on New Year's Eve 1997, Tania, my shooting star, the woman of my dreams, came back one more time. I made reservations for a romantic, candlelit dinner at renown 5 stars "Chez Queux" restaurant in Old Montreal. Tania sparkled like a ruby in her red velvet dress. At the stroke of midnight, with confetti flying and champagne popping, I took out a small, blue box, got on my knees, and said, "Sweet Tania of my dreams, my exotic bird of the islands, will you marry me?"

When she said, "Yes, I will!" we jumped into each other's arms as the revelers around us blew their festive horns. It was the coldest New

Year's Eve in Montréal's history, but as she put on the engagement ring, it was the warmest one that ever blessed this Earth.

On August 1, 1998, we signed our vows at City Hall while my cellist friend Josée delighted us with Bach's Suite No. 1 in G major. We celebrated as in Degas' painting *Déjeuner sur l'herbe* with a picnic on top of Mount Royal. The weather was picture-perfect, and the cloudless sky was a pristine, azure blue. We danced by the lake to Compay Segundo's Cuban music, drank, and ate on red-and-white checkered tablecloths. I'd never felt so blessed!

The unrelenting beeping of the medical monitor made me tumble down from my dream to the cold, hard floor reality of my dad's hospital room. I stroke his thin, gray hair and said, "Dad, when I came back, I tried to bring all of us together. I realize we didn't really have the kind of family we'd hoped for, but we came pretty close with your 'little princess', right? During my concert at church, she sat on your lap while I sang your favorite, the Lacrimosa from Mozart's *Requiem*.

"Even when I sang Beethoven's 'Ode to Joy' with the Montreal Symphony Orchestra for the 100th anniversary of the Canadian Hockey Club, and you told me how proud you were of me, I knew in my heart that your beloved little princess was your pride and joy. And you know what dad," I added as I gently squeezed his hand, "seeing you so happy and proud was a thousand times—no, a million times— better than living in Paris. That's how much you mean to me, Dad. After all, she's your first and only grandchild."

I looked up at the lone drawing left on the wall that his little princess had drawn. It was a castle for the "King of Neurology." I closed my eyes and cried.

Chapter 35

THE LITTLE PRINCESS

Are you still with me, Dad? I leaned over and listened to his raspy breath. *He's holding on.* He had a living will, rejecting "futile and aggressive treatment." Even though he'd been a man of science, he was still a farmer's boy and wished to die as Mother Nature intended.

"I'm sure not having any grandchildren was such a disappointment for you, Dad. I can't believe I'm the only one of your kids who even got married and, sadly, also the only one who divorced. I'm sure it broke your heart." I tenderly placed my hand over his chest. "Oh, my poor, sweet Papa. You look so terribly exhausted. When you visited me in Amsterdam, you told me how much you hated the divorce. You'd wanted so desperately to stay with us, and it hurt you that you couldn't. I had no idea, Dad." Tears rolled down my cheeks as I continued talking to him. "Is that why you remained so quiet around us? Was it too hard for you to share your pain?" Now that I was a dad myself, I couldn't imagine losing my precious daughter. His one and only granddaughter took years to come into this world.

"You were lucky, Dad. When you were only eight years old, you knew that farming wasn't for you. You knew you wanted to be a doctor, and you did it. I've always admired you for that." I paused briefly to collect my thoughts. "Dad, after my return to Canada, I felt this emptiness growing inside me. I know it sounds crazy with my art shows, the choir concerts, and my marriage, but I felt this void that needed to be filled." My chest tightened up, so I reached for a pack of cigarettes. Then I laughed at my absurdity because I'd quit smoking right after Tania and I got married fifteen years earlier. I had started smoking to numb my pain from the high school bullies and stopped when Tania and I moved in together.

"I was fulfilled with Tania for the first few years, so I didn't understand it when that emptiness creeped back in even stronger than before. I needed something—anything—to fill the void. Every morning, I left very early for a cup of coffee and a muffin from a local bakery. I'd sit there for an hour or two, ruminating over why my suicidal thoughts had returned. By that time, I'd become so overweight that I'd get winded walking up the stairs. I was prediabetic, but didn't realize anything was wrong until Tania screamed in the middle of the night, 'WAKE UP! WAKE UP!' She almost shook me out of bed. 'You stopped breathing!' She was right dad. For so long, I'd been stuffing myself to my feelings, and in doing so, I'd developed sleep apnea. I was suffocating and digging my own grave.

"I got mad at myself—really mad—so I started an exercise program, switched to a paleo diet, did a ten-day water fast, and even created a blog to help others. After losing a quarter of my body weight, my sleep apnea disappeared. And then, miracle of miracles, Tania got pregnant! Dad, you were so excited that you broke out the champagne! You gave us advice for each and every stage of the pregnancy and even called the midwife and our doctor. The first time you held your granddaughter, you looked her right in the eyes and said, "Why hello there, my little princess."

As she grew up and we came to visit him, he'd always hide gifts in the living room cabinet. He'd open the drawer with a jubilant smile and hand her a toy or a card with money when she got older. He'd offer her Whippets, his favorite chocolate-coated marshmallow cookie, and for dessert, strawberry pie with ice cream, strawberry shortcake, or strawberries swimming in cream and sugar. He'd say, "Here, have some more with your papi, my little princess."

Everyone on his staff knew how his little princess had changed his life. Her framed portrait hung on his office wall, and a smaller one sat on his desk. They often told me "He sure does love his granddaughter. He can't stop talking about her!" That's why I never told him that he almost lost her forever a few years ago.

"Happy birthday, dear Guuuuy! Happy birthday to you!" Hooplas all around as they sang in dubious harmonies! My wife, our four-year-old daughter, Aïyana, and her godmother Ruth could barely move in the small Lebanese restaurant. I blew out a small candle on my scrumptious piece of baklava. With my belly full of Arabic goodness, I was more than happy to get bundled up in my heavy coat and escape into the quiet narrow streets. The night had a magical feeling to it, with snowflakes dancing to a mad jig in the wind. As we made our way hand in hand to the nearest bus stop, Aïyana joyfully surfed on the undulating waves of the snowy sidewalks.

At the bus shelter, I decided to stand outside for some fresh air and to feel the falling flakes tickle my skin. "If you stick your tongue out like this, the snowflakes taste just like marshmallows!"

"Daddy you're silly!" Aïyana said with a giggle.

Finally, the orange lights of the bus appeared, but it was coming fast—way too fast! Just as the girls stepped out of the shelter, an ear-piercing screech sent a shiver of electricity through my spine.

Sliding on the slick road, the bus had plowed into the shelter. The sound of metal crunching and glass shattering filled the air as the shelter exploded into a million pieces. I quickly swept Aïyana into my arms and backed away just before the shelter's lighted billboard toppled toward us. I barely managed to sidestep it as it loudly crashed at our feet.

Aïyana and I were safe, but the shelter's curved roof was still in motion. I watched in horror as my wife fell down right in its path. "Tania, no!" I cried. But she remained frozen in fear, her eyes transfixed. Still holding our daughter, I threw myself in the path of the falling roof, and it hit my shoulder with a loud thud. Summoning all my strength, I managed to nudge it sideways, and as it hit the ground, it missed my wife by a hair. I landed on one knee with Aïyana still under my arm. She never touched the pavement. Miraculously, we were all safe.

That was four years ago, and I never told my dad about it. Since his hospitalization, Tania, Aïyana and I had been visiting him regularly. His face lit up whenever his princess was around. The walls of his room were covered with her drawings of bright rainbows, giant sunflowers, and self-portraits. They hugged, held hands; she loved her papi, and he loved her. They had a special healing bond, so it broke our hearts when the nurse intervened on our way to see him one day. "Children are not allowed in the intensive care unit!" she barked. "They'll contaminate the patients!"

"What's wrong, Daddy? What's wrong with Papi? I want to see my Papi!" Aïyana cried. She knew he was just down the hall and didn't understand why she couldn't go see him.

"Children aren't allowed!" the nurse repeated, giving me a scornful look and paying no attention to my daughter's anguish.

I tried to console Aïyana as I picked her up and carried her toward the lobby. But it was no use; her whole body convulsed as she sobbed on my shoulder. In the lobby, we sat at a table and I gave her some markers and paper. "Let's make Papi a drawing so he'll know you're here," I suggested.

She stared blankly at the white sheet as tears silently trickled down her cheeks. "Why can't I see Papi? Is he OK?"

I was choked up, but I was eventually able to say, "I'll bring your drawing to Papi, and he'll know that you're here. He'll be so happy!"

She sniffled then hesitantly removed the cap from one of the markers and started to color. The more the image took shape, the more excited she became. First a castle appeared, then a throne, and a king wearing a golden crown. Finally, she drew a little girl and handed me the sheet. "That's me, Daddy. I'm sitting on his knees." By this time, she was smiling. "Tell him that's me, OK, Daddy? And tell him that I love him."

When I entered my dad's room, he was surprised that Aïyana wasn't there. "Where is she?" he worried.

"She's just outside. The nurse wouldn't let her in your room. She said to tell you that she loves you."

He picked up the drawing and, with tears in his eyes, stroked the rosy cheek of the princess in the picture. "Please tell her that I love her too, and we'll see each other soon." He put the drawing right next to his bed so that every day he could reach out and caress his little princess.

They never saw each other again.

Chapter 36

A Good Boy

I heard some footsteps outside the corridor, then the door creaked and a nurse walked in. "Oh sorry," he apologized. "I didn't know you were still here. I have to check the monitors." He looked at the machines then prepared to exit the room. "I'm sorry about Dr. Giard. He's such a great man. Take all the time you need. I won't be back for a couple of hours."

I looked at the princess and castle; it was the only drawing left. In it, Dad sat on his majestic throne wearing a golden crown as "The King of Neurology."

"You know, Dad, you've successfully created a kingdom all your own. The staff, your colleagues, and your patients love you. But I look at my life—I'm married to a beautiful woman, have an exceptional daughter, and I have my exhibits, concerts, lectures, and my work in museums. I even own our condo. So why do I still feel so empty inside?" A pall of silence fell over the room. Except for the beeping machines, it was so quiet I could hear a fluorescent light in the hallway buzzing. The sound evolved into a long painful whine then ended in a brief metallic click.

"Neurology's been your passion, Dad, your mission in life, but what is mine? Ever since I survived the bus crash, I've wondered what's the point of it all? Why even bother? Am I really living my life? Or is it what my wife or what society expects of me? What do *I* really want? I just don't know anymore, Dad.

"You once told me after a concert that I have a beautiful voice and you could hear me above the other tenors. Maybe you were trying to tell me something then, Dad. Music has always been my passion and I would have played piano for you if you hadn't left home. I also took violin lessons, sang Gospel, did music improvisation and even played the gong and the kendang in a Balinese gamelan ensemble. But I wanted to do my own thing, just like you, and for me, that was singing. I was just too scared to go solo."

I did get closer to my dream when I founded my own choir, Les Chants Marins de Montreal, which specialized in classic sea shanties, songs written to synchronize the hard work of sailors on tall ships. The songs were joyous, sometime vulgar, but always full of gusto. They weren't made for singers but for men of passion. I was one of them. I even taught sea shanties classes at a cultural center, made my audience sing during talks, and sang duets in concert. I loved it. But I had to confront my demons to get there.

It all started when I wanted to write down the scores of my childhood compositions. I started taking music theory classes at night and bought a keyboard to practice at home. I composed new poetic pieces such as *Je suis car j'essuie la suie dans le noir*[1] for four voices and Ô rage ("Oh Anger") for two soprano soloists and chorus and applied to the music department at the University of Montreal. I was admitted to major in music writing. *Yes, this is it, this is my life, this makes sense!*

I excelled at all my classes except for one: atonal ear training. I was failing one damn class, and it was preventing my dream from coming

---

1   A play on words based on the sound of *suis/essuie/suie*. Literal: I am/ wipe/soot. Meaning: I am as I wipe away soot in the dark.

true. I studied harder and sat for hours at the piano. Even so, my grades failed to improve in that one class, and without passing it, I couldn't continue my studies. My dream of a career in music became a nightmare, and my panic attacks resurfaced.

"I'm late again! I have to hurry," I muttered to myself. The snow was coming down hard and the sidewalks were slippery. As I left the house, tormented and exhausted, I rushed like a madman to pick up Aïyana at day care. That's when it hit me. *This is insane! It's just a stupid course. There's no bus flying toward me, threatening to wipe out my family. I'm not going to die. What is wrong with me?* At that moment, my view of the world stopped as if in freeze-frame. It was like the snowflakes stopped in midair and the squirrels were suspended in flight between snow-covered pine branches, only the wind whistled in my empty head.

Then, I finally saw it. I let out a big sigh as I admitted to myself: *I have a problem!* With that, the squirrels landed on the branches, the snowflakes reached the ground, and I heard the whizzing tires of cars stuck in the snowbanks. Saddened yet relieved, I reached the daycare and devoted my full attention to getting our daughter dressed for the walk home. I knew I had to ask for help.

Help came in the form of Marguerite, a middle-aged woman with spirally, pitch-black hair that she fought a constant battle to tame. Comfortable in her maturity, she wore an elegant burgundy blouse and welcomed me into her office with a firm handshake and a warm smile. Patches of autumn sceneries decorated the emerald green walls. A massive bamboo palm far too large for its corner extended its huge leaves near a window. The trickle of a water fountain and the languishing pan flute melodies filled the air. Everything about the room was about nature. I instantly felt safe in her presence.

I'd tried conventional talk therapy before, but after my experience with Blanche, I knew body work was better for me. I continued with massotherapy and osteopathy and reached better relaxation and restful sleep.

Sitting behind her desk, Marguerite explained that she would help me process my memories through a variety of techniques based on my needs. I began by telling her that I hardly slept, and I'd been having panic attacks after flunking one of my music courses. By the end of the session, I felt confident enough to dig deeper. Her recommendation for PTSD was Eye Movement Desensitization and Reprocessing therapy (EMDR), a technique in which the patient recalls a traumatic experience while the therapist directs him to focus on external stimuli such as hand tapping or eye movements.

Toward the end of our second meeting, as I lay on the shiny, black leather couch, I confessed, "I'm a workaholic! I have to perform, to work—no, I have to excel—at everything I do! I'm an obsessive perfectionist."

"I see," Marguerite answered. "Do you suppose you have this tendency as a form of escape?"

"Maybe. I also use muffins and pastries to avoid feeling my emotions and my void."

"Tell me, Guy, what is this 'void' you keep mentioning?"

"I don't know." My body tensed up. Perhaps I was getting too close to an unspoken truth.

At our subsequent meeting, Marguerite started with a calming meditation. "Now Guy, I'd like you to close your eyes and breathe easily. Tell me about a place where you feel safe."

"I see a beach, an infinite stretch of golden sand. The sky is clear and sunny, and an incredibly blue sea stretches to the horizon."

"Very well. Feel yourself there. Take your time. When you feel ready, tell me what's happening. Do you see anything on this beach?" Marguerite asked as she lightly tapped on my knee, anchoring me in the safety of the room.

"On the horizon, I see black clouds. A storm is brewing. It's coming toward me!" I called out as I let myself drift deeper and deeper.

"You are always safe, Guy. Tell me what you see now."

"The beach is completely dark, and I hear screams all around. I want to scream too. I feel nauseous, my jaw is clenched, and my teeth are as tight as a vise. One hand is on my cheek, another on my throat. More screams. I'm choking!"

Marguerite's calm voice interceded, "Just breathe, Guy. Everything's going to be OK. I'm right here next to you." She continued rhythmically tapping on my knee to make me aware of her presence. "What's happening now?"

"There's a weight . . . it's crushing me! I can't breathe!" My heart pounded like it was going to burst out of my chest. "I want to run, to fight, but a pain on my neck is paralyzing me. There are fingers all around my neck! Someone is strangling me!" I broke into a sweat and then I saw it. "No, it's not a hand! It's a knife! Someone's holding a knife to my throat and is about to slice it!"

"Just breathe, Guy." Marguerite's voice was as solid as a rock. "Tell me about the knife. Take your time. You're safe."

"I see the knife. I hear other kids. I'm at Boy Scout camp. The knife is long, pointy, and shiny silver. I hear a man's voice. He threatens me, saying: 'Shut the fuck up, or I'll kill you!' I grab the knife and feel rage surging throughout my body. Through clenched teeth, I shout, 'Not this time! Not this time, you fucker! Never again!'

"The knife in my hand is losing its shine. It's turning into rust! It's disintegrating into dust and spilling through my fingers." I held my hand in the air and looked at it. As the rusty dust vaporized, so did my rage. It was all over.

I gasped for air as I sobbed uncontrollably, liberating the millions of tears I'd suppressed over the years.

Marguerite leaned over and offered me a box of tissues. "Congratulations on the work you've done today, Guy."

"I've been so terrified all these years. I always felt like I was about to die. When I was a Boy Scout, the troop leaders were the authority. If I disobeyed or dared to speak up, I was afraid they were going to cut my throat." I stopped and looked away as I cried some more. "I was going to die, so I let my brothers do whatever they wanted to me. But I was so scared. Every day I expected my throat to be slit open. I felt like any rule I disobeyed was punishable by death! I was so afraid of doing anything wrong that I did everything in my power to be a Silent Good Boy!"

"Yes, Guy, I believe you've nailed it. Bravo!" Marguerite praised. "It was this so-called Silent Good Boy, not you, who panicked after failing your music class. You were a defenseless little boy and you had a knife to your throat. You created this other persona, the Silent Good Boy, while you hid away." She paused for a moment and let this sink in. "How do you feel now that you fought back like a true warrior, grabbing the knife and pulverizing it?"

I smiled when she unwittingly referred to my sculpture *The Warrior*. I realized then that I'd always had this power to defend myself within me, I just didn't know it. "I feel a warm glow coming from here," I admitted as I pointed to my chest. "I no longer need to be scared."

As I got up off the sofa, it was like a weight had been lifted off me. I felt taller, lighter, and stood up straight. I took a chocolate from the bowl on Marguerite's desk and pocketed it for the bus ride home. I wanted to hug her goodbye, but instead, I simply paused and smiled as I shook her hand.

On the bus, I reflected on all that I'd learned: the knife, my throat, and regaining my power. *I don't need to be the Silent Good Boy anymore. So what if I failed that class. Who cares? I'm going to make my own music!* Right then and there, I decided to create Les Chants Marins de Montreal.

Back in Dad's hospital room, I started to hum the traditional sea shanty "Blow the Man Down." I saw us both on a tall ship, with the sun in our eyes and the wind in our hair as the sails billowed in the breeze. Large waves sprayed us with cold, salty water and pushed us toward the horizon.

I wondered if my dad, with all of his achievements, had ever reached his port. He was so honored when he was presented with the Lifetime Achievement Award from the Quebec Society of Neurologists for his long list of achievements: outstanding clinician, research on epilepsy, head of his department, board member, and so on. And when he showed me his name in the book *History of Neurology in Quebec*, it was like a small child saying proudly to his parents, "Look what I've done!"

"Dad, when you lost your mom, were you forced to become a Good Boy like I did? You always told me that life is about hard work, and you've worked so hard all your life. You told me that you hated the divorce and being away from your children." A deep current of sadness welled up inside me. "I needed you, Dad!"

I burst into tears as words I never knew revealed themselves to me and to my dad. I leaned over his bed and brought his hand to my cheek and up against my tears. "I need you, Dad," I sobbed. I felt his grace as we shared a moment together in silence.

"I realize you've always been there for me. I'll take good care of my wife and your little princess. I'll guide her as best I can. I promise. You're a healer and you've lived a full life. Your loving heart and your brilliant mind have touched thousands. You don't need to be a Good Boy anymore. You can rest now."

I stood up slowly, carefully bent over the bed, and kissed him on the forehead. "Goodbye, Dad. Rest well." Before I left the room, I turned one last time and said, "I love you, Dad."

A few hours later, a chorus of angels sang the sea shanty "Leave Her, Johnny" as my father peacefully passed away and reached his final port.

Chapter 37

TEARS OF LAUGHTER

The little princess sobbed quietly, nestled between her mother and me in a church pew. I put my arm around her and whispered, "He loved you."

"Yes, Daddy. I loved him too."

In the portrait atop the closed casket, his sky-blue eyes glimmered and I felt his presence. In my mind, I heard him say, *"I love you, son, and I will always be with you. Now go follow your heart."* I knew exactly what he meant. It was my turn to break the cardinal rule of all 'good boys': Thou shall work all the time.

For forty years, I'd never stopped working: lawn boy, newspaper delivery boy, pool and skating rink attendant, night watchman, janitor, waiter, salesclerk, window display designer, the list went on. Even while studying as an artist, I worked feverishly in my studio on weeknights and weekends. So I felt the time was right: I took a leap of faith and quit my job in Spring of 2013.

Twenty-three years prior, at my first *Family Show*, I had discovered my passion for public speaking. Since then, I'd written new speeches merging art, music, and humor like *A Thousand Years of Art History on One hand*, also *From Bach to Rap: A Thousand Years of Music* and *The Magnificent Adventure of Sea Shanties.* My audiences loved how I danced and even sang while they learned, and many of them demanded return engagements. It pushed me beyond my comfort zone, and now I decided to take a chance and follow my gut. *I want to help change the world as a public speaker!*

But after only a couple weeks, anxiety and doubt crept in, and I often woke up in the middle of the night in a panic. *Did I make the right decision? What if I fail?* The Good Boy even threw in his two cents. *What have you done? I told you to stick to the rules? You need to shut up and do as you're told!* I'd go the kitchen and wolf down a couple of *chocolate covered marshmallow whippets* just like Dad used to do.

But like my *Warrior,* I forged forward. Realizing that I needed some additional skills, I scoured the Internet, bookstores, and libraries for all I could find. My thirst was unquenchable. When I decided to reach out for assistance like I had in Paris, I logged onto my laptop and, within minutes, found a free entrepreneurship program at "YES Montreal." "Never do anything alone" became my motto.

After being assigned an adviser, I covered her desk with piles of documents. "This is all me: exhibits, catalogs, concerts, compositions, classes I've taught, talks I've given. What can I do with it?"

The counselor was flabbergasted at all I'd accomplished, but she was also perplexed. "This is truly impressive, Mr. Giard, but with all of this, why are you here?"

"Well, I don't really know what to do," I admitted, averting my eyes. "All of this must be worth something. My entire life I've worked hard and put in long hours, but . . . ," I hesitated. I couldn't tell her about the Good Boy. "But I've always placed the cart before the bull, work before passion. Yes, I've achieved amazing things, but I just don't know where to go from here. Do you know what I mean?"

She smiled with compassion. "I get it Mr. Giard. Don't worry, you're not the only one. Now let's organize this and start with a business plan. What are your goals?"

My goals? Nobody had ever cared or showed any interest in my own personal goals. Tears of relief flooded my eyes as I realized, *I'm finally acknowledged.*

I did the exercises she suggested, but the Good Boy wasn't having any of it. I was plagued with insomnia at night and headaches and shortness of breath during the day. I tried reading, writing, and going for nature walks, but I couldn't concentrate and had no energy. Burned out and white as a sheet, the Good Boy pushed me into a depression. My wife insisted that I see a doctor, which I did and was prescribed some antianxiety drugs. But I didn't want to take them.

And then I remembered something that had always intrigued me that I was too scared to try: people getting together to laugh. I figured I had nothing to lose, so I decided to break another rule from the Good Boy's rule book: Never try anything new because you might fail.

I found a laughter yoga workshop being offered at an old factory that had been converted into multiple studios. As I walked up the old, wooden stairs, flamenco music blasted in the hallway as young women in colorful leotards and long hippy hair sipped kombucha. When I arrived at the top of the stairs, a young receptionist with neon green hair directed me inside the dance studio. Mirrors covered one side opposite a wall of windows overlooking the city.

After taking off my shoes, I joined a mix of young and old gigglers, no dress code seemed in order. "Hi, I'm Jonathan," a tall, skinny, twig of a guy with overflowing unkempt hair announced. "Don't be shy. We're here to have fun. If it's your first time, don't worry, you can't go wrong." Then he erupted with a big belly laugh.

He had us arrange ourselves in a large circle, then we imitated animals, threw invisible balls, swam on the floor, mimed, and walked imaginary tightropes. In between, we took breathing breaks and clapped our hands to the rhythms of "HO-HO-HA-HA-HA, pretty good pretty good, YEAH!!!!!" throwing our arms up in the air.

After an hour of this, I was sweating, my sides were splitting, and I had made new friends. I felt a sense of exhilaration like I hadn't experienced for the longest time—if ever. *This is exactly where I belong!* On my way home, I walked with a spring in my step, sounds were crisper, and colors were more vibrant. Right then and there, I decided to become a Laughter Yoga leader. That night, I snored the house down as I slept so deeply that my wife and daughter couldn't wake me.

In the following weeks, a chain of events so amazing unfolded that it felt like destiny. I completed my certification as a Laughter Yoga leader with Liliana De Leo, joined the first Canadian Laughter Yoga Conference in Toronto, met the founder of Laughter Yoga, Dr. Madan Kataria and his beautiful wife Madhuri, and entered Laughologist Albert Nerenberg's first annual Canadian Laughter Championships. I competed onstage wearing my Les Chants Marins de Montreal T-shirt and a captain cap as the crowd enthusiastically cheered, "Captain Guy! Captain Guy!"

Never in my life had I been surrounded by such positive people. I felt like I'd finally connected with and belonged to a community. I had pulled myself out from the undertow of the Good Boy and dropped myself into a sea of laughter.

I tingled all over as I felt myself getting closer to my life's purpose. Wanting to bring this powerful energy into my public speaking engagements, I enrolled in a six-day clown workshop. Most of the students there were in their early twenties and were part of a two-year program. Our teacher, Francine Côté, was petite, but she had the presence of a towering giant. As part of our training, she suggested our costumes. She looked me up and down and decided, "You'll dress in plaid as a golfer from the 1930s!" I was as giddy as a kid in a candy store to rent my first costume.

Francine embraced the old-school European style of clowning. She demanded excellence and believed in tough love. "Don't insult our intelligence! Do you think we're stupid?" she'd growl if we tried too hard to be funny. "Don't act," she'd advise. "Show us who you really are and let your inner clown emerge." Like Charlie Chaplin, it was about vulnerability, not putting on a show.

But I struggled with that. Many times, I swallowed my tears as I constantly failed at just being me. Until recently, my whole life had been devoted to being invisible, the Silent Good Boy. *How can I just reveal myself? Who am I?* Still, I kept trying.

In the final hours of the last day of the workshop, I thought, *If I'm going to fail, I'm going to do it with flying colors and be the best failure of all time!* I straightened my costume, fixed my tartan bow tie, and put on my red nose. I came out onto the stage riddled with shyness, fear, and self-doubt, but instead of fighting these feelings, I freely improvised them. I fumbled over my own two feet, tried to run away, and pretended to be invisible. I was just being who I'd always tried to hide my whole life, but Francine and the students giggled—outright laughed—and applauded. Overwhelmed because I finally got it, just being myself, I let the tears of joy flow out of me.

Transformed by laughter, I wrote a new talk titled "The Health Benefits of Laughter" and presented it at cultural centers, libraries, and to schoolteachers at their annual convention. That inspired me to write a book on healing through laughter. I was so excited that I emailed the founders of several different schools of thought: Dr Madan Kataria in India, Corinne Cosseron in France, Steve Wilson and Sébastien Gendry in the US and Linda Leclerc in Canada for interviews. They all graciously agreed to share their stories for my book.

For the clowning chapter I thought of one of my heroes, Dr. Patch Adams. I knew of him from the biopic about his life, which starred Robin Williams. I cried during the movie when he became a clown to entertain kids in a pediatric cancer ward. He was changing the world with humor.

I bought his book on the Gesundheit Institute, and through the magic of the Internet, I watched many of his interviews, which he always closed with a warm and heartfelt invitation: "Write to me, and I will answer. I've never missed a letter in the last forty years."

I hesitated many times, doubting myself. *How can I write to him? I'm nobody.* But I had to do it, so wrote him about Laughter Yoga, my clowning workshop, my talks, and my book. I asked him for an interview, and thought, *Whatever happens happens!*

In the Fall of 2013, I got a call from Dr Madan Kataria at the Montreal Alzheimer's Association. "We're having a get-together on November 4 to thank our volunteers and participants. Would you be interested in holding a Laughter Yoga workshop?"

"I'd be delighted!" I said. "Thank you for thinking of me."

On the day of the workshop—my 54th birthday—I met the group, which included many senior citizens and their family members. After showing them HO-HO-HA-HA-HA, I gently started with some light movements and laughter, which quickly escalated into an explosion of belly laughs and tears from laughing so hard.

In the space of a few months, laughter had totally transformed my life from depression to a new life's purpose: to be a healer like my dad.

Chapter 38

I WANT TO GO!

Every day I wrote for my book on healing through humor—on my balcony, in public parks, and, as winter arrived, in coffee shops. As if leaving for work, I'd fill my backpack with my journal, laptop, lunch, and headphones.

On the morning of December 7, 2013, I picked up my mail on my way out and found a single postcard. I pocketed it, put on my stocking cap and gloves, and ventured out into the falling snow. Sitting next to my favorite window, I placed my tools on the table and set up my office, as I jokingly called it. Then I pulled out the postcard. One side showed a child's colorful drawing of a sprawling city with the caption: Maria's Children of Russia. The other side contained a bunch of illegible scribbles, but I was able to make out a name in the right-hand corner: Patch Adams. I was so surprised that my knee hit the table, almost spilling my coffee. *It's really him, the Gandhi of laughter! He actually wrote to me!*

Dear Guy,

I've just returned from my 29th annual Russian clown trip with 40 people from 11 countries ages 16–70 (we don't require any experience). I was tickled by your material and dreams. I'm on the road 300 days/year for 29 years trying to build and spark a love revolution. I've clowned every day for 50 years. The best way to get me would be for you to come on our next trip.

In peace #Patch

Already in a sweat from the shock that he'd written to me, I choked from reading his words. The other patrons turned to look at me with worried looks on their faces.

Me? Join him on one of his humanitarian clown missions? Who am I to do this? How dare I? What about my family? How is this going to affect us? Doom reigned over me. *It's impossible, unthinkable, insane.* And yet, I felt elated that the universe had showed me a path to follow.

His next trip was to Guatemala in March 2014, which seemed like a dream come true. But the Good Boy inside me was full of apprehension, doubt, anguish, and fear. *How dare you even consider doing such a thing, you irresponsible lowlife. First you quit your job and now this!*

Torn between my negative thoughts and my dream, I shared the idea with friends. They just laughed and said, "Are you serious? It's perfect for you. Just go!" But I wasn't convinced, so I discussed it with Tania. Ten days apart didn't seem like much, but for my wife, after fifteen years of marriage, I might as well have been going to the moon.

"You don't even speak Spanish!" she argued. "How will you manage?"

For weeks, I weighed the pros and cons, like a dog chasing its tail. Exhausted, I finally turned to Marguerite for help

"Why am I so anxious?" I asked her. "I feel it's important for me to go, like it's my calling. But I'm scared. Why am I so hesitant when it all seems so obvious?"

After half an hour weighing the pros and cons, Marguerite

commented, "These are all fine and reasonable, but tell me, Guy, right now, at this exact moment, what do *you* want?"

This was the first time in my life that anyone had ever asked me—in all seriousness—what I want. For most of my life, I'd felt like I didn't even have the right to exist. Now I was being encouraged to put myself first without trying to explain or justify it.

"What do *I* want? Am I even entitled to want something?"

Marguerite nodded her head and patiently waited. Seconds went by, then minutes. The pan flute music went on piping and the trickling waters went on splashing. My inner Good Boy desperately wanted to escape, but I held my ground. *Should I go or not? For once in my life, I have to think about myself. What do* I *really want?* Anxiety and darkness closed in until my light suddenly burst through. "I want to go!" I shouted.

As I sat in Marguerite's office and shed tears of relief, every cell of my body was charged with electricity as if I'd leaped off my childhood swing and catapulted into space. *I'm going to join Dr. Patch Adams as a humanitarian clown in Guatemala, and I'm going to dedicate my mission in memory of my dad. It's because of him that I can do this. I love you, Dad.*

I paid the participation fee and bought my plane ticket. Tania was pretty upset at first, but she and our daughter soon became my biggest supporters. And I needed their moral support when I launched a fundraiser, which made me completely uncomfortable. My whole aim in life up to that point had been to be invisible: never be seen or heard. I always felt unworthy and would never have dreamed of asking anyone for anything. But as soon as I let go of my fears, classmates I hadn't heard from in years joined in to support my dream. Love was just pouring in!

Other donations came from members of AATH, the Association for Applied and Therapeutic Humor. I became a member, enrolled in their Humor Academy, and planned to attend the next annual conference, which was being held in Indiana a couple weeks after I was scheduled to return from Guatemala. I then shared my fears with two Montreal-based clowns, Guillaume and Steve, who'd already volunteered with Dr. Adams. "Don't worry. It's going to change your life!" They answered as Steve lent me a shaggy fluorescent green parrot hand puppet.

But still, the Good Boy didn't give up. Finally, I told him, *Look, I'm going there for the children, not for myself. Maybe I'm not worth it like you want me to believe; maybe I'm no one. Fine, then I'll be a citizen for everyone, and my clown name will be Citizen Clown!* As if to fulfill my new resolution, I miraculously found a red checkered jacket in my size at a second-hand store for my costume. It all seemed to be happening so quickly, but it also felt magical, like it was fate.

On the morning of February 27, 2014, my wife and daughter braved a snowstorm to take me to the airport. For Tania, the separation was too painful, so she decided to say goodbye near the entrance. I understood as the three of us hugged on one of the coldest days of the year. "Take care of yourself, honey bear," Tania said. "We can't wait 'til you get back."

Aïyana added, "I love you, Daddy! Come back soon—sooner than soon!"

After one last kiss and hug, we blew each other kisses as they went back into the snowdrifts.

"Bye-bye! I love you! I love you!" I called out, waving until they fully disappeared. I turned toward the large glass doors of the terminal and paraphrased Neil Armstrong's most famous words: *That's one small step for Guy, one giant leap for Citizen Clown.*

Chapter 39

CAFÉ CON LECHE
CALIENTE, POR FAVOR

Unbelievable . . . it's happening. I have enough butterflies in my belly to fly me there directly! I dared to don my red checkered jacket and make a first clown appearance at the airport. Dr. Adams suggested that we wear our full attire, but that was farther than I could go at this point. I did get a few looks, but most travelers seemed preoccupied by their flights. I understood when I saw that my own flight had been delayed.

My butterflies became sticky, slimy slugs as one hour morphed into two. I felt my heart racing as the blood left my face. *So much for keeping calm. I'm going to miss my connecting flight in Atlanta!* I practiced a HeartMath breathing exercise for five minutes to calm myself: inhale for five seconds then exhale for five seconds. Once I felt better, I turned my attention to the whining children in the passenger's lounge. I put on my red flowered hat and handed balloons to their parents. They thanked me with smiles of reprieve. *First step for Citizen Clown.* I felt a warm glow inside knowing that I could bring them some joy.

When we finally boarded, I raised many eyebrows walking down the aisle. I'm sure some people were literally thinking: *Who's this clown?* I placed my journal in the compartment on the seat ahead of me while listening to "You Can't Always Get What You Want" by the Rolling Stones on my MP3 player. I clutched my flight envelope, which contained photos of Tania and Aïyana, and support messages from my donors. They believed in me more than I do! *If only they knew how much they're helping me on my journey.* Giving one last look at snowy Montréal I repeated the following in my head like a mantra: *I can do this. I can do this*

While checking our seat belts, the stewardess smiled and asked about my colorful clothes. When I told her that I was going to care for children in orphanages and hospitals, she was so moved that she later returned with double drinks and snacks for me.

Across the aisle, Hugo, a very talkative young man, told me that he was going to Guatemala to visit relatives that he hadn't seen in fifteen years. He was very excited but was also worried about missing our connecting flight. His concern made me nervous, but the extra drinks calmed me a bit.

Unfortunately, because of the delay getting out of Montreal, I literally had only minutes to catch my connecting flight. While waiting to collect my checked luggage, I inspected the gate numbers. *I'm at Gate 4 and have to get to Gate 24, so that's not too bad.* I started to walk, then jog, then run as I hadn't even reached gate 5 yet!! Atlanta terminal was as not tiny as in Montréal, it was insanely humongous!

I suddenly doubled over in pain as I ran. *No! It's those extra drinks from the stewardess! I'm going to pee my pants!* I did the unthinkable and stopped in the bathroom with a mixture of relief and dread. When I was done, I jumped back to my race. Imagine seeing a clown running through an airport with his luggage flying in midair behind him. Finally, I saw the stewardess desperately waving her arms like a windmill. I broke into a mad sprint, and we both let out a huge sigh of relief as she closed the door behind me. *Whew! I just made it! I will not have drinks on this flight!*

Three and a half hours later and well past midnight, the plane made its descent in pitch-black darkness. As I stepped out of the cabin, I was hit by a chocking fiery wall of humidity. It was like walking into a tropical greenhouse. A second shock came when I realized that we were still on the tarmac. I felt like I was in one of those old black and white movies like *Casablanca* with Humphrey Bogart, and as I descended the stairs, I imagined him greeting me with his signature hat and overcoat, "Here's looking at you, Citizen Clown."

"Guy! You made it!" Hugo declared with a grin when we met at the luggage carousel. "There's no way our luggage made it here with our short connection. Come with me." Hugo explained our situation to the baggage handlers and offered to help me find my awaiting driver. "There he is, with a sign with my name!" *Another movie classic!* After we found him, I gave my savior Hugo my first official clown hug.

I followed the short old man in his white shirt. His face was scarred by the sun and with a few teeth missing wished me a good night, or so I thought. All I could say was *si*, meaning yes, and he soon realized the extent of my vocabulary. *A stranger in a strange land who doesn't speak Spanish. I'm at the mercy of the taxi driver who has a broken nose like De Niro.*

At two o'clock in the morning, the streets were dark and dusty. A hot wind kissed my face as we flew through the maze of Guatemala City. As I watched the few streetlights punctuate the nocturnal calm, each one seemed like a signpost along my journey: Amsterdam, re-pressed memories, *Family Shows*, Paris, divorce, marriage, daughter, my father passing away, and now, Citizen Clown. I was actually here. *Incredible, I did it, I really did it, I've made it to Guatemala!*

Stopping in front of a crumbling, old facade, the driver got out, reached through an iron fence, and rang the bell; windows also had bars. A tall, skinny man with slicked-back hair and a Clark Gable mustache emerged from the shadows with a huge grin. The two ex-changed joyous salutations as I got out of the car, groggy from the long day of travel. "Welcome to Posada Belen Museo Inn, mi amigo. I'm Nilo," the tall man said as he warmly shook my hand. "You had good flight, Mr. Guaille, yes? This is the key to your room, number eleven. You no luggage?"

I gratefully accepted the key and told him that my luggage would be arriving the following day. I soon taught him that my name was pronounced Guy as in guitar, which worked well.

My room was beautiful with pastel yellow walls. One was decorated with a traditional blanket that matched the bedspread. There was a light musty odor in the room, which gave it an air of authenticity. The room also included a huge wooden wardrobe, an old chest, a table, and a water pitcher. I undressed for a quick shower and washed away the stress of the past twenty-four hours. After I was squeaky clean and dried up but lacking a change of clothes, I placed my photos of my wife and daughter next to the bedside lamp. I kissed them goodnight, switched off the light, and tried to fall asleep but morning couldn't come fast enough.

I awoke to the sounds of chatter and the clanging of dishes. *Breakfast, mmmm yes!* I sprung out of bed and peered through the lace curtains of my small window. Nilo was sweeping the inner courtyard and talking to his colleagues. A blue-and-white striped polo seemed to be their informal uniform. I cleaned myself up and quickly shaved before stepping into the hall. There, I met Francesca, a small, round woman with a pleasant smile. She was the owner of the inn, and she welcomed me like I was family. "Hola! ¿Cómo estás? Oh, you don't speak Spanish. Welcome. Thank you for coming to Guatemala for the children!" She leaned in and gave me a warm maternal hug.

As I entered the dining room, I was met by a fellow with a square jaw and piercing blue eyes "Guy my brother, there you are!" It was Rob. Dr. Adams had put us in touch through social media prior to the trip.

Rob, who worked as a policeman in Washington, looked me straight in the eyes then gave me a bear hug as he said, "I'm so happy to finally meet you!" He would turn out to be my rock on this trip.

One by one, new faces trickled in: Emily, Chappo, Pamela, Carmen, Dee Dee, and Christy, among others. *I've never hugged so much in my life, and it's only been half an hour!* Many were already in their clown gear, while others were still in their pajamas. I felt a warmth like I'd never experienced before. *These are my sisters and brothers, my new family. So much love!* Finally came our leaders for the trip: the soft-spoken Peruvian Pedro and smiling Ash with her tight, red curls and radiant, apple-red cheeks. Their devotion to making sure that everyone was well taken care of and listened to was boundless. As Ash said that first day "We're here to give love to the children, patients, and staff, but we're also here for each other, so if you need anything, just ask."

They explained what a typical day would be like: breakfast, head to our first visit, come back for lunch, and then go for a second visit. After dinner, we would give feedback and share our experiences. "We are the only ones in this hotel; this is your home for the week!" There were about sixteen of us from all over the world, including Australia, Germany, Iran, Italy, and Mexico. We ranged in age from twenty-one to seventy-three, with a few couples and even a one-year-old boy. Most of the volunteers shared rooms, but I ended up having my own space. English was the universal language, and so during our stay, a local clown group called Fabrica de Sonrisas (The Smile Factory) helped interpret for us.

"Patch is landing late this evening, so let's relax and get to know each other." Ash encouraged.

We sat in a circle and introduced ourselves. A handful were experienced clowns, for some, it was their second or third trip, but the other half of the group was like me: they weren't clowns and had never done anything like this before. "Great, this is your first time, your life is going to change, I know, and don't worry I'm always here for you brother" Rob added sitting next to me.

After breakfast, I got another coffee and sat in the courtyard with my journal, enjoying the shade of a leafy tree while the birds sang. Flowers, cacti, and even a small turtle offered a peaceful oasis within the confines of the hotel. A few feet away, Rob and Carmen giggled as they tried to get in and out of the hammock: a real loving family! I had left the icy, winter cold of Montreal for a heat wave of love, friendship, and brotherhood. Although we were volunteers, we'd paid quite a sum of money to take part in this trip, but it was worth it to bring joy and relief to the sick.

The next morning, a hotel worker named Francesco, short and round face like a watermelon and all of smiles, taught me to say, "Café con leche caliente, por favor," which he then victoriously brought to me. The staff members were more like uncles to joke with and were thankful for our devotion to the happiness of the children.

A few minutes later, a giant stumbled in. He had a pointy mustache and long, white hair with a streak of bright blue, and he wore red glasses and a happy grin that extended beyond his face as he greeted us in his baritone voice, "Well, hi there good friends!"

"Patch!" everyone replied excitedly in unison.

Hugging Patch was like being engulfed in a mushy, warm beanbag. At six feet five inches (2 m) tall, he was as big as his heart. His devotion for everyone and his mission of building a free hospital— the "Gesundheit Institute"—was evident. His vision for humanity was nothing less than a love revolution. He was born in 1945 while I was born in 1959 and always felt like I'd come into the world too late. I felt like I should've been part of the Hippie and Flower Power era. I felt like I never quite belonged in our modern society, but in humanitarian clowning, I had found my community.

"OK guys, it's so great that you're all here," Patch began. "Now let's all get together in a circle so we can see each other."

As we excitedly assembled for our first clowning mission, Patch led the introduction. "Love is the most powerful emotion in the world, and to give it—to share it—is a gift. So let's bring joy to the ones who need it the most. I love all of you for being here today." When he looked each of us in the eyes like a father gazing at his newborn baby, I felt his love and warmth. "For many of you, this is your first experience, so how you are feeling?"

I usually stayed quiet, following my rule to be invisible and unheard. But this time, the love I was receiving gave me the courage to openly share, "I'm scared!"

"Why Guy? Why are you scared?" Patch asked with concern.

"Because I'm afraid of the unknown. In my past, the unknown has always meant danger."

"Well, I find the unknown exciting! It brings me joy! It brings me energy!" Patch responded.

How can the unknown mean such different things to different people? I wondered.

The other clowns smiled in support. "You'll be fine," Rob assured. "It's going to be awesome!"

Just then, the bus honked outside, and everyone jumped up and clapped with glee. But I felt queasy and my head started spinning. *I've made it this far. Do I go or stay behind?* What was I to do?

Chapter 40

THE LOVE BUS

"OK clowns, last chance for the restroom," Ash announced. "Check your noses, stickers, and accessories." This was it! Pedro picked up his accordion, and everyone chanted, "Clowns on the bus! Clowns on the bus! Clowns on the bus!" They danced, laughed, and hollered, and we weren't even out the door yet. My new family members had lent me some colorful clothes and accessories to wear because my luggage still hadn't arrived. I was jittery with joy but also afraid as I let myself get swept up by the fervor of the group.

Outside the metal gate, a small, beige bus was waiting for us in the blazing sun. "¡Hola payasos!" Juan our driver with frizzy short black hair greeted us with a huge smile. The windows had brown curtains to shield us from the sun, but the green vinyl benches reminded me of the shuttle bus in my university days. My chest felt like it was in a vise as I remembered the panic attacks of my school years. *This is different,* I reminded myself. *We're all friends here.* I sat beside Emily, a young yoga teacher with long, silky, blonde hair and a flowing gypsy dress. We'd had a great talk at dinner the night before, so I felt comfortable around her. Plus, she reminded me of my friends from art school. *I'm going to be fine.*

Ash strummed on her ukulele and sang the classic song "You Are My Sunshine." Everyone joined in while others stuck their brightly colored faces out the windows and blew bubbles. There was so much joy inside the bus that it spilled out into the city and passersby, both young and old, smiled and waved. But suddenly the colorful clown costumes transformed into green Boy Scout uniforms. Pressure built up around my eyes and it became hard to breathe as a traumatic memory surfaced. *I took a bus like this when I went to summer camp and . . . the horrors. There was no escape. I wanted to die.*

My eyes filled with tears. *How can I be on a bus filled with love and happiness when it was such a nightmare at that camp?* I turned to Emily and said, "May I please hold your hand?"

In her eyes, I saw understanding. As our fingers entwined, my body convulsed with deep silent sobs; Emily leaned over and rocked me in her arms. More tears flowed as I trembled in the aftershock. "Tell me Guy, what's wrong?"

I shared the horrors of my youth with her as I took in her gentle kindness. *It's over. I'm safe now.*

After an hour on the bus, we arrived at our first destination: Anini, a shelter for kids with physical and mental disabilities who had been abandoned or lived in extreme poverty. Emily and the others exited the bus, but I was paralyzed with fear. I observed the exit and thought of the two little steps I needed to descend. *What will I find after getting off the bus? Will I be funny? Loving? I'm nobody. Who am I to do this?* Time stopped as I stared at the gray floor in silence, feeling hopeless.

Suddenly, I could just barely hear the echo of a child's laughter. Noticing the red rubber nose in my hands, I took a deep breath, slid it on my face, and took those two final steps off the bus. Outside, the clowns were joyfully running around. Across from me, a young boy in a wheelchair flailed his arms about with his mouth agape. Unable to speak, he moaned as I approached, and his arms slowed as he tried to look at me. I knelt by his side, and when our eyes met, my fears, doubts, and pain all vanished. *I'm here for you!*

As we played, he clapped his hands and I inflated balloons. His face lit up with cries of happiness. This was the happiest moment of my life and probably his too. At that precise moment, Citizen Clown was born.

I pushed the boy's wheelchair to the main courtyard so we could join the others. Patch was running around chicken hat on his head, holding a fish, and with fake snot dangling from his nose. My brother Rob was close by and always ready to lend a hand. Clowns from Fabrica de Sonrisas in their white doctor's coat tattered with of multitude colorful badges showed us some games. They were like the cousins I never knew, and their love seemed boundless. At the end of the visit, we formed a large circle, held hands, and sang songs of thanks for everyone's presence. Before we knew it, it was time to go, we took pictures and hugged the children.

Back on the bus, we shared our experiences. Some cried because they had also been transformed. Everyone had a different story, but love was the common theme. We were one on a mission to bring love to the abandoned and suffering.

At dinnertime, there was even more laughter, tears, and sharing. *It's like my support group, but instead of sad stories, we're sharing happy ones!* I remained quiet, though, because I hadn't yet learned to share my happiness.

After dinner, we hugged, some remained to chat, but I was too shy and returned to the solitude of my room, where I shared in my journal:

March 2, 2014

Emily is a friend who helped me get in touch with my hurt. Ash gives compassion, and Rob gives love and support. The hurt and rejection I feel is mine and has nothing to do with the friends who help me get in touch with my feelings.

I have to own my feelings. My feelings are who I am. This is who I am. From there, I will discover my dream and my mission. I am not shy, I was with the wrong crowd, environment, and family. I never was in an environment where I could show myself and feel safe, where I could own my feelings.

> *What I feel is inside me.*
> *I am my wounds, my ghosts and my past.*
> *I should not try to banish them,*
> *Or bury them or hide them.*
>
> *The pain will pass.*
> *It hurts now, but that too shall pass.*
> *Time heals, time needs time*
> *I will forgive and forget.*

My family is here; it is possible for me to love and to trust. My suffering is the basis for my compassion. I am not alone to suffer, and this is why I am a clown: I laugh at the absurdity of holding back suffering instead of living equally between love and suffering.

What I feel now is fatigue. I'm exhausted. Is it mainly because of letting my bruises, my wounds, rise to the surface? Or is it the first clowning experience? Probably both! Today I opened up, I let go, but I did not replace and create a new space, and that is OK. Now I'm going to play with my family and give my gifts and talent.

I closed my journal, and kissed my wife and daughter good night. Just as I turned off the light, a little, green lizard slithered across the wall. It emerged from a dark crack and revealed itself in the light. I looked at it with admiration. *Like my suppressed memories, you came from a dark place into the light. You are as much a part of me as I am part of this new family. Bless you. Sweet dreams. May tomorrow bring more light.*

Chapter 41

YORBELI

I soon learned that the clown costumes, humor, and games were only tools to initiate human contact. Sick children and adults were powerless to their diseases and doctors, but us clowns listened to their needs and let them know that they were not alone and were loved unconditionally.

I understood this as we visited a cardiac surgery ward, first bringing joy to a young girl who had recently underwent an operation. Her torments were over, and her life was on the upswing. We sang, danced, and drew pictures. The little girl read poetry to us, and I gave her mom a red nose. Thirty minutes later as I walked into the waiting room, I saw a six-year-old girl sitting alone on the floor. Balloons, clown noses, stickers—nothing could make her smile. She had just learned of her upcoming hospitalization, so her needs were entirely different. She didn't want to play or laugh; she needed to be held and rocked, which I did. As a humanitarian clown, I offered my presence, held hands, and brought reassurance with gentle caring.

At other times, we were confronted with our own fear of diseases, like when we visited Psiquiatrico Zona 13, a children's psychiatric and neurology center. It was home to kids with Down syndrome and other heavy pathologies. Our mission was to be there for their needs, which can change from one second to the next. And at the San Jose Hospice, we met wonderful children who'd been rejected from society for having HIV/AIDS. It was gut-wrenching to know that they'd been abandoned in their hour of need. We were there to play and make them come alive as innocent kids full of life and joy.

Each new experience was like a petal on my blossoming flower of love. But at night, my roots of abandonment, abuse, and rejection were unearthed. Razor-sharp memories shredded my soul, drowning me in pools of blood as my stained sheets drew maps of despair. I never slept more than three hours, but I was alone in my room, so nobody knew of my suffering. *Love exists, dammit! It does! It's here! I'm living it now. I didn't know it existed. I thought that with my marriage and daughter I had achieved it, but it's nothing, nothing compared to this. I'm starving in an ocean of love!*

On our third day, my suitcase finally arrived, and I was reunited with my toys, stickers, and, most importantly, my fluorescent green parrot puppet. Jackô, as I named her, became my partner in overcoming the language barrier. A squeaker was hidden in her orange beak, and she constantly babbled to the delight of the kids.

That day, after a long bus ride up winding mountain roads flanked by wild palm trees, we arrived at a massive redbrick building. The Valle de Los Angeles school and orphanage was home to more than two hundred children. With short, graying brown hair, Father Michael wearing a brown cassock greeted us with hugs and smiles. "The kids have been waiting for you all year. They're so excited and have prepared a special ceremony for you. Come." As he led us to the refectory, we could hear shouts of joy even before we opened the door. "PAYASOS! PAYASOS! PAYASOS!"

As soon as they saw us the children sang, jumped up and down, and proudly waved huge banners they had made, which read: "Welcome!"

"We're so happy you've come to visit us!" "We love you!" A chill ran through my body and tears welled up in my eyes at the outpouring of love. Jackô squawked with joy as the children danced and recited poetry. When some of the children came over to pet her, I noticed a shy, six-year-old girl in her white-and-navy-blue uniform had her sparkling eyes fixed on me. Small and delicate with glistening black hair, she was mesmerized by Jackô.

"Cuál es tu nombre?" (What's your name?). Her name was Yorbeli, and we played Patty Cake Patty Cake and they all tried to catch me as I started running. Exhausted, in sweat, I sat down next to little Yorbeli. Jackô in her hand, she helped me distribute stickers and explained (in Spanish) the different games I showed. *What an amazing little helper!* I thought.

I took my journal from my backpack, sketched a map of the Americas, and pointed. "This is where we are, and this is my home—Canada." They fervently wanted to write loving messages of their own: "Take my heart. It's yours forever. Love, Erika." "I love you, Yuliza." "You and me together forever. I love you so much!!! You are beautiful. Jolissa." "Lo quiero mucho, feliz viaje que dios lo acompañe, Yorbeli." They had so much love in their little hearts.

DING! DING! DING! When the dining hall bell chimed, it startled us. All the kids ran to the cafeteria, except little Yorbeli. As I stood up, she grabbed ahold of me, looked up with tears in her eyes, and said, "¡No te vayas! ¡No te vayas!" I didn't need to know Spanish to that she didn't want me to leave her. She burst out crying, so I picked her up and walked around while gently rocking her and whispering soothing words into her ear. I knew she couldn't understand me, but I hoped she would sense my care.

Luckily a staff member came and gave me a hand. "Please tell her that we're only breaking for lunch and that I'll see her afterward." Slowly Yorbeli loosened her grip, so I gently bent down to let her join her friends. Sniffling, she gave me one last big hug and walked away, turning every few steps to wave and say, "Bye-bye."

As Jackô and I waved back with a smile and loud squeaking, my heart filled with love for that little angel. Then all of a sudden, I felt a lump in my throat and like a thousand-ton weight had fallen on my chest. Teary-eyed I could hardly breathe. *This wonderful little girl is an orphan. At the end of the day, I can go back home to my family. But for her, this is it. She's just going to stay here.*

Feeling hopeless, I spiraled into a dark void and faded into oblivion. There was nothing left of me but one final cry: *I CAN'T ABANDON HER!* A dazzling light suddenly shone from my heart as I thought, *Yorbeli, I may not be able to change your world, but today, I will give you all of who I am to bring you joy, care, and love!* I was lifted from my void and at that precise moment, I became a "love clown."

I looked up to the blue sky and embraced the sun, feeling that my inner light was in harmony with the outer universe. After lunch, Yorbeli came running over as soon as she saw me. Jackô cheered as she hugged both of us, almost falling to the ground. The rest of the day, we ran, jumped rope, and sang "You Are My Sunshine." *She certainly is,* I thought, feeling a warm glow in our hearts.

At the end of the day, the children accompanied us back to the bus, radiant with joy, laughter, and smiles. After one final hug, all the children held hands and serenaded us with a farewell song. As we drove off, I stuck my head through the open window, waved, and shouted, "Farewell kids! I'll never forget you! You'll always be in my heart!"

On the drive back, half the clowns snored in deep sleep, but I watched the palm trees stream by. I bathed in a warm serenity until we crossed the bridge into Guatemala City and the slums on the slopes jolted me back to reality. I imagined my life there with no running water or electricity, the crime, the poverty, the violence, the desperate fight for survival. *Yorbeli is safe at the orphanage. Hopefully with a good education, she'll create a new life for herself.* I closed my eyes and prayed for her.

After our evening meal, I was restless as I tried to reconcile the void I'd felt with the love that had suddenly emerged from it. "I've always lived with this hole inside me, so why did love suddenly come pouring out? Was it always there?"

Rob listened and offered some words of wisdom. "Guy, it sounds like you really opened up your vulnerability and compassion. What you gave to that young girl, you can give to yourself. Have some compassion for yourself."

"I've never allowed myself to feel vulnerable or feel compassion for myself, so this is all new to me. Thank you for saying that, brother." We hugged then went our separate ways for the night.

Back in my room, Rob's words echoed in my mind. *I always demanded the best from myself then hated myself for not achieving it. Compassion for what? For having been vulnerable as a baby? For having being raped?*

I realized for the first time in my life that a crime had been committed against me: I'd been raped! I'd never admitted it to myself or anyone else. I did admit to having been sexually abused, the politically correct expression. But I'd never uttered the word *rape* with its raw power out loud with the pronoun *I* in front of it. It was the dagger of light in *Mack the Night*, the sharp blade of Jack, my girlfriend Sophie's angry father, and worst of all, it was a knife held at my throat when I was a Boy Scout. This time it felt real and covered with my blood.

I HAVE BEEN RAPED! With my heart opened, I was vulnerable and a knife was plunged into it. I screamed in agony but buried my face in my pillow so as not to be heard. *There was a crime committed against me, and I didn't even know it!* The album cover for Supertramp's *Crime of the Century* came to mind. *The title itself denounced it: CRIME and those two hands behind bars, they were mine all along. I'd been imprisoned in my void, my heart closed off because of the fucking crime committed against me.* I'd never told anyone and had a lifelong fear of the authorities, but Rob was a policeman, an authority figure. *He's a cop, but he's a clown. He's an authority figure, and yet he's a clown—a love clown like me!*

Torn apart by indecision, I pummeled the mattress with my fist and bit the sheets as I plunged headfirst. *I've never been in a safer environment to denounce this crime. What should I do?*

The next evening after dinner, I worked up the courage to ask to take the floor. Everyone looked at me attentively in respectful silence. A void formed beside my chair as if calling me as I heard my inner voice say, *Come down here, Guy. It's safer. No one's going to hurt you.* But I refused. *NO, I love these folks and want to stay with them, go away!* It closed. With my voice trembling and gasping for air, I opened my heart, "I . . . I . . . I was raped at three years old by my cousin, and when I was eight years old, I went away to Boy Scout camp. I'm not entirely sure what happened, but I recall having a knife held to my throat by some of the counselors."

Everyone was shocked and wept along with me as I told my story. This time, I wasn't afraid that they would laugh, run away, or abandon me; I simply shared who I was, and they thanked me with hugs.

"We love you, Guy!" many of my fellow clowns called out.

"I love you," Patch added. "We're a family, and you're always welcome in our home."

First, I had found a family of caring friends in Amsterdam, then a spiritual family in Regina, and now a family of love. The home I'd always longed for was here in Guatemala.

Chapter 42

BUT WHERE'S BRIAN?

As our voluntary clown mission came to an end, we laughed, danced, cried, and several of us climbed into Patch's giant white underwear while we brought relief to hundreds of kids, parents, and caretakers. *Love does exist and it is limitless! I've experienced more love in a week than I have in all my fifty-four years.*

We gathered around the table for our last dinner together as a group, but I was still unsure how to join in, so I remained quiet. Across the table, Jerry, Rob, and Chappo were competing to see who could come up with the best pun: "What do you call a boomerang that doesn't come back? . . . A stick!" We all groaned and exploded into laughter.

Then a scrumptious surprise was delivered as chocolate cake was served along with a farewell song from our new adoptive Mom Francesca, Nilo, Francesco, Juan, Maria and Marcelino of the Posada Belen Museo Inn. Then some members of Fabrica de Sonrisas joined us. It was like having the entire extended family that I never really knew all under the same roof. For the first time in my life, I felt like I had a complete family, and it made me tingle all over.

Sitting in a circle after dinner, we enjoyed our last group share session. I took the opportunity to confess my regret, saying, "I'm sorry if I didn't speak to many of you. You see I am scared and awkward with relationships."

My new friends nodded and smiled, accepting me for me. This was so incredibly different from what I'd experienced as a child. I melted in a cocoon of warmth as we finished the evening with a group hug. Sadly, it was time to say our goodbyes because some of the clowns were leaving in the middle of the night.

The next evening, Rob and I shared a cab to the airport. We talked about what was waiting for us back home, exchanged our best memories from our time in Guatemala, hugged, and then went our separate ways. I was overwhelmed with sadness knowing that this wonderful journey was coming to an end. But then, at the last moment before I boarded my plane, I heard someone calling my name. I turned around and there was Carmen, the sunniest Mexican clown I knew. After one last hug, I boarded and the door closed on the happiest week of my life.

As a love clown, I was overflowing with emotion. I could hardly wait to see Tania and Aïyana, but a fourteen-hour layover in Atlanta stood in my way. I was more than ready to try out new experiences, so I decided I'd sleep in the terminal. Plus, I figured I might be able to bring some joy to weary or stressed travelers as a clown. But first I had to get through customs. By this time, it was the wee hours of the morning as I stood in line with hundreds of zombies. I was still dressed mostly as a clown, so my colorful clothes made everybody else look muddy brown and drab. I quietly waited and, in my head, I heard Ray Charles's deep and resonant voice singing "Georgia on My Mind."

The two women agents in gray polyester shirts were stone-faced and dead serious. *More authority figures,* I thought. *I'll be fine, though. Rob is a policeman, and he's my friend. I have no reason to fear authority figures.* Still, I didn't dare clown around with them. Even so, they raised their eyebrows at me in suspicion.

"What were you doing in Guatemala?" one of them asked. When

I responded, she said in a desert dry voice, "Clowning? What's that?" Neither she nor her colleague were impressed.

"You know, like Patch Adams from the movie with Robin Williams?" I responded, but the name was only vaguely familiar to them.

So I decided to own it by putting on my red nose and my flowered hat. When I did, they both started to laugh and their faces lit up. We joked so much that their supervisors, who were at a desk quite a distance away, shouted, "Hey! Quit clowning around over there!" It was contagious and spread!

As one of the agents handed me my passport, she said, "Here you go. Thanks for making me laugh. I can't wait to tell my kids that I met a clown today. She wiped away tears from laughing so hard and added, "Take care of yourself, sir. God bless you for the wonderful work you do." I thanked them both now convinced of the power of love from a clown.

I made my way to the food court. The large lounge was mostly empty but a few counters were opened. I ordered some fried rice, garlic ribs and egg rolls. *My favorite, so hungry.* As I waited for my order, the cashier called "Brian!" No one got up, so she continued, "Brian? Brian?"

I, too, started to call for Brian then two guys sitting at a table joined in. We all got a big laugh out of it. Apparently, the Brian in question had actually picked up my order. After finally getting my meal, stomach growling, I politely asked to join the other fellows.

"Hi, I'm Constantino and this is my brother Alexander." Slender, angular, well-tanned and in their early twenties, they were on their way home to Germany from a weeklong vacation at muscle beach in Miami. Overjoyed that I was a clown, they asked to have their picture taken with me. I happily obliged and put on my nose and hat. As I shared stories about the orphans and the hospitals the conversation became more relaxed and open.

When I saw other lonely or bored travelers in the food court, I called them to join us. First, there was brother and sister Tim and

Diana, both nail stylists from Vietnam, who had just missed their flight to Las Vegas. As we talked, I made sure to bring humor to the table, making up ridiculous stories about why we were here, why'd they missed their plane, and on and on. It was like a live-action Monty Python sketch—the sillier the better.

Next was a young woman sitting by herself; dressed in an elegant blazzer she was a young Argentinean architect. "I'm waiting for a friend of a friend to pick me up, but I don't know what he looks like. I've never met him!" I made up a skit that she was the most intelligent one of all of us, and how was it that "You are getting in a car with strangers while you're abandoning your friends and family here?" We had a ball as more strangers joined us. And my clowning soon transformed a dreary waiting lounge into a circle of laughs.

Tired, I took a family photo, hugged everyone and left to find a couch to spend the night. I ended up pushing some chairs together and making a nest under a house-sized black Yangchuanosaurus dinosaur skeleton. I was so cold that I piled all my clothes on top of me and tried to rest for a while.

A few hours later, I was abruptly awakened by a family squabble next to me. They were stunned into silence when a clown unexpectedly emerged from the crumpled, colorful, chrysalis. Unshaven and dazed, there wasn't much clowning left in me. I limped my way to the boarding gate as my legs were still crawling with sleepy ants. I found my gate and warmed up in the radiant rays of a glorious sunrise. Like a colorful butterfly, I could feel my wings extend back into their full shape.

I was shocked and amazed by my metamorphosis. *I've been scared my whole life, but yesterday, not only did I ask strangers to join me, I actually led the conversation. I didn't hide behind cigarettes, food, or music or leave like a ghost. I was just me. I love myself, and it feels good!* Recharged with hope and love, I boarded the plane with a huge grin on my face.

I'm blessed to have shared love and humor at the airport, and in a few hours, I'll do the same with my wife and daughter. Life is so amazing!

Chapter 43

FAMILY CRISIS

Finally! After hours of traveling, I was thrilled to reunite with my family. I waited to deplane, waited for my luggage, waited at the customs but when I saw them, I no longer waited. I ran to meet them, threw my arms around them, kissed them, and then . . . nothing. Tania spoke about current events, what I'd missed. *It's all superficial and disconnected,* I thought.

I had just lived through the most heart-wrenching experience of my life, cried oceans of tears, drowned in the abyss of my loneliness, made myself vulnerable, held hands with and gave countless hugs to strangers, and now this. The conversation felt as cold as the ice on the slippery roads.

"What the hell is wrong with you?!" I shouted.

They froze, shell-shocked by my outburst while hundreds of strangers stared. A suffocating silence descended upon us as we sat on the bus, which plowed through the dirty fallen snow on the road, the ashes of our love.

When I entered our apartment, it all seemed foreign, out of sync. I felt like I'd been away for six months, not ten days. Nothing had changed for Tania and Aïyana; they were the same. But I was a different man. Time, like a mirror, had broken, and its shards made us bleed. "It's all wrong! It's all wrong!" I hollered, trying to make sense of what was happening. I wanted love, peace, hugs, and understanding, and yet, here we were having the worst drama I'd ever experienced. *What just happened?*

Tania screamed in tears, "What do you want?! This is a nightmare! It's not real!"

Aïyana, not knowing what was happening, raised her arms and shrieked, "STOP! STOP! STOP!" Horrified by the despair in my daughter's eyes, I hugged her and my wife, and we collapsed on the sofa still shaking. We were spent, but we could breathe again. The whole scene seemed so surreal, like a soap opera. It didn't make any sense: *We love each other, so why does this feel so wrong?* It felt like the end of the world.

As we sat in silence, I saw balloons and signs that said: "Welcome home, Daddy!" This was the worst scenario any of us could've imagined.

"What do you want from us?" my wife finally asked, surely afraid of how I'd react.

How could I explain love? It was an experience, not words. I went from a starving life of loneliness to a full love awakening and back to starving again. My little family was not violent or abusive like the family I'd grown up with, but they also weren't open or vulnerable. I felt like we were strangers living together. *How can you put the love genie back in the bottle?* I wondered. "I'm sorry for what happened," I answered then hugged them again.

In the coming weeks, we walked on eggshells around each other. There were no arguments or crying, but we had lost our bearings. *Who am I? Was my mission in Guatemala just a dream?* Stuck in a whirlpool of emotions, we needed to create a new equilibrium. *Can we make it?*

Patch and the other clowns had warned us: "Be careful when you get home. Be gentle with yourself and others around you. Some families can't get around it, and they struggle. The last thing we want is for this trip to drive a wedge between you and your loved ones and cause separations or divorces. We're here for you, always. Remember, we're a family, so don't hesitate to reach out."

Christy, one of the clowns I'd met in Guatemala, started a social media group. *It wasn't a dream after all. I'm still part of the family: Rob, Jerry, Dee Dee . . .* they all lent a hand and a virtual shoulder to cry on. And then something miraculous happened: I began receiving calls from journalists wanting to interview me about the humanitarian clown mission. It suddenly all felt real.

Meanwhile, I could no longer wear my usual clothes because I'd become a different person—a humanitarian clown. I had a new teaching contract and introduced music improvisation at a primary school dressed in full colors. And "Captain Guy, the Shanty Singer" made his comeback, leading the public in song at a cultural center. I tried to clown in hospitals, but since I wasn't a "professional clown," they rejected my offer.

Not deterred by their exclusion, I kept bright red, foam noses in my pockets and gave them to people walking down the street, taking selfies and writing of their transformation on my new blog "The Amazing Adventures of Citizen Clown."

Shortly after I returned from Guatemala, Patch came to town. He was playing wheelchair field hockey at a local charity event. Everyone was after him, so when I finally got to talk to him, appearing out of nowhere, it took him a few moments to recognize me, then he exclaimed, "GUY!".

As I kneeled down, we shared a long hug and stared lovingly in each other's eyes. "It's so great to see you again! How've you been?" Patch asked.

At a loss for words, I could only thank him for changing my life.

He replied, "No, Guy, *you* changed your life . . . *you* did!"

These were very wise words from a very loving man. Journalists took photos of us, then I left Patch with a long line of fans who wanted to meet him. Thanks to those thirty seconds with him, I finally felt that I was really myself again. I was back—back in Montreal, back home.

Two days later, I saw Patch again—by pure coincidence—at the airport. I was on my way to the AATH conference and Humor Academy in Indiana.

"You know, Guy, I'm only home two months a year with my partner, Susan. She's so patient with me. The rest of the year, I give talks and go on clown trips—all to raise funds to build my hospital. After more than fifty years, I've never stopped. I think it's going to happen really soon!" His eyes lit up at the thought of his institute opening. After one last hug, we parted ways. It was my turn to become a messenger of love.

After a short flight, I arrived at the hotel in my full Sunday best clown attire and greeted everyone with a big hug and smile. After leaving my clown family in Guatemala, I was meeting more extended family members, like Barbara, Mary Kay, Maïa, Harald, Julie, Olga, Bron, and Kathy. I felt ecstatic and camera in hand, I transformed everyone in clowns with the gift of a red nose! The best compliment was when they said, "You must've been clowning for years!"

I was still insecure, so these words affected me deeply. "Actually, I've only been doing this a few weeks!"

"Guy, you're a natural!"

At the conference, I finally got to meet Lenny Ravich, the director of the Gestalt Institute in Tel Aviv, Israel, who looked a bit like Baloo from *The Jungle Book*. He had awarded me the Shalom for World Peace scholarship to attend the Humor Academy. We got starry-eyed and had the longest, warmest hug the first time we met and every time we crossed paths during the conference. Like Mowgli, I asked his advice. "I don't know what to do. I find it so hard just to be myself."

Surprised, Lenny looked at me with infinite compassion. "Tell me, Guy, what happens when you want something?"

"My inner critic judges and censures me."

"Then move your ear away and flush him down!" Lenny said with a mischievous grin.

"But when I do, I feel sad."

"That's normal because it's a part of yourself that you're letting go of."

Knowing that letting go always left an emptiness, a vacuum, I asked, "Then how do I deal with my sadness?"

"Just accept yourself as you are because, you know something, Guy? Today is the best moment of your life; there is no other moment like it." Then he added with a huge smile and a twinkle in his eyes, "Out of the millions of sperm, you are the one who won the race! You're already are a winner, Guy!" We both exploded in laughter and hugged.

After I returned to Montreal, I reached out to Marguerite. "Who am I, really?" I questioned. She nodded mindfully behind her paper-covered desk. "In Guatemala, I discovered that as an art teacher, I give the best of myself only 5 percent of the time, but as a care clown, I give my best 95 percent of the time. As a clown, my life has meaning and a purpose because I bring healing joy. What I didn't expect was the reverse in my relationships. Coming from the abuses I lived through, I thought I was getting 95 percent of the expression of love from my wife and daughter, but, but compared to the open communication in my clown family, it's actually a paltry 5 percent. That's why we experis enced a crisis when I came home; I'd opened Pandora's Box."

"And what do you feel about your 95 percent you give as a volunteer clown today?"

"To be honest, I feel a calling to join a new mission for three weeks in India. It happens to coincide with my fifty-fifth birthday. But after what happened when I came home from Guatemala, my wife doesn't want me to go. For her, my going on a new trip, it's just over the top. I don't know what to do."

"Guy, I understand that your family situation has been your greatest concern, but what do *you* feel?"

"I feel like I've emptied my barrel and I'm scraping the bottom. I see light shining through the slats, but I don't know what's down there. In my gut, I know going to India is the next step, but I'm afraid."

"Afraid of what exactly?"

I'd long known the answer but was afraid to admit it. "I'm afraid of my wife," I confessed, baring my soul.

I expected Marguerite to give me the same response I'd gotten from the school counselor or the therapist in Paris, "Man up, Guy. Don't be such a doormat!" But she stayed quiet and just waited for me to continue.

"I'm scared of her. I've been scared in all my relationships—scared of being judged and rejected, scared of someone lashing out and hitting me." I paused for a moment to collect my thoughts. "At the bottom of the barrel are all my relationships. But after Guatemala, I now see a new light coming through the slats—a glimmer of hope."

"I see," Marguerite said. "And this light, this hope, . . . what does it tell you?"

I remained silent for a few minutes, and then as if a splinter of wood broke off from the bottom my barrel letting a light shone through, I sat up straight and firmly stated, "I'm going to India."

The Good Boy inside me freaked out: *How dare you spend three weeks away from your wife and daughter?*

Standing firm in my decision, I replied to him, *Ok, I'll make a deal with you: I'll take my family for a special vacation—something unique that we've never done before—just the three of us to give us a chance to reconnect.* The Good Boy agreed, so I explained my idea to Marguerite and later to my wife.

A couple months later, we were off to the islands of Guadeloupe in the Caribbean, where we swam in the ocean, relaxed on the beaches, and ate fresh passion fruit and avocados right off the trees. I also brought along foam noses to entertain the locals, and lo and behold, my wife and daughter started to appreciate my gift of bringing love and laughter to those around me.

"You know, I'm still basically the same husband and daddy, there's just more of me now. And I'll always be here for you both." With my family reassured, I learned the Tamil language and bought my ticket to India.

Chapter 44

MARIA

At midnight on November 4, in the hot and dusty city of Vellore, India, there was a mysterious knock on my bedroom door. *Who's there?* I wondered. I padded over in my PJs and opened the door. "SURPRISE! Happy Birthday, Guy!" A group of joyous clowns showered me with dozens of colorful balloons next to a huge banner that read: HAPPY 55th BIRTHDAY GUY! They took out ukuleles, squeakers, whistles, and sang "Happy Birthday" to me. *What an amazing start to my mission in India! I am blessed to be here.*

When I'd registered for the trip, I'd mentioned that it coincided with me turning fifty-five. I wanted to show that I'm living proof that change is possible at any age and under any circumstances—that it's never too late to create a new life.

Later at lunch, they brought out a birthday cake with a unique twirling, singing candle. Giri Dharan, our local coordinator for this trip to India, had the honor of serving me the first piece of cake according to their tradition—by ceremoniously squashing it all over my face! It was also his birthday, so I had the pleasure of returning the favor. Chocolate cake flew around the room to the delight of everyone who joined in the fun. I'd just arrived in the state of Tamil Nadu, in southern India, and was already overflowing with love.

The newest members of my clown family came from Australia, New Zealand, Thailand, Italy, and the United States. A few local Indians also clowned with us to help with the language barrier and the cultural differences, one of which was no touching between men and women. I found this custom to be most difficult because I don't do tricks; I bring joy by holding hands and giving hugs. Luckily, I'd brought some flutes and harmonicas to connect with the kids.

This time we rode to our destinations in clunky, noisy, windowless tuk-tuks. Three of us squeezed into each of the tiny auto-rickshaws like sardines. Riding the dirt roads at breakneck speeds, I saw poverty and misery on dirt streets littered with trash and homeless people while hundreds of temples adorned the cities. Everywhere we went was busy and congested. The mass of people, the heat, and the thunderous roar of motorbikes, trucks, and tuk-tuks crazily zooming by overwhelmed my senses. Chickens ran wild, female dogs just flesh and bones with their empty darkened tits hanging in the dirt scavenged for food. Cows lay by the roadside while buses raced past, just barely missing them.

The first place we visited was a shelter for homeless aged men and women rescued from the streets. Their desiccated bodies were garbed in simple, beige cotton robes. They lay motionless on concrete beds, and the pungent smell of urine was etched in the floor. These poor abandoned white hair souls did not have much time left in this world, but for a moment, we showed them that their lives mattered and they were loved. One very old man made my heart twinge. With his eyes closed and skin as thin as tissue paper, he reminded me of my dad. "I am here for you," and prayed for him, "May your struggles be painless and your journey filled with love."

Back in the tuk-tuks, many of us were moved to tears. We huddled together, shared our sadness, and brought each other compassion and support. Our next stop was a huge hospital for lepers. The doctors told us that they have to clean the patients' lesions, but they don't have enough sedatives to ease their pain. As we entered an overflowing ward with forty beds, a nurse waved us over. Along with two other clowns, I proceeded to the bedside of a young mother, where a nurse was slathering a bright orange disinfectant ointment on her raw wounds.

With no medication, the poor woman was writhing in pain, her eyes turned upwards as she squeezed the metal bars of the bed and screamed. We sang her songs while a female clown lightly caressed her arm. For a moment, the patient calmed down and smiled—until another wave of pain sent her screeching again. We cried tears of empathy but remained by her side until the treatment was completed and she closed her eyes out of sheer exhaustion. There was a limit to what we could do, but to go beyond our limit was the greatest gift of all.

Another day we visited a school for children with speech and hearing impairments. I wondered if I should bring my instruments and, at the last moment, I decided to do so but kept them in my backpack. The kids in their red-and-white checkered shirts started to frantically point at the flute sticking out of my bag and politely gestured for me to take it out. "Oh, you want to see, sure!" As I played, they formed a circle around me, touched the instrument, and imitated my movements.

I handed it to a tall boy beside me, but when he tried to play it, nothing happened. I took his hand and showed him by blowing on his palm; he felt my breath; and I asked him to do the same thing on mine. He understood that he needed to blow into the flute. Overjoyed, he pranced around like Pan, feeling the vibration of the notes. Others kids gathered around him as he tried the harmonica, and he showed them how to play. *Wow, so much about my preconceptions, this is so beautiful* I gave him two thumbs up for being my mentor!

Because clowning in India was so intense, we had a few days off to take care of ourselves. Some mornings I walked for hours off the main road just to take in the local culture. One time, I came across a multitude of small chapels surrounded by colorful chalk drawings and dozens of tattered, old bags hanging from trees. I was told that they were to help the dead on their spiritual journey. I could feel the presence of and love for the departed ancestors.

Other days I joined Zoe from Australia and visited the Sri Jalagandeeswarar temple in Vellore. Leaving our shoes at the entrance, we witnessed various chanting ceremonies as we moved from one tiny stone room to the next, each home to a different deity. We respectfully kept our distance, but feral monkeys with not such respectful thoughts scavenged all around us. I closed my eyes and whispered prayers, thankful for my health and the love I was bringing here.

As Zoe and I made our way back, we traveled along the busiest, noisiest, and most polluted street in the city and had to cross an overpass to get to the market on the other side. On our way, we saw a woman sitting by herself on the stairs, her white dress stained by dirt and blood. She begged for handouts, bringing her fingers to her mouth in the universal gesture of hunger. Her voice was so weak I could barely make out what she was saying, but in my heart, I understood: "Please help me."

Everyone ignored her, but we kneeled down next to her. We didn't see poverty or disease; to us, she was a beautiful woman. Zoe touched her shoulders to let her know we were there for her. *When was the last time she was touched by a loving hand?* I wondered. Despite the language barrier, we let her know that we were going to the market and we'd be back. We crossed over and got some green grapes, bananas, water, and a garland of jasmine flowers.

When we returned, we crowned "Maria" with the garland as we sang "Amazing Grace" and other songs of love. As we kneeled down and prayed together, she covered her toothless smile and flowing tears with her bandaged hands. Leprosy had claimed many of her toes and fingers, but she reached out for our hands and prayed for us in return. Most passersby still ignored us, but a few stopped out of curiosity and one or two actually thanked us. However, Maria's prayer was the most beautiful gift I received in India.

When we parted, I carried this encounter deep within my soul. Something inside me had been stirred as I recognized parts of myself in Maria. In everyday life, I never would've dared to stop and sit with her. But as a humanitarian clown, I could open up my heart and give love as part of an organized group on a world mission. But there was still one person I couldn't give love to: myself.

I have been lonely all my life—lonely in my family, at school, in my relationships. I knew I wasn't the only one because even people living in big cities and in a world connected by cell phones, social media, and video-chatting apps can feel terribly alone. I was the homeless in my paintings, the observer and the victim in *Mack the Night.* Like so many others, I could function for decades alone, but I almost fell through the cracks like so many Marias of the world. Yes, loneliness is a real disease even in the technologically advanced twenty-first century.

Thank you, Maria. Thanks to you, I am no longer homeless, an observer, or a victim. I've stepped out of my paintings to become an agent of change, one heart at a time.

Chapter 45

A GOOD MAN

Leaving Vellore, we continued to the megalopolis of Chennai, formerly called Madras, the capital of Tamil Nadu. In the evenings, as I didn't dare venture too far from our hotel, I'd walk to a closet-sized tea shop and watch the deafening and ceaseless traffic.

I'd order a chai tea served in a tiny glass and sit on the dusty sidewalk under the yellowish glow of the streetlight. I observed many dogs wandering in the streets, but one stood out to me: a frail-looking pooch with dirty, sand-colored fur. With his tail hidden between his bony legs, he'd clearly been the victim of countless beatings. Sadly, I'd often witnessed mean-spirited street vendors bait stray dogs only to kick them when they approached.

Staying in the shadows, he was hesitant to approach me. I was usually afraid of dogs, especially strays, but not this one. "Come here, buddy. It's fine."

He bowed his head and scampered closer. I'm sure he was wondering if it was a trap like the ones he'd survived many times before.

"Come on. It's OK." As he got within arm's reach, I gently stroked his head. Reassured, he finally sat down and leaned his sad, scrawny body against me. "You're fine. Just rest. You're safe here with me. There, Sebastian. That's a good boy." And just like that, I'd christened my doggy soul mate.

Over the next few nights, we shared teatime together. He'd be waiting for me by the shop, then we'd sit and play. He'd take my hand in his jaws but would never bite. If other dogs showed up, he'd get protective, jump up, and bark at them to go away, then he'd return to lay his head on my lap. I came to India for the children, discovered the invisible street "Marias," and now had found Sebastian. All were creatures of the world who needed love.

Less than a week before the end of the trip, we spent the weekend in Mahabalipuram, a small coastal village. It was a dream come true as I'd always felt a calling to the seas. I took long walks on the sandy beach, marveling at the fishermen's boats, and rested on the terrace of the Bob Marley Café writing my journal. As I put pen to paper, suddenly the high-pitched voice of a young woman called to me, "Hey, good sir. You buy nice necklace, yes? Good price!"

I looked toward the beach and discovered two young women with dark complexions, jet-black hair, and arms full of brightly colored necklaces. I politely declined and returned to my journaling. When I left the terrace, they followed me to the village where I sat with a bunch of kids, offering them balloons.

"Give one to me, yes?" one of the two women asked sweetly and sat down beside me. As I gave her one, I noticed that she had the highest cheekbones I'd ever seen and a sunburst of a smile. As we talked, I soon discovered that she and her sister were members of the Narikuravas, a class of indigenous tribes in the state of Tamil Nadu. I proposed that my new friend do a video interview.

"My name Aspni," she said in broken English. She went on to describe her aspirations of riches and marriage "I want only two children, one boy and one girl. I speak French, English, and I want to live in Europe. I want to marry very rich man."

"Well, I'm already married, and I'm not rich at all!" We both laughed.

"No, you rich . . . rich of heart," she said, pointing to my chest.

When I ask if she knew any songs, she sang with an amazing and cheerful voice about the eyes of a lover. There was so much peace, love, and hope in her voice I could tell that her circumstances did not define her life. Aspni was an image of hope that remained forever etched in my heart.

When I got back to the hotel, Zoe extended an amazing invitation. "I'm going to the beach tomorrow morning to see the sunrise, if you want to join along!" How could I refuse!

"Yes, of course, four AM no problem I'll be there!" I set my alarm but could hardly sleep. Finally, in the inky, black darkness, I got up and flashlight in hand found my friend. She had rented a scooter, and off we went as a few dogs barked in the night. The road was empty and the fresh air grazed my face as I held on tight so as not to fall off. Half an hour later, we turned onto a narrow dirt road just as a sliver of sky was revealed.

The cold sand spread between our toes as we made our way to the beach. When we dipped our feet into the freezing water, it sent shivers up my spine. As we sat in silence witnessing the incredible birth of a new day, the only sound came from the waves lapping along the shoreline. Glimmers of orange brushed up against a whisper of clouds, forming a celestial glow until a magnificent red sliver of sun appeared and started to slowly rise above the horizon. Imperceptibly, the subtle tones changed from pink to yellow as the sky's palette gradually turned to a brilliant cerulean blue. My whole being fluttered in awe at the heavenly spectacle.

This is so amazing! I'm in India, sitting next to the ocean, watching the sunrise with a friend, and giving love as a humanitarian clown. This is one of the happiest moments of my life!! I've made it! I've made it! I've finally succeeded!

But my Good Boy, who couldn't stand for such happiness violently stepped in. *You were raped, bullied, abandoned. You can't have this! You can't!* For a moment, I wasn't sure which voice to listen to because both were true. *I am here in this magical place, but I can't be happy. I'm here, yes, but the rape . . .* These thoughts raced through my brain like a skipping record, tearing my soul to shreds.

And then, as I felt the first warm rays of sunlight on my face, both voices shouted in unison: *It's over! It's finally over! I'VE WON!* I was elated. I breathed in the rising sun and burst into tears. "It's over! I'm free! I've won!" I said out loud.

"Are you OK?" Zoe asked. "What's over? What do you mean?"

"Just give me a moment," I muttered between sobs of joy, taking in the beauty of the moment. The sun purified all the pain I'd been living through, and in between breaths, I started to tell Zoe my story of abuse, doubt, and loneliness, and how this was one of the happiest moments of my life. "So, you see, I've won. It's really over!" I told her about all the risks I'd taken to get to this moment and that I was still scared and unsure of the future, but at least my past was finally behind me.

"I see. Tell me, Guy, do you think you're a good man?"

"A good man?" *What a strange question. No one had ever asked me that before. Am I a good man?*

I was fucking raped, my body was the enemy, my entire self was guilty. *Am I a good man?*

I used to be nothing more than a doormat, and now I was a humanitarian clown. *Am I a good man?*

With all the love I was giving, couldn't I look within myself for once? *Am I a good man?* Finally, I admitted to Zoe and to myself, "Yes, I am. I am a good man."

As soon as I said those words, I felt engulfed by a pure, white light of love glowing from inside myself. "I am a good man!" I repeated. *I am finally at peace.*

On the plane ride home, I carried Maria, Aspni, Sebastian, and all my clown family members in my heart and left my Good Boy at the Bob Marley Café on the beaches of Mahabalipuram.

After I returned home, I contacted Giri Dharan, my birthday brother in Vellore, and sent him funds for his Third Hand Foundation, which provided food and clothing to needy families and was building a school for tribal communities like Aspni's Narikuravas.

As I settled back into family life, my daughter's schoolteacher was organizing a knitting drive to donate scarfs for the homeless people of Montreal. I went with them to distribute the warm garments on the snowy streets. "Daddy, this is so great! It's like giving them a Christmas gift!" Then her teacher also set up a letter exchange program with schoolchildren in Ouagadougou, the capital of Burkina Faso in Africa. I contacted their director Mrs. Francelline Nakoulma, who also planned to build a school for orphans and poor families. I made it my personal mission to send her school supplies and grants for her students.

In March of 2015 I volunteered on my second clowning mission to Guatemala. I reconnected with Rob and met new clowns like Patti and Domi from Mexico City. They later invited me to their home, and from there, I organized my first clown visit for kids at a police shelter. After that, I went to Cancun, where I met Lou Rodriguez, who had founded an association for clowns hospitals. She taught at the Del Mar Waldorf Initiative, a school for kids with Down syndrome. And although she was recovering from an operation, we gave clown tours together. She was the most amazing, loving, and caring clown I'd ever met. Finally, I made one last stopover in Panama to give a talk on humanitarian clowning. My mission was as clear as day: bring as much love as I can.

My next big challenge came when the following summer I boarded a flight for South America.

Chapter 46

MUD ANGELS

Peru was worlds away, literally. In the mid-August tropical heat, I joined Patch and more than a hundred clowns—most of them professionals—half from the capital city of Lima and most of the rest from all over Latin America. Included among them was Dr. Carl Hammerschlag, another giant-sized humanitarian clown with his signature pink flamingo outfit.

Unlike my trips to Guatemala and India, where I basked in the safety of an intimate group, this time I was drowning in a sea of native Spanish speakers. We were subdivided into groups of twenty participants (known as families) to plan out the volunteering. Every morning we signed up to assist in either giving workshops or preparing a show. There were no organized communal meals, and we were on our own for lunch. I was rarely with the same volunteers, so despite the kindness of the organizers, because of my shyness, I found it nearly impossible to connect with my fellow group members.

Suffering from isolation, I shuddered at a realization that if this had been my first volunteer trip, I never would've become a humanitarian clown, never would've experienced real love in Guatemala, and never would've discovered my true self in India.

Our hotel was located in Iquitos, a small, modern city nestled in the Amazon rain forest that couldn't be reached by roads, only by riverboat and airplane. At first light, I sought refuge on the rooftop overlooking the river, pouring my heart out in my journal in the company of pigeons and cats. The warm purr of a cute, little black-and-white kitten on my lap reminded me of the comfort I received from Taffy. The early golden rays were a balm to soothe my loneliness and gave me the courage to seek advice from Dr. Hammerschlag. "I don't get it," I confessed to him. "I discovered so much love and joy on my previous missions, and I want to share it here, but I just don't know how. I'm hurting, and I feel lost."

"Well, Guy, I'm going to let you in on a little secret," Carl replied in a warm, deep voice. "What you experienced is magical and precious. And it'll be part of you no matter what happens—so cherish it. Sure, we're a bunch of very different individuals here, and some of us haven't discovered what you have because they aren't ready. But that's our greatest asset. You feel like you're all alone—and I get that—but believe me, Guy, you're anything but. Be patient with your comrades and especially with yourself. Never forget that what's in your heart belongs to you and will always be there, regardless of whether you express it or not."

Moved to tears by his compassion, I gave him a big hug. *I know I can do this,* I assured myself. Then I went to my room, put on a bathing suit, and plunged into the hotel's small pool. After reconnecting with my element—water—something magical happened: I was finally able to make new friends like Moira from Chile, and Alyx and Rebecca from the US.

Our mission was down the hill to the muddy streets of Belen, an old shantytown populated by natives from the rain forest, which was regularly flooded. The contrast between the city and the shantytown was like a punch in the gut as you walked from the flashing neon lights of stores selling washing machines to a mad puzzle of houses on stilts with no electricity, sanitation, or running water. Another major difference was that on our other clowning trips, we'd visited children in different care facilities, but this time, we were actually in their village.

We'd been warned to bring tall rain boots, mosquito repellent, and lots of disinfectant. I soon understood why: We were walking in the mud amidst the worst sanitary conditions I'd ever experienced. Dog feces and garbage floated in the green slime of putrid rain puddles infested with mosquitoes while the children ran around barefoot.

As we arrived at our destination—basically a large rectangle of bare earth where kids played soccer—ominous, dark clouds suddenly appeared and the sky opened up as a thundering downpour dumped buckets of water on us. The kids huddled together under my tiny orange-and-pink polka-dotted umbrella and squealed with delight, even though we were all wet as fish.

As soon as the rain diminished, the children ran to the soccer field and did the strangest thing I'd ever seen. They lay on the ground and opened and closed their arms and legs, pushing the mud away. My heart skipped a beat as I suddenly saw myself in them. *As a child, I did the same exact thing in the snow! They're making mud angels!* It was so inspiring to see how they transformed their bleak environment into a field of joy.

I also noticed little groups of kids scattered all around the wet field. A young girl, who was maybe six years old, was holding hands with a boy and girl who looked to be four and two, respectively, while a slightly older girl tended to a baby in her arms. Although I was still cold and wet from the rain, I felt my heart warm just by looking at them. Then it hit me: *All the kids are smiling. They all take care of each other and are filled with love!*

As an art teacher, I had guided thousands of kids, and most of them had had their inner light snuffed out. *They had everything: food, shelter, education, and yet their eyes were empty. But these kids have nothing, and look at them—they're glowing with love!* At that precise moment, I realized: *This what humanity feels like. This is who I am! I get it.* My link to the universe, which had once been severed by the abuses had been reconnected. *I belong to the human family, and these are all my brothers and sisters, even the ones who abused me. I love you all.*

I flew back home with the gift of humanity blooming in my heart. At this point, I was more determined than ever to reach out to the world on a mission of love. Even so, I wondered how I could bridge the language barriers. I remembered how much joy my flutes and harmonica had brought to the children in India and how singing soothed "Maria" and that woman suffering in the leper hospital. Deep down, I knew the answer: *I'll sing!*

I ached to sing, but it had taken me decades before I found the courage to join a choir and even longer before I dared to start my own sea shanty group. But my dream had always been to be the lead singer in a rock band. I went to the music store and bought my own sky-blue soprano ukulele and decorated it with hearts and flowers stickers. I ditched my red rubber nose because I wanted the human connection and vulnerability of someone like Charlie Chaplin. *Thank you, Citizen Clown, for bringing me this far. Now Ukulele the Humanitarian Clown, or "Uku" for short, is my new messenger of love.* I was ready to join Rob and Patch on my third mission to Guatemala.

First, I learned a few Spanish favorites, such as "La Bamba," "La Cucaracha," and "Estrellita." known in English as "Twinkle, Twinkle, Little Star." Then I added a couple of personal picks like "Tonight You Belong to Me" and Monty Python's "Always Look on the Bright Side of Life."

When we arrived in Guatemala in March 2016, I improvised with the amazing Dr. John Glick on the bus and in the wards to comfort the children. Back at the Valle de Los Angeles orphanage, I reunited with Yorbeli, who, by this time, was eight years old. After a long hug and many tears of joy, we surrounded ourselves with dozens of her classmates and improvised zany, animal songs.

Once my mission with Patch and the others ended, I stayed in Guatemala a little longer and continued clowning by myself. I set out for San Pedro La Laguna, a small mountain village on the shores of Lake Atitlán. I strummed my ukulele through the quaint streets, handed out foam noses and stickers, and brought joy to the shopkeepers as we sang together. I felt a sense of peace emanating throughout my body.

One day, a young woman approached me and said, "Hola, I work at Somos Hijos Del Lago, a community center for kids with disabilities. Tomorrow afternoon, we're having a celebration for Holy Week for the kids and their families." She paused then asked with a smile, "Would you play for us?"

"Yes! It would be my pleasure! Thanks for the invitation!"

The next day, I made my way up the hill to the community center. The activity room was decorated with multicolored balloons and filled with dozens of children—some in wheelchairs, others on crutches—along with their parents and siblings. I made the kids and their parents sing, exchange hats, participate in Laughter Yoga while I performed acrobatic dances. I was sweaty from bouncing all over the place, but it was worth it as we laughed and clapped.

Then I noticed a frail-looking girl with long, black hair and a bright purple sweater sitting up front. She tried to clap along as I sang, despite her physical disability. Nevertheless, her enthusiasm warmed my heart, so I threw myself at her feet and asked her parents her name. When they told me her name was Rosalia and she was nine years old, I improvised a song for her.

Rosalia, Rohhh-sahhh-leeeahhh
With your eyes so kind
You make everyone's heart shine
Rosalia, Rohhh-sahhh-leeeahhh

You're a little angel
Bringing joy with your smile
Rosalia, Rohhh-sahhh-leeeahhh.

Her eyes sparkled while her parents cupped their hands to their hearts. She held out her arms to me, wanting to be picked up. When her father nodded his permission, I gently lifted her in my arms and carefully waltzed her around. She leaned her head on my shoulder in bliss while everyone cheered and applauded.

After a good two hours of jumping, singing, and dancing, I was exhausted. I gave Rosalia, her little sister, Maria, and her parents, Pina and Cristoval hugs. Their little angel had given Uku a new set of wings. His next stop would be Eastern Europe.

Chapter 47

KOLYA

For my fifty-seventh birthday in November 2016, I joined Patch and the clowns in cold and snowy Russia. Patch felt very special about this trip because it was one of the first places he'd visited more than thirty-five years earlier.

"*Здравствуйте, где я могу купить пиво?*" Russian wasn't that complicated as I managed to ask the taxi driver where I could buy beer. He was impressed that a foreigner spoke Russian and kindly offered to take me directly to the store. I admittedly knew nothing of the Russian culture, except what Françoise, my former landlady, had taught me. But I found the Russian people to be friendly, extremely honest, and straightforward—no small talk, just directly to the point. It took me a while to figure this out, though.

For Russia I prepared two celebrated music themes: 1985's children's science fiction television series "Гостья из будущего" (Guest from the Future) and their most revered holiday movie; 1975's "Ирония судьбы, или С лёгким паром!" (The Irony of Fate, or Enjoy Your Bath!) I strummed classics like "Petrushka" and irreverent rock hits such as В Питере пить ("Drink Up In St. Petersburg") by the rock group Leningrad, and Пей пиво ("Drink Beer") by Discoteka Avaria. They gasped open mouth as I surprised them with these and some even danced traditional Russian folk steps. But the best part was when I taught children to play the ukulele. They clapped and danced along, but more importantly, they forgot their pain and became kids again.

Everything in Moscow was huge—the streets, the traffic, the buildings—and when we finally arrived at the central hospital, I was awed by its size. As we made our way to the neurology floor, I thought about my father. *Thank you, Dad for seeing me all the way through. I know you're always here with me. I love you.*

I joined with my new clown friends Marleen and Kees from the Netherlands, and we brought our crazy theatrics to a mother and her fourteen-year-old bedridden daughter, Nina. Every movement seemed to be extremely painful for her because her limbs were contorted with acute muscular dystrophy. Her mother clapped as we sang, danced, laughed, and wiggled on the floor like giant worms. As I got up, I kneeled next to Nina and offered to make her sing. Her mother interjected in Russian that it wasn't possible but I trusted my instinct.

And so I strummed a simple melody and gently did "ooooh" while encouraging Nina to repeat after me. At first came a shy, wispy voice, but the more we sang, her voice became louder and clearer. She was singing! Her whole face lit up, and her mother, tears streaming down her face, beamed in bliss.

When our duet ended her mother thanked us profusely for the small miracle that had just taken place. "Спасибо, спасибо!" Marleen, Kees, and I just looked at each other with wonder. We knew it wasn't a miracle; it was the healing power of our caring love.

I left the room and, as I explored the long corridor, I noticed an eight-year-old boy all by himself in a dorm room with ten other beds. He sat motionless, hunched over his bed, with a sad, empty expression. I tiptoed into his room while strumming a few chords. His name, Piotr, was written above his bed. Dark circles ringed his eyes like he'd endured hundreds of sleepless nights. *I suffered from nightmares and insomnia at his age, and nobody was there for me, so I can't abandon him now.*

I continued to move closer to him but got no reaction. When I was standing right beside him, I placed my ukulele next to him and pulled one string, then another and another. He noticed and timidly imitated my movements. Then he brought the ukulele to his knees and for the next twenty minutes, he was totally transfixed, playing a melodic suite of notes. I watched in awe as Piotr came to life.

As I left the room, he smiled so brightly that the dark circles seemed to have faded away. George Harrison's inspirational song "My Sweet Lord" played in my mind as my heart glowed with joy and my tears flowed.

If parents were reluctant to sing, my little helper, a pink rubber piglet named Tocino, would come to the rescue by oinking so loudly that it was impossible not to laugh. They'd squeeze him to the rhythm of the music or pass him around and squeak him at each other. He also had the amazing gift to make people laugh far across the room: I'd point Tocino, oinked, and they burst out laughing.

On one special occasion, I was playing with a big family of children with their mother and aunts. At first, they were quite shy—until hospitalized little six-year-old Amir ran around with Tocino. He giggled with glee, squeezed the piglet, and had each of his family members do the same. The joy on Amir's face was so palpable that I gave Tocino to him. His mother glowed and confided in me, "Thank you for the joy in this difficult time. I was very tense and nervous at that time. But when you arrived, a miracle happened, I felt light and well, and we could feel the happiness! I am very grateful to you and I am happy that we met. It was a huge relief for me! Especially when you see how your child laughs and rejoices. Thank you, God brought you to us!"

One of our last stops at the hospital in Moscow was at the preemie ward for newborns with disabilities. It was painful to see these deformed shells of infants encased within glass incubators with the constant thrum of beeping, buzzing, and suction noises. The contrast of technology with their fragile, pale skin was heartbreaking. Each station held the baby's chart: Marina—fifteen days old; Igor—three weeks; Anya—four weeks. Life expectancy appeared to be limited. I felt a pang in my soul.

As I looked down at little Marina, she was blind as her eyes were hardened with an opaque white cornea. *She can't see anything. Can she even hear?* I wondered. Her frail body twitched as the respirator brought air to her underdeveloped lungs. I longed to hold her close. When another volunteer came by, her gentle gaze met mine. Feeling connected to each other through our concern for this child, we held hands. In silence, we kneeled, closed our eyes, and prayed. As if we were the parents of Christ in a Nativity scene, a current of love bonded the three of us for eternity.

After having given our united love to Marina, we stood up and hugged. As we regrouped, I felt like pieces of my heart belonged to all the infants in the ward. *Peace be upon them,* I silently prayed.

Apart from our visits with Patch, I wanted to meet Russian hospital clowns. I had reached out through the Internet before my arrival and asked them to meet up. Not only did they accept, Margarita from ANO Hospital Clowns took me along on some visits in Saint Petersburg, and Alexander, the director of Clown Care, asked me to accompany him on his regular visits to families in their homes.

After an hour drive, Alexander and I arrived in a suburb filled with rows and rows of monolithic apartment blocks that all looked the same. It was pitch-black at eight p.m. when we trudged through the snow to the lobby of a bland-looking building. After taking a rickety, nondescript elevator, we arrived at the apartment. Alexander put on his red nose then knocked on the door while I strummed my ukulele.

With a welcoming smile, Alexey, a tall man with short, brown hair invited us in and escorted us to the living room where his lovely wife,

Nataliya, and their seven-year-old son, Kolya, awaited us. The blond boy was strapped to a raised chair with a respirator connected to his throat and pumping rhythmically. Paralyzed, only his eyes could track our zaniness as the four of us threw balloons and made universal animal sounds: *Quack-Quack! Woof-Woof! Meow-Meow!* Sometimes he winced and groaned if we were too intense.

I handed Nataliya my ukulele and she started to strum and dance while I sang simple songs with Alexey and Alexander accompanied us with his flute. As the four of us twirled in front of Kolya's chair, we were all in tune, but all of a sudden, Kolya knitted his brow, coughed, and moaned as a ear-piercing beep signaled a sense of urgency. Nataliya immediately cleared out his throat and checked the dials on the respirator while Alexey regained his composure.

It was hard to fathom the total devotion Nataliya and Alexey had for Kolya—the constant pressure they must've felt needing to be on guard at all times of the day and night. My heart ached for them even as I witnessed with awe their deep love for their son.

As we hugged goodbye, I understood that even though we'd come to bring joy to their son, we were there for them as well. When we got back to the car, Alexander and I both had tears in our eyes. Even though we'd just met, we'd shared something so real and special.

In their youth, my mom was a nurse in a premature babies' ward and my dad made his rounds in the neurology department. I had just clowned in those same floors in Russia as Dr Clown Uku! We now shared a healing bond by leaving so many pieces of our hearts to the children.

Chapter 48

BEYOND GOOD AND EVIL

*B*ack in Montreal, connected with humanity and the healing spirit of a Love Clown, I was ready to get started on my book. I headed to Chicago for a weekend workshop by comedian Judy Carter called "The Message of You." Geared toward public speakers, it proposed digging deep inside to bring out your unique message in order to make a difference in the lives of others. With her kindness, soft-spoken voice, and boisterous humor, she gave me the courage to publicly—on stage—talk openly about my abuse. The participants and I were in tears. It was a healing experience for all of us, and many of them came forward and hugged me afterward, saying, "Guy, you are so courageous! Thank you for sharing."

Like my dad on his tractor seat at eight years old, I'd reached my moment of clarity. *My book won't be about laughter; it'll be about healing from sexual abuse—from abuse to happiness, a healing memoir. I want it to be like a North Star for other survivors who are silently suffering alone. The book I couldn't find when I needed it most.* I wrote through the winter and spring in cafés, and when summer arrived, I moved outside to write in the parks. The company of strangers and the hustle and bustle spared me from the loneliness of the writer's task as I devoted myself to my life's work: being a messenger of love. This also included being present for my wife and daughter, and I looked forward to some precious family time.

In the summer of 2017, we decided to take a family vacation to attend the Buddhist Mandala and Compassion Workshop, which was being held in a small town in the countryside. By this time, Aïyana was twelve years old, and the one thing we all had in common was a love of reading and a curiosity for learning new things, so this was right up our alley.

We left the crowded city for Ayer's Cliff, an enchanting little village along a secluded lake surrounded by forests, and made our way to an old wooden church with its country smell and creaky floor. Our gracious hosts—five bald, Buddhist monks in long, burgundy robes—embodied peace and serenity. In the mornings and afternoons, their deep guttural chants resonated through my core.

The three of us sat on folding chairs in the front row as the monks began working on a sand mandala, a centuries-old Tibetan Buddhist tradition. They drew a three-foot (1 m) circle on a piece of plywood as one of them explained, "This is the Temple of Compassion to bring blessings and spiritual insight on the creator as well as you, the audience. All the symbols of the mandala represent the different steps of the path to happiness, to Enlightenment."

Three young monks in their twenties meticulously rubbed long, thin, copper funnels to allow colored sand to fall into architectural patterns. Every door, staircase and window was predetermined, and each color had a symbolic meaning reminiscent of the First Nation's medicine wheel.

As they worked, the head of the delegation, Lama Samten instructed us in the "Great Wisdom of Compassion." With a melodious ringing accent, he asserted. "You are the creator of your thoughts and feelings.

You are free to choose your attitudes, so choose compassion and happiness." His laugh was contagious and as fresh as a mountain spring.

During the three days of the workshop, he repeated his catchphrase at every occasion, even adding French to it: "Happiness, *le bonheur*, all the time, anywhere, *tout le temps, oui!*"

In the afternoons, Jason, a young monk from Quebec, led meditation sessions. He was a tall, angular, stick figure of a guy with a clean-shaven head that protruded out of his burgundy-red robe like a lollipop. His smile was addictive as he kindheartedly welcomed my clown hugs. His meditation workshops were very peaceful and grounding, except for one talk that set my mind ablaze.

As he sat cross-legged on a cushion, he mentioned that he introduced Buddhism and meditation in schools. While he spoke, I whimsically imagined him levitating with his legs crossed above a teacher's desk. In this vision, I saw a small crucifix hanging behind him on the wall. This was typical for the '60s as the Christian religion played a fundamental role in my education.

The message of dying for your sins came to mind, so it made me wonder about the place of forgiveness in Buddhism. I had yet to hear that word uttered at the workshop. At the end of the session, I politely asked Jason, "What's the stance on forgiveness in Buddhism?"

His answer floored me. "There are no words for forgiveness, guilt, or shame."

I couldn't compute. "Really? No words for those?" I questioned, bewildered.

"We are about accepting all there is and choosing happiness, but there is no equivalent to shame or guilt."

These concepts simply didn't exist in Tibetan Buddhism! Instead, the religion focused on the inner life and letting go of desires rather than your relationships with others or your past.

"You are 100 percent responsible for creating your life," Jason clarified.

I was speechless. How can forgiveness—a concept so fundamental to my healing journey— simply not exist?

Then I remembered Lama Samten's reaction when I'd pointed to the iconic red nose on my Fabrica de Sonrisas T-shirt from Guatemala and said, "I volunteer in humanitarian missions as a clown."

He gazed back at me with a look that told me he was totally clueless. When I mentioned this to Jason, he validated Lama Samten's response. "There are also no words for *clown* in Tibetan Buddhism." I was stunned.

After three days of constant work on the mandala, an amazingly detailed and colorful palace emerged, surrounded by luxurious gardens with fountains. After the usual morning chant, the monks donned dazzling, ruby-red robes and bushy, bright yellow headdresses to officiate the "Passing of Compassion." Lama Samten led us by reciting the mantras of respect and acceptance that we dutifully repeated: "Namo ratna trayaya. Nama arya jyana. Sagara vairochana. Byuhara jaya tathagataya."

The ceremony culminated by sweeping the sand drawing into one central pile. Once all the colors were mixed, the monks sprinkled the grayish remains into each of our palms. Afterward, they led us to the lake behind the church. Lama Samten recited a final prayer as we let the grains of sand fall into the lake. "Life is impermanent like this temple's creation."

As the dust sifted through my fingers, the moment felt poignant. *My life is like this dust. I've gone through so many passages, but now I must let them go.*

I returned to Montreal still puzzled by what I'd learned about Tibetan Buddhist. *No sins, no guilt, no forgiveness, or even clowns. How can that be?* I opened my laptop and researched Tibetan Buddhism and one name kept popping up: Swiss psychiatrist Carl Jung. According to Jung, each person hid an unknown, dark side of his personality known as "the shadow." *Maybe I'm troubled by my own shadow?*

And then I found a recording that blew my mind. It was from Alan

Watts, the philosopher whose many books I'd read over the years. In the recording, Watts paid tribute to Jung's work and called the dual concepts of good and evil an "absurd hypothesis." He theorized that society was being driven insane trying to resolve this impossible conflict. *Good and evil a hypothesis? Impossible! But this is Watts and Jung, so what if good and evil are actually just a hypothesis? No good, no evil, no shame, no guilt, not a thing to forgive? Could this be possible?*

For three days and three nights, I feverishly listened to the recording over and over again. My gut told me something was hidden behind this hypothesis.

It's like a cat playing with his image in a mirror. As soon as he reaches his paw behind the glass, he realizes that there's no other cat. It's just an illusion! They're just different sides of the same thing I shouted, "Good and evil simply don't exist!"

I experienced the world as if for the first time. *Without good and evil as a dividing mirror, then Lama Samten was right! I am free to choose happiness. My Taffy never had to jump over the wall, and I could have pushed my brothers away, and I—*

But just then, the phone rang, interrupting my train of thought. "Marc died in his sleep last night." my sister informed me.

My brother, who'd endured the role of the Joker during our childhood and battled his inner demons his entire life had passed away at the age of fifty-nine. I was devastated. For years when I'd phone him to meet for coffee, he'd answer, "I can't. Let's do it in a couple weeks." I'd heard of his failing health and was always looking forward to seeing him, but he still kept putting me off and putting me off. Now there was no more time. There were no more chances. He was gone.

I helped clean out his apartment, a sad, dusty spectacle of solitude filled with overflowing ashtrays and hundreds upon hundreds of piled-up books, comics, CDs, and cassettes. Among his things, I found a few typewritten sheets of paper. He once mentioned that he wrote poems, but he also said that he burned them and threw them away in frustration. I was able to salvage a few of them that he hadn't disposed of.

The path she spits in my face.
At each of her violent turns,
Shakes me a little, certainly, even,
Disfigures me in spite of all these omens
Projected in this pale reality.
One perceives it in all its allure.

Our young cruelty dictates however,
More than the opposite of the misguidance,
Which is invented in this curious void.
Let us forget these futile moments.
Let us tire of these acid movements.
This cry must remain subtle.

This one was dated November 21, 1984, at five o'clock in the morning:

And I'm still standing
Even when it cried on me.
Longing for you, never knowing the true you.
Longing for something.
Longing for someone.
Is it you?
How often do our days end the same way they began?
Cycle after cycles, repeating themselves again
and again.
WHERE IS THE DAMN LOVE???

I knew he was haunted by solitude and the lack of someone special in his life to love, but he never shared his suffering. Instead, he'd launch into unnerving laughter like in the song "Speak to Me" from Pink Floyd's *Dark Side of the Moon*, the same album that saved me from my night terrors. Marc had chosen Pink Floyd's "The Great Gig in the Sky" and Lynyrd Skynyrd's "Free Bird" to be played during his funeral. We all wished him a peaceful voyage to the Rock & Roll Hall of Fame of the Great Beyond.

First Dad and now Marc. It hit me how they both never opened up around the family table. For most of my life, I'd remain silent and suppressed my feelings anyway I could—with cigarettes, alcohol, sugar, and relationships. If my emotions still pushed through, I filled myself with coffee to force myself to work. During the daytime, I was Dr. Jekyll, high on caffeine, fidgety, and fast-paced; at nighttime, I became Mr. Hyde, needing alcohol to get some sleep.

I imagined Marc, Dad, and I at the dinner table, sharing our feelings and smiling. *How amazing that would've been.* I emerged from that daydream knowing what I had to do: give up caffeine, the stimulant that had made me a workaholic for the past forty years.

Caffeine withdrawal was nothing to joke about. The first time I stopped, I suffered days and days of irritability with migraines so bad I felt like my eyeballs were going to pop right out of my head. I wanted to die. But if I took painkillers, I couldn't concentrate or speak and wandered around like a zombie. If tempted, I'd drink one measly cup of coffee. I was in heaven for a few hours, but the next day, the pain would be unbearable.

Eventually, after I was able to kick the habit, I entered a world of quiet bliss, waking up in the morning so refreshed from a deep sleep and beginning my days with a calm I'd never known.

After breaking free from caffeine's clutches, I immersed myself in research on the Buddhist belief that good and evil don't exist and found its roots in the ancient texts of Taoism, Buddhism, and Hinduism. What we desired became "the good" and what we rejected "the bad," or Jung's "shadow." Breaking that illusion was called nonduality. In the 2008 documentary *The Dhamma Brothers*, I found an even more intriguing proposition.

This film documented an experimental meditation program offered at Donaldson Correctional Facility in Alabama, in the United States. For ten days, inmates—many of them convicted murderers—participated in a strict regimen of pure silence and introspection. At the end of that period, the film showed the transformation of sad, hardened, and closed-off criminals into radiant, soft-spoken individuals. I'd never seen anything like it. I was instantly hooked.

The technique they learned was called vipassana, which loosely means "direct perception of what is inside." It was an old tradition passed down through the ages, kept alive in Burma, and reintroduced to the world in 1969 by a businessman named Goenka. I studied dozens of videos on the technique and borrowed books at the library. *Could I undertake such a transformation?*

Then, packed away in a box of drawings, poetry, and a teddy bear that had been given to me by a dear friend, I found a treasure: *The Art of Living: Vipassana Meditation as Taught by S.N. Goenka.* My friend had given me her own annotated copy, and I'd had it all along! I couldn't believe it.

In the book, I read the summary of the ten-day retreat and was ecstatic when I viewed videos of Goenka's lectures online. Within days of these discoveries, I found a meditation center offering this practice just a few miles away—and the next retreat coincided with my fifty-eighth birthday! *Dare I do it?*

Like writing to Patch the first time, this seemed like a crossroads that was bigger than life itself. After Guatemala, India, and Russia, was I willing to take a journey that went further than anyplace I'd ever traveled but, at the same time, was closer than home: an expedition to the inner core of my soul? This time I didn't have to wait for an answer. I knew I had to do it.

Chapter 49

THE GREAT DISCONNECT

I arrived at what used to be a private school hidden among a lush forest. It was the autumn of 2017, and the leaves were golden yellow and the air cold and pure. The sun played hide-and-seek between the tall trees. Feeling at one with nature, I drank in the musky energy with deep breaths and thought, *This is going to go well.*

Walking into the reception area, I was directed to a table to fill out some forms. By signing the last one, I committed to stay for the whole ten days and respect the five precepts:

- abstain from killing any being;
- abstain from stealing;
- abstain from all sexual activity;
- abstain from telling lies;
- abstain from all intoxicants.

We also weren't allowed to access the Internet, use phones, radios, or tablets, read books, or write in journals. Speaking was also prohibited—for ten days! This was referred to as "the Noble Silence." In this age of social media and interconnectivity, this was going to be quite an adjustment. I'd suffered from loneliness since childhood, lived for years disconnected from other people and unable to make connections, and now, I was willfully plunging into the heart of pure isolation.

I was asked to surrender any valuables, including my wallet, for the next ten days. I was surprised and felt deprived of my identity, but I obliged. I entered a long, dark gray corridor with identical, unmarked doors on either side. Since we were not allowed to bring any personal possessions, there was no need for locks anywhere. In a way, it was comforting not having to worry about security.

My room was a stark shoebox with empty walls, two sets of basic bed, chair, and an old office desk. Luckily, my bunk was by the window while an old self-standing grey padded divider separated the space. As a hypersensitive sleeper who is easily awakened by the slightest noise, I hoped for a quiet roommate.

As I set out to explore the grounds in the gathering dusk, I saw a sign warning of bears as I came across two footpaths: one for men and one for women. The one for men made a small loop, going up and down the rocky mountain slopes. When I returned to the main entrance, the other guests had gathered. There were about sixty men and forty women, and some had come with friends or partners. The ambiance was charged and the large wooden halls resonated with excitement. *I wonder when "The Noble Silence" starts?*

DONG! DONG! DONG! Two tall, skinny figures banged on a gong then introduced themselves. When they did, the mood instantly morphed from happy-go-lucky to an ominous silence. They instructed us on the basic guidelines, which began at four in the morning and ended at nine thirty at night. Interspersed between our meals, we would be constantly meditating—either on our own or in groups—and there'd be a teaching session late in the afternoons. For the next ten days, the chiming of the gong would regulate our lives.

The rule prohibiting conversation also applied to mealtimes and even to our facial expressions. "Look at the floor, a wall, or off in the distance when you walk and never meet the eye of any other participant," we were told. Large curtains were deployed as we left for our rooms—like a Berlin Wall dividing the room into two separate dining areas. I thought about the couples who began this journey together and now, without warning, were being kept apart until the last day of the retreat.

When I returned to my room, I was relieved to see that I was still alone and wouldn't be bothered by a roommate. I sent silent kisses to my wife and daughter, turned off the light, and immediately fell asleep.

DONG, DONG, DONG! At four o'clock in the morning, I was awakened from a deep sleep. It was still dark, and everything seemed too quiet and eerie. I drowsily lumbered out of bed and dragged my limp body into the corridor to go to the bathroom. In the hallway, when I encountered a few other guests, we dutifully avoided looking at each other.

Back in my room, I turned on my electric shaver and watched it vibrate in my hand for a few seconds before deciding not to shave. *It's not like anyone's going to say something about it,* I chuckled to myself.

We had the choice of doing the first meditation of the day either in our rooms or as a group in the gymnasium. While most people stayed in their rooms, I preferred being in the company of others, and the gymnasium was just a short walk away. I stepped outside, gazed at the charcoal sky, and drank in the freezing yet pristine October air. As a gentle wind rustled the leaves, I exhaled misty clouds. It made me think about the first time I saw a real night sky. It was in Greece in 1984, and it literally looked like thousands of scintillating diamonds had been tossed upon a black velvet blanket.

I shivered and made my way up to the gymnasium's upper floor to settle in and warm myself. A few amber light bulbs lit the large room, which had a raised podium at the front with a cushion and a bedside lamp for our teacher. Six rows of ten cushions faced the teacher with a few chairs off to the side. I got an ideal spot, in the last row, off to the side right next to the exit and only had one neighbor.

After the first hour, our teacher, a tall fellow in his seventies, shuffled in, sat down, then turned on a recording of Goenka. The walls vibrated as he slowly and melodically chanted Hindi couplets in his deep, bass voice. His rich tone silenced my thoughts and warmed its way through my core. I was ready to plunge into a magnificent ten days of inner exploration

Chapter 50

THE CHAIN MAIL

The first three days were devoted to a breathing technique called anapana. "Take note of your breathing," the teacher advised. "Focus all your attention on your upper lip, directly under your nostrils, and nowhere else. Feel the air coming in and out, observe the sensations that arise without holding or reacting to them, and maintain perfect equanimity."

Equanimity—to be detached from any sensation, pleasant or unpleasant—was a word I'd encountered before with the Stoics, and it was the embodiment of nonduality. The aim of the practice was to increase the mind's ability to concentrate and discover that we could control our train of thoughts. I'd heard the expression "monkey mind," meaning the constant chatter of the mind, but I was wrestling with a whole a troop of monkeys!"

What am I doing here? Am I doing this right? I can't do this! I should've completed my music degree. Yorbeli was so happy the last time I saw her! When I get back, I have to write down all of this for my book. I need choco-late right now! And on and on and on. My mind just wandered all over the place, spewing endless noise of the past and the future, but rarely the present.

After an hour and a half of this incessant inner chatter, it was time for breakfast, then the rest of the day was spent in my jumbled mind with meditation, meditation, and more meditation, with brief walks in the woods in between. If ever there was a time that I considered running away from the retreat, it was at the end of my first full day there.

DONG! DONG! DONG! Is it four a.m. already? Did I even sleep?

Since my arrival, my eyes and temples had been burning in the gym's semidarkness. As a child, I'd always been afraid, waiting for the next shoe to drop. As a result, I became hyperalert and supersensitive to noises, lights and smells. At nighttime, I was always on the watch, so this constant vigilance prevented me from falling asleep despite my exhaustion.

I dragged my unshaven self out of bed, got ready, and breathed in the chill air as I walked to the gymnasium in darkness. The ultimate goal of the anapana technique was to anchor oneself in the present moment, so I allowed my thoughts to jump around for a while until I was able to concentrate on my breath and empty my mind.

I returned to my chair and cushions but dreaded the prospect of resuming the exploration of my mind. However, as the session progressed, the labyrinth of thoughts inside my head gradually became quieter. As reflections on my past and speculation about the future became less frequent, I was finally able to focus on the present moment. I embraced an inner peace that I'd rarely experienced before. While envisioning myself by the shores of a calm ocean, my mind opened, deepened, and expanded as time slowed to a crawl. Instantly, I recognized it as the beach I'd frequented in India. I'd always believed I'd once again find the peaceful calm I'd experienced there. But I'd always looked for it outside myself when, in fact, this serenity was always within me.

I ordered myself to sit up straight. I wanted my body in its natural posture as it should be, but I watched with fascination as others took a good ten minutes to place a bunch of cushions to support every nook and cranny of their bodies. It didn't make sense to me, though, because the purpose of our stay was to accept our pains, not deny them. Keeping that in mind, I decided to sit without any physical support, but within minutes, my whole back was on fire! So I chose to have a talk with my sensations. Rather than judging my body or denying my pain, I simply asked my back: *What are you trying to tell me?*

"I am your body armor here to protect you," my aching back informed me. It made sense. All those years of living through the abuses, my body had kept me safe. Like my sculpture *The Warrior,* I had been a knight locked away in his armor. That was how I had survived.

I took a series of long deep breaths, unbolted my armor, dismantled the chain mail, and thanked my body: *My dear, loving back, today the dangers are over and long gone. I'm so grateful you took such good care of me, but I am no longer a defenseless child, so you . . . I . . . we can let our guard down.* As I let go, my pain was replaced with an array of purifying white lights beaming from over my head. Liberated, my arms floated in midair and my hands vibrated with energy. The warmth extended throughout my entire body. I felt weightless! With my eyes closed, I continued to take deeper breaths, then suddenly, I felt a radiance cocooning my whole body. I smiled from ear to ear in bliss as I floated in velvety joy, finally experiencing pure equanimity.

Goenka's recorded chants signaled the end of the session. Others groaned loudly because of their painful postures and sighed in relief as they walked toward the exit. However, I didn't move. I was enveloped in a sense of peace that I never wanted to end. From my reading, I knew this was the "traps of bliss." They wanted us to experience pure equanimity but not develop a dependence on it. So, as good as it felt, I realized that I had to end my session. I just hoped I could build on it the next time.

As I finally joined everyone outside, I admired the perfectly blue sky. But I was the only one looking up with a smile. The others crept along with their heads down as if their armor were three times heavier. In an effort to conceal my elation, I ran into the forest out of view and hopped and jumped like a rabbit, filled my lungs with the nippy air, and sent my exuberant smile to the heavens. I wanted to sing, dance, and, most of all, write it down! *What if I forget? How will I be able to remember everything that's happening!* But I'd sworn to obey the rules, so I knew I couldn't steal a pencil, even if I knew where to find one.

Troubled with a mixture of excitement and frustration, mealtime was the most excruciating part of my day. We are allowed in the dining room only at specific hours and for a certain length of time—and not a second longer! The food was strategically placed so no interaction was needed. We plodded along next to a set of tables lined up end to end with cutlery, plates, food, condiments, and hot water for tea or a coffee substitute. The offerings were plentiful and very tasty.

Heavy wooden tables flanked by benches filled the dining hall, so you ended up sitting face-to-face with someone that you were not allowed to greet, communicate with, or even look at. Inevitably, everyone sat hunched over their plate, gobbling up their food as fast as possible to escape the uncomfortable situation. *CLING-CLANG* is all you heard as pieces of cutlery brushed against each other and scraped the ceramic plates. From the other side of the curtain, you could only tell the women were there because of the same sounds along with an occasional cough or sneeze. It was hard enough for me to sit across from strangers in a normal situation, but with the imposed silence, it was pure torture.

I can't do this! For the last three years, my healing journey has been all about opening up and connecting with people. Now I'm being forced to shut out the people sitting next to me at the most convivial moment of the day. This is insane! I understood why everyone wolfed down their food; they couldn't stand it either!

After the morning meditations, I started taking walks before going to the dining hall for lunch. I soon discovered that by the time I arrived to serve myself, half the people were finished, so I could find a seat without having to face anyone. My favorite spot was near a window so I could commune with nature and give thanks for being alive. But in the reflection of the window, I could see others crouched over their food in despondency.

I wonder what Patch would make of this place. I've seen hospital wards with less despair than I see here! I imagined our colorful bunch of cheerful clowns taking over this place, handing out balloons, squawking rubber chickens, and singing "You Are My Sunshine" accompanied by me playing my sky-blue ukulele. *How blissfully different that would be!*

I have just discovered the power of love, and here I am—of my own free will—practically institutionalized in utter disconnection. Perhaps I'm more like Patch than I thought. In his youth, Patch had also pondered taking his own life, had been devastated by the death of his father, and had isolated himself by visiting a mental retreat.

Well, what's next, Patch? I thought.

In my head, I heard Patch answer unequivocally in his powerful voice, "You don't kill yourself, stupid; you create a revolution—a love revolution!"

I couldn't help but wonder what my response would be.

Chapter 51

THE WORMHOLE

By the third day of the retreat, I now had my objective: sit straight with no back support whatsoever as nature intended it.

I closed my eyes and let the few remaining thoughts fade away. Breathing in, breathing out, I bathed in waves of peace. We were now introduced to vipassana through "body scanning," going slowly with a concentrated mind's eye up and down the whole body to become aware of our sensations. As I did this, I was surprised by some pressure points, warm spots, and some numb areas. My calm ocean transformed into a tsunami of faces. To my amazement, first appeared my parents, brothers, and sister, then girlfriends, employers, coworkers, and finally anyone I'd ever had a relationship with.

Wave after wave of emotions, I relived the burning of hate, the rotting decay of shame, the bottomless pit of sadness. Thoughts of self-hatred and suicide pierced my body and bloodied my soul. One after the other they came, carving deeper into my wounds. *How long is this tempest of horrors going to last?* I practiced breathing exercises, restored my sea of tranquility, and was amazed to find myself resting alone on an immaculate golden beach. *All these people are only ghosts from my past. They are not in my present, and most of them have likely forgotten I ever existed.* And then a realization hit me: *If they are long gone and forgotten, they can no longer affect me. That means I'm creating my own hurt! I'M THE AUTHOR OF MY OWN SUFFERING!*

I recoiled in horror. *I'm the author of my own suffering!* I kept repeating this truth as Goenka's chants signaled the end of the session. Heading downstairs and walking out, I didn't see anybody. I stared at the ground, alone in the sad clarity of my realization: *I was wrong, I've survived by censoring my emotions, but I was always haunted by these ghosts, carrying them inside me all this time. Is there no hope?*

With the ground littered with rotting yellow leaves and the pathway muddied from the morning's rain, I made my way through the forest, fallen branches cracking under my boots. My suicidal tendencies, my cousin, the Boy Scouts—all my sufferings came rushing to the surface. I had fled to Europe trying to escape my feelings, but now everything was catching up with me.

Hopeless, I saw myself amidst the decaying corpses of fallen leaves until the musky damp air pulled me out from my deep void. I avoided stepping on the pine cones and, instead, picked them up like I did as a kid. Most were compressed into a perfect conical shape, like the ones I'd planted in my favorite sandbox at the park. The larger, more opened ones reminded me of hanging them on our Christmas tree. These happy childhood memories were a balm to my raw soul.

I picked up an acorn and caressed its smoothness between my fingers. I loved their funny, little hats and the shiny brown husk. *This one has a tiny wormhole in it. Too bad,* I thought as I chucked it to the ground. I picked up a second one then a third, and they all had holes. Frustrated, I set out to find a perfect one. I searched up and down the hills, plucking acorns from the ground and scrutinizing them, but ended up throwing them away again and again.

Exasperated, I was about to throw away my thirtieth acorn when it hit me: *None of them are perfect. Each acorn has a hole, but it's still an acorn; it's still beautiful. It's perfect in its "acorn-ness."*

Suddenly, it all made sense: *I have my own blemishes, made mistakes in my past, but I am still me, beautiful me! I don't need to be perfect to be a good human being; in fact, it's just the opposite. To be human is to be imperfect, warts and all! I'm not defined by my past but by the choices I make today! I can simply be myself.*

A breath of fresh air lifted me out of my misery. As I intently looked at the tiny hole in the acorn, I was filled with gratitude. *Like me, you are so minuscule and fragile, yet you produce the strongest tree on earth— the oak tree. You are magnificent!*

As a new day dawned, from far on the horizon, a sunbeam pierced the fog and shined its warm light on my face. It was then that a second wave of understanding shook me: *I am human, just like the people who hurt and abused me. They also did their best with what they had. They didn't know any better. They ached for peace of mind, but like me, they were haunted by their past hurts. They acted out in the only way they knew how and suffered the miseries of their choices.* Flooded by compassion, I realized that I was the lucky one because I'd found my way back home. They didn't and were still suffering.

After pocketing some acorns, I rejoined my colleagues on this amazing retreat. I wanted to share my joy, but I only saw misery, hoods covering faces that were staring at the ground. Others were slouched over the tables, their heads buried on crossed arms and drowning in despair. I erased my smile, slowed my steps, and opened my heart: *I've been where you are. Peace to you, brothers.*

Chapter 52

FANTASTIC VOYAGE

On the fourth day I swapped out my chair with armrests to a simple stool. *I need to get rid of all support in order to have freedom of movement and sit straight as an arrow.* Getting into position, I pulled my shoulder blades all the way back and down but immediately felt pain. As I was trying to get myself to a peaceful state of mind, ghosts of the past soon manifested. I was like Ebenezer Scrooge watching my life unfold in A Christmas Carol.

What am I feeling? Was I hurt by these people? Did I hurt them? Is this event happening at this present moment, or was it long ago?

I took deep breaths, welcomed my ghosts, and thought to myself, *Thank you for having been part of my life, but I'm letting you go now.*

When they didn't leave, I used an ancient Hawaiian technique of reconciliation and forgiveness named Ho'oponopono and slowly recited: *I'm sorry. Please forgive me. I love you. Thank you.*

Tears streamed down my face and tremors shook my body as they finally left. With my inner light extending well beyond my body, I felt alive and saw a kaleidoscope of colors and shapes. Wanting more, I inhaled even deeper and stretched my back until it seemed like the top of my head could touch the sky. *Is this nirvana?* I wondered.

Goenka described in his book that we are the four elements: air, earth, fire and water and suggested that we go beyond matter and molecules to see reality for what it really is, a mere illusion. I felt like I had lost my body and that time and gravity had stopped as I plunged into the quantum realms of Dr. Strange and the Ant-Man from the Marvel movies, then turned into the half-human, half-plant Swamp Thing creature from the comic books of my childhood. Eventually, like the actor William Hurt in the movie Altered States, I regressed to a single-celled life form. *I'm an elemental.*

When the session ended, I floated down the stairs in an otherworldly space. I looked for my jacket, *those are my shoes, that's my coat, wow!* As I stepped outside, the entire universe seemed new to me: the sky, the air, the colors. I knelt down and passed my hand through the blades of grass. It was a delight just to feel the cold and moist morning dew. In the forest, I touched everything. I picked up stones and sand and communed with them, staring for what seemed like an eternity.

I want to keep these feelings! I don't want to let them go, but more importantly, I don't want to forget! I have to write them down and share them with the world. But I quickly moved from ecstasy to sheer frustration because I didn't have a pencil or any paper, and I couldn't steal them. I stomped on the ground like an annoyed kid and gave a rock a good, swift kick that sent it tumbling down a slope.

That's when Mother Nature hailed me. *Hey Guy, pick me up!*

What???

Hey, open your eyes! Down here, I'm right here in front of you, Guy! she insisted.

All I saw were twigs, leaves, and pine cones. *My pine cones! That's it! What I need is all around me. I will select items from the forest that best embody my experiences! Thank you, Mother Nature!*

My heart throbbing with excitement I immediately recalled what

I'd learned since my arrival. *Let's see, first there's the monkey mind and then the discovery of peace. After that follows the revelation that I don't need to be perfect—and that IS perfect—and that everyone shares the same imperfectness. Then the ghosts bubbling up from the past, and yes, this is also everyone's challenge. That's six things already. And finally, a seventh: I am an elemental, whatever that means. All of this in less than four days!*

There are no wild monkeys in North America, but since arriving at the meditation center, I'd been greeted by brown-and-white striped squirrels. The leaves rustled as the little creatures endlessly foraged for food, jumping from limb to limb and scurrying across the ground at lightning speed. *They are the perfect symbol for step #1: the overactive mind.* As I looked for the tiny, flat seeds the squirrels scavenged, I discovered that they came from unopened pine cones. All the seeds were released as they fully opened into an elegant pine cone. *The symbolism is just too perfect for step #2 that we are all perfect as we are!* I jumped in glee like a child, clutching my newfound treasures to my chest.

I rapidly gathered stones, seeds, and flowers for the five remaining steps. Once I was back in my room, I cleared the desk and placed the items in chronological order. I recalled my experiences and delicately touched every object to make a mental imprint. *This is my recollection. I can now free my mind and go even deeper on my inner journey.*

Returning to the meditation hall I took a deep breath in and a deep breath out. There were no monkeys or squirrels to distract me. I was so much in the zone that I started the afternoon meditation perched at the edge of my stool with minimal contact, my back totally straight, and my head reaching to the stars. My energy was so free-flowing that I took off all the blankets, my sweater, and my scarf, but I was still hot. I must've stood out from the sixty-odd others in the meditation hall, many of whom were buried so deeply under mountains of blankets that they might've only been faking their presence. With my eyes closed, I thought, *I don't care. I am here for* my *journey!*

Goenka also suggested looking deeper into every living segment of your body: the skin, the eyes, the brain, the lungs, the liver... even your bones, your blood vessels and your lymphatic system. Everything that makes you YOU in this universe, if it's there, it's you.

This reminded me of my favorite movie, *Fantastic Voyage* from 1966. Being a devout science fiction fan, the image of a shrunken submarine navigating through the bloodstream was fascinating to me. Giant cells and sticky organs were out of this world special effects for those days. The threat of being digested by stomach acids, sucked away by the tempestuous lungs, or finally coming out triumphant through the tears of an enormous eye—well, let's just say it was an instant classic in my book. But now it was my turn to embark on my own fantastic voyage.

As I scanned my body, I was totally shocked to uncover parts of my family members deep inside me. My dad, a lifelong smoker, was in my lungs. I painfully remembered the choking stench and nausea of the interminable car rides stuck between my unruly brothers. I could still hear Mom shouting from the front seat, "Stop it! Stop it! You boys behave!" as she hopelessly tried to tame caged lions. And so, Mom was lodged in my throat, symbolizing my inability to express myself.

Other abuses resurfaced as I scanned my liver, kidneys, and heart. *The bullying, the insults, the knife attacks—it's all here!* It was like I was hosting my own version of the television show *This Is Your Life*. Anchoring myself in equanimity, I recited, "You are the past and have no reality anymore." I repeated this mantra with each new story because that's what they were to me at this point: stories.

As I opened my heart to myself, my compassion extended to them. *They didn't know any better. They couldn't have done any better.* I remembered my acorns and thought, *No one is perfect. We are only human.* So, I told those parts of my family members buried inside me that it was time to go.

I prayed, wished them well, and filled the vacant spaces with light and health. *This is my body, my beautiful body. I own it, I love it, and I'm going to take care of it from now on.*

I came out of this session filled with peace. No longer inhabited by my past abuses, I wanted to celebrate but felt compassion for the others who were still entangled by their ghosts. As I made my way through the forest with its richly luminous amber, orange, and crimson leaves, I basked in the sunlight. With a grateful heart, I was truly appreciative of how blessed and lucky I am to be able to forgive and let go.

My steps were so light that I wanted to run and play with this new body of mine, so I piled up a huge ball of leaves and threw them toward the sky. I giggled as they danced to the ground, because I could finally feel all the joy and spontaneity I was denied when I was young. I could be silly, have fun, and be playful.

At fifty-eight years old, I had finally felt the freedom to be a child.

Chapter 53

THE BARE TRUTH

On the fifth day of the retreat, my body unashamedly suggested that I get fully undressed for meditation. It was four thirty in the morning and very cold, so everyone was hiding under mountains of blankets—everyone except me in my T-shirt. With my back straight as a rod and my head reaching toward the ceiling, I breathed in perfect equanimity.

Still considering getting naked, I opened my eyes and peered around. I was sitting in the back corner, and the handful of meditators in the early morning session either had their eyes closed or were lost under their self-made tents. So I took off my shirt and sat half naked. While everyone else in the room seemed to be freezing, I was enveloped in a warm energy. And then, out of nowhere, it happened: I start swaying!

The teacher had repeatedly warned: "Do not move! Let the pain come and go. You see, it will pass. Remain equanimous!"

Until that moment, I'd applied this commandment religiously, but now my body was asking me to do otherwise. Stretching in all directions, I began with an imperceptible sway from the bottom of my spine to the top of my head. When I felt sharp pains in my lower back, I attributed them to the ghosts of past unhealthy relationships rattling their chains. *Thank you for being part of my life. Now you can go away.* Immediately, the pain was gone.

I thought it might be over, but the swaying got even stronger as my neck joined the dance. Rocking from side to side, my ears desperately tried to touch my shoulders. *SNAP! CRACKLE! CRUNCH!* my achy muscles creaked as if made of gravel and sand. Having lived under paralyzing fear of imminent threats, my neck, shoulders, and upper back had absorbed all the stress as if they were cast into reinforced concrete.

Suddenly, I heard footsteps. I glanced to my right where one of the meditation assistants angrily stared at me as if saying, "Hey, have you lost your mind?" He then gestured that I needed to get my T-shirt on immediately. I simply complied with a smile.

Even though I'd been admonished for my actions, I felt a small victory for listening to my body and being spontaneous. After the session, I went back to my room, closed the curtains to only let in a sliver of light. This day was particularly cold so I sat near the radiator inches from the windows. I thanked my lucky star that no roommate ever showed up. I propped the second chair against the door. *I want my privacy and to feel safe.* In the Noble Silence all was too quiet and I felt very vulnerable.

I ceremoniously undressed completely, carefully folding my clothes and laying them on my bed as in a ritual. Then I sat, took deep breaths, and let myself be guided. Ever so slowly, my body began to sway again. I felt a warm embrace, a gentle caress as I gave in to the movement. After a while, it grew stronger and transformed into a hypnotic swirl. From a gentle mother's rocking it was now a threatening tornado! Scared, yet I stayed true to myself and trusted the process.

Suddenly, my head violently whipped from side to side, again and again. With each crack, my neck let loose a geyser of pain. In my mind I screamed, *AAAARRRGGGHHHH!* As if some primal force was tossing me around, my entire body shook under the unbearable pain. I wanted to howl, but the paper-thin walls censured my urge let it all out.

Then all of a sudden, in my mind's eye, I was transported back in time. I saw myself at Boy Scout camp. It was the middle of the night, everything was pitch black, except for the red light of the flames of a campfire.

I was eight years old, and a group of young men imprisoned me in a circle, cheering as they violently shoved me around. They hit me, insulted me, showed me their dicks, and thrust them in my face. Then they pulled my hair and yanked back my neck so they could piss and masturbate on top of me. *I'm a big, long, empty hole.*

As I relived the violence, I choked and wanted to vomit. Belches spewed out from deep inside my entrails. I flung myself off the chair, dropped to all fours, and started to spit. Over and over, I raw heaved as a watery, whitish puddle of phlegm formed near my face. I wanted to cry, but I was still kicked around. I choked and spit some more then finally fell over in a heavy thud where I lay quivering on the cold floor.

After a moment, a soothing calm took over. *It's over; I'm back in the room.* Still jittery, I gently pulled myself off the floor and returned to the chair. *I know what this is,* I thought. *My body has just released the sensations that it remembered all along, but I was unaware of.* I thanked my body for protecting me from these memories for so long.

Raw, exhausted, and still nude, I sat there motionless. I had just relived one of the most horrendous moments of my life and there was nothing to do and nothing to be done. *It's over. I have the tools to let it all go. I can forgive, forget, and love myself and those who wronged me. How much did they suffer to be capable of doing something like this to another human being?* With compassion, I understood that they had been hurt too.

What now? I look at the puddle and knew right away what it represented: semen. *I've just spit out my rape. Should I just pick it up with a tissue and throw it away?* It was disgusting, and yet, precious: *It's my truth finally out.*

I grabbed the garbage bin, sat on the floor, and stared at the puddle as I remembered the nagging urge I'd always felt to lick the spit of other men off the ground. This revolting image was carved into my soul. My stomach would painfully contract whenever I thought about it or saw spit on the sidewalk. I had never understood why until I'd shared this feeling with Marc, the only family member I could openly discuss it with. He had agreed that it most likely signified semen.

I want to get rid of this sickening impulse once and for all! So instead of wiping it up, I kneeled down, licked up some of the "semen" off the floor, and expelled it into the trash can. When I bent down again, I felt a boot kicking my head so hard that I collapsed on the floor. With my face slammed against the floor submerged in the spit and my cheek achingly scraped the floor, I thought, *The rapists are back!*

That's it—the missing piece—the fullness of their violence! That was their final degradation, the insult added to the injury. Now, it's finally over!

After that, the puddle was merely a puddle. *I am free of their abuse, free of their violence, free from their attack. I've shown them that I am no longer afraid.* But more to the point, I'd shown myself that I could own and face anything they threw at me. *There is no shame, no guilt, no need to even feeling dirty. I've won! I am my* Warrior *sculpture without any armor. I have arms to defend myself, eyes to see the injustice, and a mouth to denounce the evils and declare* Victory. *I am free! I am beautiful! And I am powerful!* I sat down and bathed in the warm glow of serenity.

After I cleaned up the floor, I had the urge to reconnect with nature. The earthy smell grounded me, and I felt gratitude for my life. I scavenged for artifacts to add to my recollection of what I'd just relived: the horrors, the rape, and the liberation. *I need to remember everything so I can pass on the experience for others to heal. I'm so fortunate, and I want others to live their freedom too!* I kicked the ground in frustration as I couldn't find any objects and I ached to write down my story.

Supplicating to heaven, I saw that dark clouds now covered the skies; *A storm's coming.*

I returned to my room empty-handed but felt like I was inside a cold operating room where a surgery had taken place. I decided to take it easy for the rest of the day. I put on my green, heavy wool sweater—my favorite—and gave myself a long overdue hug. *I love you.*

As evening fell, a storm raged outside. My windows shuddered from the howling winds and branches cracked under the driving rain. For three days and three nights, nature unleashed wicked waves of water over us.

Like sailors adrift in a tempest we lost our port of call.

> *The wind howled like sirens*
> *And rattled the portholes.*
> *For three days and three nights,*
> *An ocean of tears poured from the heavens*
> *To save our souls or drown our sorrows.*
>
> *Mariners amidst the breakers,*
> *Our ark drifted aimlessly*
> *Lost in the valley of waves.*
> *Poseidon split the mountains*
> *And tossed them into the sea*

As if we weren't already isolated enough, then the power went out.

Chapter 54

THE HOLY GRAIL

At four thirty in the morning, in total darkness, my windowpanes groaned as branches flayed in sinister lamentations. As I made my way to the first meditation session, my flashlight, like a lighthouse overlooking a cliff, guided me through the storm. With the wind whipping all around me, I clung to my umbrella for dear life as I carefully stepped over the cadavers of mutilated branches like they were fallen soldiers on a battlefield.

As I entered the gymnasium, the roar of generators assured us that we weren't marooned. The dimly lit hall was blanketed in a cavernous glow, and even though we had all taken a vow of silence, the clickety-clack of raindrops pelting the tin roof was deafening. The atmosphere was melancholic and damp as we plunged into the abyss of our thoughts.

Seated on the edge of my stool, I allowed myself to be cradled in Mother Earth's warm and tender arms. I was still feeling frail from the previous day's inner journey, so I wanted to be gentle with myself. I closed my eyes and started to sway again, but this time a soft, swinging, side-to-side motion replaced the violence I'd felt the day before. *What's this about?* No answer, my body was mute. The rocking nevertheless continued, never getting any harsher or threatening. *Just a calm soothing side to side motion.* I scanned my body. *I feel pressure on top of my left eye, and my cheek feels numb.* The sensation spread until half my face was frozen.

I visualized the dozens of aggressions I'd been the victim of: bullying at school, the nasty remarks made by my teachers, the knives, my brothers. The list went on and on. As the rocking accelerated, my body urged me to be quiet.

But still, the numbness continued making its way further down my left side. Then, in an instant, I saw my three-year-old self curled up in a ball and crying, alone in my room. I was rocking myself. *I've destroyed the world! I'm bad!* I heard my inner child's voice scream as his whole body convulsed. *I'm disgusting! It's my fault that my cousin played with my penis. Mommy screamed and slapped her. Then Mommy locked me in my room because I'm bad. I have to be punished. I've destroyed the world.*

In Wim's yoga class, I had sensed the slap and the destruction, but I'd never experienced the bodily sensations. *That's it, when I was three years of age I etched deep in my soul that it was all my fault, that I was the guilty one! That's where it all began.* After holding Yorbeli, caring for "Maria," and praying for Marina, I was ready to welcome my inner child into the warmth of my heart. I cried as I saw myself holding Little Guy and whispering, *It was never your fault. You're not guilty, and you didn't destroy the world. You will never be alone again. I will always be here to protect you. I promise.*

When the meditation session was over, I went back to my room, thinking: *What another amazing breakthrough! First, I made peace with my rapists at Boy Scout camp, and now I'm healing my shame and guilt. I'm rewriting my life!*

But I quickly became frustrated because I wanted to write everything down. *I need to remember all of this. It's too important! I can't just let it fade away! It doesn't make any sense! Why won't they allow us to write down our thoughts and feelings when we're here to make breakthroughs like this? Why can't we have a pen and paper?* I paced back and forth, forward, backward, eyes open, eyes closed, even counting my steps.

Too many emotions, I need to clear my head! I made my way down to the restroom to splash some cold water on my face. Then I looked at myself in the mirror. *Didn't I promise to take good care of you and assure you that you're not alone anymore?* As I looked in the mirror, I saw it hanging on the wall behind me: *A marker! My holy grail!* I hadn't paid much attention until now, but throughout the retreat center, there were clipboards posted with cleaning tasks for volunteers to sign up for and check off when complete. And there was one right behind me, just an arm's length away.

Can I borrow it without being seen? I'll hide in the cabinet, but the pen is tied to the board, can I write my stories in a few seconds? And what am I going to write on? On the wrapping paper of the toilet rolls! My plan was born. I felt the excitement of Martin Landau from TV series *Mission: Impossible* as the theme music played in my head. My heart raced as I unpacked a few toilet paper rolls and carefully folded my precious parchment. *Ready for my mission Dan!*

Time to regroup for the evening instructions. The room seemed empty as many participants had left the center and the mood was as the leaves, wet and falling apart. *Maybe there really are bears lurking in the woods! It isn't just the howling winds!* Writer Stephen King would have loved our setting: isolated in a forest, no electricity, savage beasts, disappearing people and a vow of silence. The novel practically wrote itself!

My heart pounded as I was prepared to break my vows for the sake of my child! *I'll always be there for you, I promise.* I waited, waited for the session to end. Finally over, I took my time before standing up as the others hurriedly went downstairs, dressed and disappeared into the storm. I listened, *Nothing! Finally, I can put my plan into action!*

Flashlight in hand I tiptoed down the stairs and lit the way to the bathroom. To my surprise the restrooms in this building were individual cubicles: one door, one lock, one clipboard! *They are different here, I don't need to hide or be stealthy to borrow a pen! This is just too perfect, thank you!!* I was still in the dark but a light shot out from my heart!

My hand nervously reached for the door handle. I opened it and sneaked a look over my shoulder. *No one!* Drums pounded in my chest as I locked my secret hiding place. On the verge of hyperventilating, blood rushing in my eardrums I felt dizzy and terrified as I considered betraying the dictates of the center but I knew I had to do it. *I don't care—my story has to be told.*

I turned to the wall, the tablet and marker were there. *Excellent!* It hung next to the paper towel dispenser. *WHAT!* I gawked at if it was Michelangelo's masterpiece "La Pieta": *The universe is giving me paper at will!* I ripped a first piece of brown hand paper, unhooked the clipboard, sat on the toilet's seat cover and stared at my hands. *Where do I start? So much has happened in just a few days! The most urgent: the spittle on the floor!* The felt marker so frantically scratched the rough surface that I could barely make out my own handwriting. A few minutes in, I heard a noise. *Oh no! Someone's here! I'll be caught!*

My heart stopped, as I heard footsteps outside the door of the stall I was in. The doorknob rattled. Locked! More footsteps. The door to the other toilet creaked open and slammed shut. Water flowed, the dispenser creaked, the toilet flushed, papers crumpled, the door opened and closed, more footsteps, then silence. *Safe!* I breathed a sigh of relief.

I noticed with horror that my flashlight was shining under the door! *How could I not have seen this?* I felt like young Anne Frank writing her life story concealed behind a moveable bookcase in Amsterdam during World War II. My life wasn't in danger like hers, but we both secretly hid in the dark journaling about our lives on whatever we could find. I urgently scribbled the rest of my testimony then dutifully numbered, dated, and meticulously folded the papers and hid them in my pocket.

I listened carefully: *All is quiet, no one is there!* I unlocked the door, tiptoed out and ran into the sheets of rain. The freezing air made me feel alive. When I entered my room, I knew I had to conceal my make-shift diary like Anne had hidden hers from the Gestapo. I found my luggage, unzipped the bottom part of my small carry-on, and stashed away the papers. Then I fell down on my bed, relieved, thinking of all the love I'd just given myself, all the love I could now offer others.

I had just proven that I could fulfill my inner child's needs. *You are never to be alone again, never! I am here for you, always!* Tears of relief fell as I cried in silence. *I've done it!*

Chapter 55

THE TUNNEL

For three days and three nights, we were adrift like Noah, showered with torrential rain in an endless sea of darkness with no stars to guide us. And then, on the tenth and final day of the retreat—my birthday—the sun, the baby blue sky, and electricity miraculously reappeared.

I was looking forward to breaking my vow of silence, returning to my beloved family, and unloading my precious treasure chest: a dozen secret writings retracing my journey and my carefully catalogued recollections. *I am free from my past. It doesn't define who I am, or, more importantly, where I want to go.*

During the last session, I finally attained my perfect posture. I sat at the bare edge of my stool. Basically, other than the soles of my feet, only a whisper of my tailbone supported me. I didn't expect any random thoughts to clutter my mind because I'd reconnected with my three-year-old self and found peace. With my eyes closed, I breathed deeply in and out, bathing in pure equanimity with no thoughts, only silence. I waited for my light of joy, but it wasn't coming! *Love should fill me now, but it's not! Where is it?*

As much as I concentrated and breathed, I just didn't feel love. *I don't get it! I've traveled around the world as a humanitarian clown giving love! And I'm finally at peace with my past, feel oneness with my body, and yet I find no love? I HAVE TO FEEL LOVE!*

I breathed deeper, turned inward, and waited. As gently as a lotus flower opening its petals, an answer came: *Love is the return of a pendulum.* Surprised by this response, I imagined a shiny ball attached to a string and moving back and forth. Give it a push in one direction, and it'll eventually swing back in the opposite way. *So the abuses I've survived pushed the "ball," meaning me, to one side near the extreme edge of suicide, and when it swung back, I became a messenger of love through clowning. Is that it?*

I remained quiet, calm, and centered as I tried to understand. *I didn't have love before and now I give it? My journey was to give up all the stimulants and escapes—like alcohol, cigarettes, pastries and caffeine—and to add music, art, journaling, traveling, and, ultimately, humanitarian clowning?* I felt like I was getting closer to a universal truth: *These were my tools for my journey, but they would be different for someone else?*

And then every cell in my body lit up as I reached an insight: *LOVE ISN'T THE END POINT, something to be sought or possessed, it is life's journey itself!* I felt energized with the realization that being alive is being loved. *Love is in the acting, the doing, the listening. Love is evolving and changing. It's the process, not the destination!*

Love is being alive! Today I am full of love, I am *love, and I was always love.* I literally saw myself in a new light: *My mission as a humanitarian clown was not only to bring love to others, but to bring healing into the world. My life's purpose is to be a healer.* I rested in pure stillness with this newfound knowledge.

Five, ten, fifteen minutes passed, and then I suddenly vacillated like a human pendulum. *What else does my body need to be healed from?* I gently started scanning my body. *I'm numb from the left side of my face down my neck and to my arm! Most of my left side is paralyzed! I can't move!* Then I felt a presence and got the sensation that I was violently banging against something.

I tilted my head forward, turning it sideways with my mouth opened to the left. It was extremely painful at that angle. *I'm being forced! There's a hand on my head, jerking it in a rhythmic back-and-forth motion.* I saw a shadow, a dark, blurred outline.

Suddenly I saw myself sitting on the park bench in the park at eight years old with the groundskeeper. "Come here. I want to show you a game in my office," He said, so I followed. *I hadn't run away, I never did!* He led me to park's administrative building, up the stairs and he locked the door behind us. This flashback was so powerful that I could see the groundskeeper's crooked teeth and smell the rancid air and his nicotine-stained fingers in my face. Suddenly, my head hit against his dirty, old jeans. I felt like I was suffocating as he forced his penis into my mouth.

The acrid stench of his piss and the putrid mustiness of his semen overpowered me. He talked, but all I heard was the squeaking chains of the swings. I wanted to scream, but I couldn't. I was paralyzed.

I stayed with the image; I stayed with the feeling, the violence, the revulsion, the helplessness. I felt everything, every second, every hurt, every pain. And then I felt the moment when my younger self left his body to enter a tunnel and fall into an abyss.

But this time, I was on the other side of the abyss. In my mind, I called out to my eight-year-old self, *"Take my hand! Take my hand!"*

He reached up, crying, *"HELP ME!"*

He was disappearing beyond my grip, so I reached further down, gave an ultimate push, an as our fingers grazed each other a blinding flash of light merged helpless, eight-year-old Guy with fifty-eight-year-old Guy. Love, compassion, and pure forgiveness poured over me. *Finally, I am whole!*

I pulled Little Guy out of the tunnel and hugged him as he shrieked in horror: *"IT'S A MONSTER! IT'S A MONSTER!"*

I recognized his rage. I had lived with it, locked away in my abyss for the last fifty years. *"Cerberus, you can come out now. I know who you are . . . you are my rage."*

He came out of the shadows and stood right in front of me as I said to him, *"With your fiery red eyes, you were locked away within me. When I was ten years old and my brother stole my ball, it wasn't him that I wanted to beat to a pulp, it was the groundskeeper. And when my first love Suzie wanted to open the door, you only wanted to protect her from the groundskeeper. I was so terrified of my rage, of you Cerberus, that I wanted to kill myself all these years, but like Sebastian the stray dog I found in India, all you ever wanted was to protect me."* Deep sobs of relief rolled over me as I prepared to finally let go of my rage.

As his bloodred eyes extinguished, Cerberus moved into the light and snuggled up next to me. I felt all my senses coming back to life. For the first time, I felt warmed by Catherine's magical hug. I tasted my very first kiss with Sasha. I shuddered at Suzie's gentle caresses. I felt all the love they'd shared with me. Cerberus howled out of happiness.

Thank you for protecting me all these years, my friend! I love you. He gently licked my cheek as he, the tunnel, and the abyss slowly faded from my life.

I cradled Little Guy in a tender embrace, looked into his eyes, and smiled as he slowly grew to become me.

I am home, here, in the present, in my body, and I am beautiful.

Chapter 56

IT'S ALRIGHT NOW

With a final bang of the gong, our teacher unceremoniously signaled the end of the retreat by simply saying, "The Noble Silence is now lifted." He got up, picked up his book, and quietly exited the room. "Wow, we made it!" said two friends who started to laugh. The gymnasium filled with rejoicing voices and couples hugged and kissed as the curtain was pulled back in the dining room.

Back in my room, I shaved and started to sing but discovered I had actually lost my voice. I could only laugh, but it sounded more like a cackle. I packed my luggage and got my identity back with my wallet then made one last trek to the forest trails. I jumped, danced, and kneeled on the ground in the fresh, crisp November air. "Thank you trees, thank you squirrels, thank you sun, thank you nature! You have been my salvation for the last ten days. This is the best birthday present ever! I love you."

On the bus ride home, I felt like I was soaring on a magic carpet. As I admired the pine trees in the gorgeous afternoon sun, I thought to myself, *I'm whole and I can help others heal. But first I want to be with my family.*

When I got home, I ran up the stairs and threw open the door.

"Daddy, you're back!" Aïyana squealed as she jumped into my arms.

"We missed you!" Tania added, joining us in a group hug.

"Yes, I'm home. I missed you both terribly!" I excitedly kissed them as we twirled around the room.

I could tell they sensed that I was different. My wife's eyes twinkled like they did when I proposed to her on New Year's Eve. " Honey bear, you're back!" she exclaimed.

Then our little princess chimed in, "My sweet daddy is back! My sweet daddy is back!"

"Yes, I am." Those were perhaps the truest words I'd ever spoken.

"Daddy, Daddy, close your eyes!" Aïyana jumped up and down, pulling on my wife's arm and whispering to her, "Let's do it now, Mommy." I heard noises coming from the kitchen while I expectantly waited. "Happy Birthday to you! Happy Birthday to you!" they sang in unison.

I opened my eyes to a triple chocolate cake slathered in hot fudge sauce and sprinkled with stars. "Wow! I love you, my darlings! What more could I wish for?" We ate, sang, and danced to celebrate this homecoming and the most precious of all birthdays.

In the weeks that followed, I immediately got to work on my manuscript. I wanted to write down everything that had happened during the retreat. I preciously unpacked my "recollection" with my secret scrolls and shot a video about my vipassana experience for my video channel. I also collected all the recordings of my piano compositions from my youth, added those from Amsterdam, and uploaded them for my first album: *Against the Winds: Compositions 1975–2004.* I then added a second one, *Les Chants Marins de Montreal, Virée à St. Jean Port Joli,* with a new original song.

"I'm ready to sing now. It's time!" I told my wife. "I saw an ad seeking a lead singer for a Rolling Stones cover band. This is it! This is it!" My childhood dream was going to come true. After months of rehearsing, we were ready to go onstage at the Piranha Bar in downtown Montreal.

The stage was ready, and the cheers of fans exploded like fireworks. The stuffy, hot bar was crammed from the entrance to the front row.

"Five minutes, you guys. Get ready," the stagehand warned.

I peered through the door across the dimly lit bar and pictured my dad and my brother Marc drinking their beers. *They would've been so happy for me.*

Staring at the three little steps I needed to walk up to get to the stage, I thought to myself. *"Wow, it has taken me almost sixty years to finally reach this staircase, through my pain, loneliness, exhibitions, travels, marriage, divorce and humanitarian clowning - I have finally reached it, and these three steps are the last ones I have to climb to take my first steps as a singer."*

Stepping up onto the stage to a wall of heat, the public roared and stomped their feet. With mic in hand I introduced the band and shouted "Are you guys ready?" The crowd cheered back. Blinded by the lights, I caught a glimpse of Taffy perched on the speakers. And sitting at the end of the bar, Felix Leclerc and Vincent van Gogh smiled and raised their glasses in my honor. *"Here's to you, Guy! You've done it!"*

As the band strummed the first chords of "Jumpin' Jack Flash," I dedicated the song to Marc, saying, "This one's for my brother, "the Great Rock and Roll Fan". The crowd whooped and roared in delight as I continued, "'Cause it's not about where you came from or where you've been, it's about where you're going from now on!" Tears in my eyes, the crowd cheered back even more.

"So are you guys ready to rock?"

They yelled in response, but I egged them on.

"I can't *hear* you! . . . I said, ARE YOU READY TO ROCK?"

They screamed even louder and chanted, "GUY! GUY! GUY!" This was it, this was my moment. I took a deep breath, smiled, and started to sing.

Yes, everything is alright now!

Victory, a dream come true:
Guy Giard sings the Rolling Stones at the Pirhana Bar.

Patch Adams MD and Guy Giard in Russia

Interview with Patch Adams, MD

Guatemala, March 10, 2014

What role does laughter play in your life?

For me laughter is a healthy human emotion. One of the first things to go with many mentally ill people is their laugh. So it's an indicator of whether or not you are healthy when you have a repertory of funny things and you laugh at them.

An interesting thing about laughter is that sometimes jokes are horrible, racist, or sexist, but they are so funny that even though you hate laughing at them, you do. So sometimes laughter controls you, you don't control it. You laugh and then you apologize and say I think this may not have been appropriate. Laughter is just something that comes with a healthy life.

How can we put more laughter back in society?

First, you try to understand what the problem is, and for five thousand years, there has been a global value system nested in greed and power over other people. That's never funny.

I think of love as the most important thing in life, which is again another healthy emotion. But it's not necessarily special. If you are healthy, you are loving, but as a society we are so uncomfortable and untrained and thoughtless about our loving even though it is the most important in life. I have looked all over the world and have found no public school that teaches one hour on love.

All over the world, they say that laughter is the best medicine, but I actually think friendship is the best medicine, and laughter is a great grease for it. However, I also think they say laughter is the best medicine as opposed to love because many people have had horrible love experiences. Again, you can laugh at horrible moments, and it's funny when people try not to laugh, but it's like a giant sound hovering on the edge behind a dam, behind a locked door, that's ready to burst open! So, again, it's an ambivalent emotion because it is natural laughter, the volcano of love that explodes out of your body, and a healthy way probably always connected to love.

People laugh when someone slips on a banana peel or makes a mistake. There's a little bit of the devil in laughter, and, like with any devil, you work to use it appropriately, as a tool that you enjoy. If you're coming from a place of love, then laughter is love, even the scary laughter. When I laugh at jokes that are horrible, I think of that as healthy laughter. I think the phrase *comic relief* stems from the fact that laughter is often a tension release, and maybe that is what laughter at a funeral is. It's considered highly inappropriate at a funeral, and yet most of the people I know would love to have people laughing at their funeral.

You use the word *healthy* a lot. As a doctor, what is your definition of the word *health*?

Let me start off by saying that I think it's important to have a definition that suits everyone, even a paralyzed person. So I would say that health is having a happy, vibrant, exuberant life on an average day.

Health doesn't require that you have a healthy heart or a healthy kidney; it just means that your approach to life is a lot more involved. Of course, we're talking about the health of your psychology rather than the health of your organs. A wonderful Japanese man wrote a book despite the fact that he has no arms and no legs. On the cover is a really happy picture of him that shows that he has no arms or legs and yet the title of the book is *Yes I Can!* It's astounding! I have the feeling that Stephen Hawking was one of the most famous people who had a severe illness and yet had a sense of humor.

Consider the phrase, "Laugh in the face of death," which means that if I'm in front of a firing squad, I'm going to laugh, and I would love to be conscious at my death and still be laughing. I would like that to be a last memory and probably do something disgusting.

In your first book about the Gesundheit Institute, you write that loneliness is the basic disease of society.

Yes, I think it's the worst human experience. There's no more painful experience than loneliness.

The Gesundheit Institute will be the first funny hospital. There are six qualities that I strive to embody and want the hospital to be: happy, funny, loving, cooperative, creative, and thoughtful. For me, these are cornerstones of a healthy group, so I want them in my life and I want my hospital to have them—not as a treatment, but as a place where a patient arrives and that's how it is, and then we see what treatment to give.

So how can a person, somebody who has been isolated, get with other people?

I would recommend clown trips. Did you know that last year six thousand members of the armed forces killed themselves? Something dies in soldiers when they witness so much death and destruction, so we want to bring them here to this hotel in Guatemala because it's all of us, along with the clowns of Fabrica de Sonrisas, we're a family.

You've heard me say that clowning is a trick to get up close. The soldiers who want to kill themselves, they're lost souls. I want them here because most people who come on a trip end up loving themselves and relieving their suffering. They see themselves relieving suffering, they see how much the patients appreciate it, and it makes them feel great. Once they accept that they are a valuable person, they don't want to kill themselves. They realize that, yes, they went through war, but now they can spend the rest of their lives serving humanity. So my dream is for soldiers to come here for seven to ten days clowning so they can see themselves relieving suffering and connecting with humanity.

Humor is the key to making that happen. I don't know a way to do that nested in love because a lot of people think of love as sexual love with a partner or the kind of love they feel for their child. They don't relate to the love of humanity.

And then, for me, comes the much deeper experience of love. You know, you come in, you maybe make a person laugh, but then you sit down and hold their hand. I think it's humor that allows a person to re-enter the world of love by disconnecting it from the world of sex or the fact that you have to get married. Love is the name of the beautiful you have in helping somebody.

I like to say, "The mouth is the introduction to the eyes" because the mouth has lots of ways to move, you can make it into a lot of shapes. But it doesn't have the depth of the eyes. The mouth can lie easily but when you look in the eyes, they are a very powerful force, and we feel more vulnerable looking into another person's eyes than any other way.

So basically, we're talking about love and not humor?

For me the six cornerstones of a healthy community are happy, funny, loving, cooperative, creative, and thoughtful. I would never think of separating one as humor. If those qualities could talk, they would say that they work together because as clowns, we are creative, we are cooperating. There is no way to say what percentage of these qualities is the one that's making a person laugh or enjoy himself or feel safe. Maybe humor got you in the room. You may use humor, but what the patient remembers is how you held her hand. But to those on the outside, it will appear that what they remember is the laughter.

We are and live inside a community.

Photo: René de Carufel

Guy Giard and Rosalia in San Pedro La Laguna, Guatemala

Rosalia and Somos Hijos Del Lago

Founded in 2001, The Centro de Rehabilitación "Asociación Somos Hijos del Lago," is a non-political, social and educational NGO, rehabilitation center in San Pedro La Laguna, Guatemala.

Their mission is to provide help and support to disabled children and adults with physical and psychological disabilities by providing them with education and physiotherapy in partnership with the clients' families and assistance from a corps of foreign volunteers. One of the organization's main objectives is to help improve the quality of life of the disabled.

If you'd like to become a Somos Hijos Del Lago volunteer or make a financial contribution, please contact them via the information below. Any help is greatly appreciated.

https://www.facebook.com/sohilagoong/
email: somoshijosdellago@yahoo.com OR sohilago2019@gmail.com
phone: +502 7721 8139

Guy Giard with the sculpture The Warrior, 1980
Rembrandt Park, Cote St-Luc, Qc, Canada

ACKNOWLEDGMENTS

This book is dedicated to the memory of my father, Normand Giard, MD.

It is said that it takes a village to raise a child, and it has, in fact, taken a "village" to give birth to this book. I'd like to express my gratitude to Patch Adams, MD, who has enabled me to rediscover the wonders and marvels of love. I'd also like to thank the following individuals: Liliana de Leo, who certified me as a Laughter Yoga leader; Madhuri and Madan Kataria, founders of Laughter Yoga; Linda Leclerc, Albert Nerenberg, Duncan Cook, and the whole team and all the attendees at the first Laughter Yoga Conference in Toronto in 2013. Thanks to all of you for having enabled me to discover a community of hope and laughter.

Thanks also to Francine Côté, Nez pour Vivre, Seb's Projects India, Tim Webster, Carl Hammerschlag, John Glick, Guillaume Vermette, Steve Hanlin, Stacie Ashlct, Lou Rodriguez, Marleen Van Os, and the hundreds of clowns who have been so wonderfully supportive during my humanitarian missions, as well as the thousands of children and parents who I've had the privilege of helping. Special thanks to Giri Dharan and his India-based humanitarian foundation Third Hand and Francelline Nakoulma, founder of the Saint Gabriel elementary school in Ouagadougou, Burkina Faso, for her unwavering commitment to the education of children.

Thanks to my major donors Barbara, Dominique, Dr. Marie-Eve

Cyr and her team, Harald, Jason, Josée, Julia, Linda, Liselotte, Maïa, Naum, Paul, Rob, Tracey, Wendy, and many others for their donations during my fundraising drives for humanitarian aid projects. I'd also like to thank Mary Kay Morrison, Steve Wilson, and all the members of Association for Applied Therapeutic Humor (AATH), and especially Lenny Ravich, director of the Gestalt Institute Tel Aviv; Jill Knox and her family; and the Red Skelton Museum for providing grants that enabled me to become a Certified Humor Professional (CHP).

I must also thank the late Alan Watts, whose writings revived my optimism about life, as well as the following health-care professionals: Marjolaine Gosselin, Marine de Freminville, Anne Canarelli, Anne Lucas, Anne-Marie Léger, Caroline Nadeau, and a number of others who helped me through the healing process. I'm also very grateful to the various mentors who helped me over what seemed at the time like insurmountable hurdles: YES Montreal, CAPS Quebec, Marie-Michelle Fillion, Rita Baker, Christian Beaubien, Douglas Leahey, Suzannah Baum, Judy Carter, Frank King, Monique Piroth, and Robert Therriault.

The following persons have generously provided advice and enthusiasm in connection with the writing of this book: Jennifer Huston Schaeffer, Kelly Epperson, Juan Manuel Rodríguez Sawicki, and Lina Giguère. From the bottom of my heart, I'd also like to thank the various friends and partners I haven't been able to mention in this book due to lack of space, but know that all of you are in my heart forever. Thanks to my parents and siblings, and last but certainly not least, to my wife, Tania—the love of my life—and our wonderful daughter, Aïyana, for being so wonderfully supportive during my healing journey. I love you all!

ABOUT THE AUTHOR

Guy Giard, life coach, conferences and workshops

Born in Quebec, Canada, Guy Giard lived in Europe for many years and has traveled to three continents. He's a Certified Humor Professional (CHP) and a Certified Laughter Yoga leader, and he holds a Bachelor of Fine Arts from Concordia University in Montreal and pursued advanced studies at the national art academy of the Netherlands. He has received grants from the Canadian Arts Council and the Conseil des arts et des lettres du Québec.

As an artist, Guy has exhibited his work for more than four decades, and as a musician, has been performing for more than thirty years. As Uku the clown, he has provided humanitarian aid in collaboration with Patch Adams. He also presents lectures and workshops on healing from sexual abuse and creating an extraordinary life. This is his first book in English. Translations in French and Spanish have previously been published.

Guy is available as a life coach and gives talks and workshops (in French or English) on sexual abuse and his path to healing, connecting to our true selves and living our purpose, the loving art of humanitarian clowning, creativity, music and art.

For further information and to subscribe to his newsletter, visit www.guygiard.com. You can also follow him on the following social media sites:

www.guygiard.com

www.facebook.com/guygiard1
www.linkedin.com/in/guygiard/
www.instagram.com/guy_giard/
www.twitter.com/guy_giard
www.bitchute.com/guy_giard/
www.youtube.com/user/guygiard
www.tiktok.com/@guygiard